P9-AOS-671

STABILITY AND PROGRESS
IN THE WORLD ECONOMY

STABILITY AND PROGRESS
IN THE
WORLD ECONOMY

*The First Congress of the International
Economic Association*

EDITED BY

DOUGLAS HAGUE

LONDON
MACMILLAN & CO LTD
NEW YORK · ST MARTIN'S PRESS
1958

MACMILLAN AND COMPANY LIMITED
London Bombay Calcutta Madras Melbourne

THE MACMILLAN COMPANY OF CANADA LIMITED
Toronto

ST MARTIN'S PRESS INC
New York

PRINTED IN GREAT BRITAIN

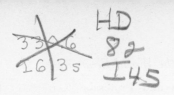

FOREWORD

THE International Economic Association, which was formally created in 1950 to promote closer relations between the economists of different nations and to contribute in that way to the development of the science of economics, had worked during the first five years of its life principally through the holding of small annual conferences of invited specialists in different branches of the subject. It was decided that in 1956, on the occasion of the third triennial meeting of the Council of the Association, there should be held for the first time a Congress, open without limitation to any member of the various national associations of academic economists affiliated to the International Economic Association. It was the purpose of the Association to provide in that way, to a larger and wider audience of economists, the opportunity of meeting and discussing with economists of other nations.

It has from the first been a tradition of the International Economic Association to organize its conferences about a single general theme. On this occasion that method was once again followed, and the theme chosen was that of 'Stability and Progress in the World Economy'. It was my task, as President at that time, to enlist a group of distinguished economists, representative of different nations and different schools of economics, to deliver addresses to the Congress on five different, but inevitably not wholly separate, aspects of our general problem. We were exceedingly fortunate in persuading Sir Dennis Robertson, representing with great distinction English economics, to give the first address. He was followed by Professor Viner, an equally distinguished and equally appropriate representative of American economics. In Professor François Perroux we were particularly fortunate in securing the opportunity of hearing one of the most eminent and original of French economists. Professor Haberler, first President of the Association, was exceptionally qualified to represent on this occasion the Austrian as well as the American tradition. Finally came Professor Lundberg, as one of the most distinguished of the great Scandinavian school of economics. To all of these we owe a great debt of gratitude.

To open the subsequent discussions we invited for each of the five sessions two scholars. The talent that we secured will be obvious when I say that those who consented to perform this task were Professor Dupriez of Belgium and Professor Keirstead of Canada in the case of Sir Dennis Robertson's paper ; Professor Vakil of India and Professor Nurkse of the United States for Professor Viner's paper ; Professor Hicks of the United Kingdom and Professor Schneider of Germany for Professor Perroux's paper ; Professor Lindahl of Sweden and Professor Papi of Italy for Professor Haberler's paper ; Professor Byé of France and Professor Lewis, representing — we would like to think — the West Indies as well as the United Kingdom, for Professor Lundberg. To all of these we would wish to extend our warmest thanks. The measure of their contribution was best seen in the liveliness and interest of the subsequent discussions, here recorded by Professor Hague.

May I conclude by expressing our special thanks in two respects? We are greatly indebted to Professor Papi as Rector of the University of Rome and to his colleagues for their generosity in putting at our disposal the buildings and facilities of his university and thus adding immensely to the comforts of the Congress. On the Sunday that fell within the Congress a number of the participants had the honour of being received in private audience by His Holiness the Pope. We are grateful for the permission that we have been given to print in this volume the address that he delivered on that occasion.

May I express my hope that, through the publication of this volume, the deliberations of the Congress may prove of value to an audience even wider than the four hundred or more, drawn from almost every country of the world, who heard them at first hand ?

HOWARD S. ELLIS

BERKELEY, CALIFORNIA,
October 1957

CONTENTS

	PAGE
FOREWORD. Howard Ellis	V
ADDRESS TO THE CONGRESS. His Holiness Pope Pius XII	ix

FIRST DAY

OPENING OF THE CONGRESS. Ugo Papi	3
STABILITY AND PROGRESS: THE RICHER COUNTRIES' PROBLEM. Sir Dennis Robertson	7
Discussion	19

SECOND DAY

STABILITY AND PROGRESS: THE POORER COUNTRIES' PROBLEM. Jacob Viner	41
Discussion	66

THIRD DAY

THE QUEST FOR STABILITY: THE REAL FACTORS. François Perroux	105
Discussion	127

FOURTH DAY

THE QUEST FOR STABILITY: THE MONETARY FACTORS. Gottfried Haberler	151
Discussion	179

FIFTH DAY

INTERNATIONAL STABILITY AND THE NATIONAL ECONOMY. Erik Lundberg	211
Discussion	227
INDEX	259

vii

ADDRESS

THE SPEECH OF HIS HOLINESS POPE PIUS XII
DELIVERED AT CASTEL GANDOLFO
ON SUNDAY 9TH SEPTEMBER 1956

ON the occasion of the First Congress of the International Economic Association, you have wished, Gentlemen, to come and inform Us of your work and give witness of your devotion. We are very appreciative and are glad to welcome you as representing the most distinguished practitioners of economic science. By your teaching in universities, by your publications and by the authoritative views which you express, you undoubtedly exercise an influence of the highest importance on contemporary society, where economic factors so greatly influence other aspects of social life.

The present Congress continues with distinction your series of yearly meetings devoted to the study of particular economic problems, which constitute the chief activity of your Association. Founded in 1949, at the instance of UNESCO, this Association aims at stimulating the development of economic science through international collaboration, and at present links twenty-five national associations from four continents. This is an indication of the interest which your deliberations will arouse in the world, among all those who strive for the best in public affairs.

'Stability and Progress in the World Economy': such is the theme which you have chosen, and this simple title is itself sufficient to evoke the difficult, and occasionally formidable, alternatives which the economist must frequently face. In the vast social organism, whose different sectors mutually influence and condition each other, it is impossible to act on one sector without disturbing all the others and being obliged to allow for compensatory measures. So, for example, it is dangerous to increase industrial output without assuring markets for the goods produced; to change the volume of money in circulation without taking into account the corresponding volume of trade transactions; to strive for full employment without forestalling the danger of inflation. And yet the law which governs all human activity, that is, the law of progress, imposes changes and improvements which cannot come about unless there is temporary

ix

disequilibrium. The great concern of the specialist must consequently be to keep to a minimum the harmful effects of the measures he advocates, to profit from favourable circumstances whilst avoiding the harsh penalties of periods of crisis. On the international plane, serious differences exist at present between the poor countries, which are becoming more and more aware of their immense economic needs, and the countries which are liberally provided with both the necessities and the luxuries of life. In these underdeveloped areas progress is desired and sought after, sometimes violently, and not without dangers for world peace.

Thus the task of the economist is demonstrably wider, more arduous than ever, and even more fraught with responsibility. On a planet where distance counts for less and less, and where ideas spread with lightning speed, the destiny of mankind becomes always more indivisible. The decisions of every statesman, and those of the experts who execute them, have repercussions on the lives of thousands and millions of men, sometimes bringing welcome improvement, sometimes dramatic disturbances. This is clearly no time for risky theories, for artificial arrangements, satisfying perhaps to the abstract theorizer, but in profound disagreement with reality, because some mistake has vitiated their original assumptions. That is why you can never weigh carefully enough the conclusions and judgments which you reach, or be sufficiently certain of their scientific accuracy, that is to say, their full conformity with the rules of human thought and behaviour and the concrete facts of economic reality. Without wishing to enter into a technical discussion, We should like, Gentlemen, to share with you some short reflections which this occasion suggests to Us.

Economic science achieves its results, like other branches of modern thought, by setting out from the observation of facts. But if the physiocrats and the representatives of classical economics thought they had produced a weighty doctrine by treating economic facts as if they were physical and chemical phenomena, bound by the determinateness of the laws of nature, the falsity of such a conception was shown by the crying contradiction between the theoretical consistency of their system and the terrible social distress which they allowed to persist in the real world. The rigour of their analysis could not make up for the weaknesses of their initial hypothesis. In looking at economic facts they had only considered the material, quantitative elements, and had ignored the essential human element; the ties which link the individual with society and impose on him not material but moral rules which determine how he should use material possessions. Taken away from their common uses, these possessions became the means of the exploitation of the weakest by the strongest under the sole rule of pitiless competition.

To remedy this failing, Marxism tried to reintroduce social values into economics and to ensure that owners of the means of production did not monopolize them for their own exclusive benefit. But, by a no less disastrous mistake, Marxism claims to see man purely as an economic agent, and makes the whole structure of human society depend on productive relationships. While he may no longer be subjected to the arbitrary play of the power of money, man now finds himself hemmed in and crushed by the social order of a society which has grown harsh through the elimination of spiritual values, and which is as pitiless in its reactions and demands as the caprice of individual wills. At both these extremes, there has been a failure to look at the economic order in its full breadth, at once material and human, quantitative and moral, individual and social. Beyond the physical needs of man and the interests which they imply, beyond his place in the social system of production, it is necessary to envisage truly free activity, both personal and communal, for each individual in the economy. He, when he produces, buys, sells or consumes goods, is motivated by a specific intention, which may be simply the satisfaction of a natural appetite, but may also be the expression of a wholly subjective attitude, governed by sentiment or passion. So, by reason of personal conceit, prestige or vindictiveness, the whole direction of an economic decision may be changed. Moreover, these factors introduce, especially into economics, disturbances and difficulties which do not come within the scope of a true science. So it is necessary to go still higher and to recognize the importance of the truly free personal decision, that is to say, the fully rational and justifiable decision, which can consequently be introduced as a positive element in the construction of a science of economics. Eminent representatives in your special field have strongly stressed the true rôle of the entrepreneur and his constructive and determining action on economic progress. Above the subordinates, who simply carry out work as prescribed, are the men in charge, those with initiative, who stamp events with the marks of their individual personality, discover new paths, provide a decisive driving force, transform methods, and raise the output of men and machines to an astonishing extent. And one would be quite wrong to think that such action always coincides with their own interest and only responds to selfish motives. One should compare it rather to scientific inventions or to works of art, that spring from disinterested inspiration and are directed much more to the whole of the human community, which they enrich with new knowledge and more powerful operative media. So, in order to assess economic facts accurately, economic theory must allow simultaneously for aspects which are material and human, personal and social, free, yet at the same time fully logical and constructive, as required by the true meaning of human existence.

Doubtless many people, in their everyday conduct, usually obey the natural and instinctive tendencies of their being. But We prefer to believe that there are few who are incapable, at any rate in critical moments, of making their altruistic and disinterested sentiments prevail over their concern with material interests. Recent events have again shown how far, even among the most humble and under-privileged, solidarity and devotion express themselves in moving and heroic acts of generosity. It is one of the most fortunate features of the present age that it increases the feeling of mutual dependence between the members of society. It leads them to realize that a human being only reaches his true stature if he recognizes his personal and social responsibilities, and that most human, or purely economic, problems will only find their solution through a sincere effort of understanding and of mutual goodwill.

Perhaps We may be allowed to extend this perspective further, recalling a word of the Gospel, which explains the Christian approach to the problem of the production and use of material wealth. 'Seek ye first the Kingdom of God and His justice, and all these things shall be added unto you' (Matt. vi. 33). Even as a subject of economic studies, man can never introduce a complete dichotomy between the temporal goals which he pursues and the ultimate end of his existence. The words of Christ have led to a veritable revolution in the established ways of looking at the relation between human beings and the material world. Do they not suggest, in fact, that as far as possible economic constraints should be cast off, to put all of man's thought and all his powers at the service of a divine order? They teach mastery over that instinct which impels men to enjoy riches without any curbs. They invite men to choose poverty as a means of personal liberation and of social service. Even in our modern times, avid for wealth and pleasure, there is no lack of souls noble enough to choose the way of detachment and to prefer spiritual values to all that vanishes with the passage of time.

If the work of economists does not touch directly on this plane of reality, they can still find their orientation in a unified concept of their science, which gives a place to such behaviour and to the principles on which it is based. They will find there, We are certain, some very useful inspiration.

We hope, Gentlemen, that your Congress will end on a confident note, despite the numberless perils which mark the path of progress with stability. If all have the courage to face these difficulties without deceiving themselves or falsifying any aspect of reality, We have no doubt that you will soon be able to congratulate yourselves on the results of your efforts, and take them up again with more enthusiasm than before, strengthening between you the bonds of a close and fruitful collaboration.

In token of the divine favours which We earnestly invoke on you, your families and all those who are dear to you, We impart to you from a full heart Our Apostolic Blessing.

THE INTERNATIONAL ECONOMIC ASSOCIATION

Presidents
G. Haberler 1950–3
H. S. Ellis 1953–6
E. Lindahl 1956–9

Vice-Presidents
L. Dupriez 1950–6
L. Baudin 1956–9

Treasurer: E. A. G. Robinson 1950–9

Secretary: Hélène Berger Lieser

Honorary Presidents

J. M. Clark	G. Haberler
L. Einaudi	A. C. Pigou
Sir Dennis Robertson	

Other Members of Executive Committee

1953–6	1956–9
W. Hoffmann	H. S. Ellis
E. James	E. Gudin
E. Lindahl	W. Hoffmann
V. Travaglini	W. Jöhr
C. N. Vakil	I. Nakayama
X. Zolotas	C. N. Vakil

Editors of International Economic Papers

A. T. Peacock	W. Stolper
R. Turvey	Elizabeth Henderson

Rapporteur of Rome Congress: Douglas Hague

FIRST DAY
OPENING OF THE CONGRESS

———

STABILITY AND PROGRESS:
THE RICHER COUNTRIES' PROBLEM

OPENING OF THE CONGRESS

BY

PROFESSOR GIUSEPPE UGO PAPI
Rector of Rome University

I AM using no mere conventional phrase when I say that it is a very great privilege for me to welcome, on behalf of the University of Rome, all those who have come to this city to take part in the First Congress of the International Economic Association. My sense of privilege is accompanied by a hope and a feeling of profound gratitude.

The hope is that those of you who are in this country for the first time will not feel strangers amongst us. We, in Italy, take pride in never regarding the citizens of other countries as far from us in spirit. This attitude has always been the foundation of our view of civilized life, and today, on this very occasion, we profess it again with much happiness.

My gratitude goes, first of all, to the officers of the Association for having chosen Rome as the meeting-place for the Congress, in response to the invitation of this University, which considers itself fortunate in playing host to such distinguished representatives of economic science in many countries. To meet old friends again and to learn to attach faces to names which are already familiar, this is a pleasure which, I trust, will outlast your presence here — in the memory of these encounters, which offer all of us the chance of enrichment through new friendships.

I should also like to thank all those who helped in the choice of the subject. Its scope is such that all those who are here, whether their interest lies in the field of theory or practice, will be able to compare the conclusions emerging from the discussions with the fruits of their own experience. The study of the subject is so advanced in almost all countries, that we are bound to achieve a true meeting of minds on a number of matters. Indeed, the very names of the lecturers and the participants guarantee a high standard of debate, even in a Congress where, perhaps, it may not be possible to follow up all aspects of all questions — but where the fundamental ideas will not fail to stand out clearly, to be qualified and developed in the discussion.

Nor must I fail to express the warmest gratitude to the authorities and distinguished people who have made this Congress possible, and who, by their presence here this morning, are underlining the importance which they attach to its results. I thank, too, those who are dealing with the thousand and one problems of organization, especially the ladies, who have lavished on them their intelligence and their many talents beyond anything that we could have imagined. We, in our turn, must prove that their efforts were worth while.

We, in this country, are very keen to learn. We are, like so many others, a country trying to improve its condition and to discover the best means for achieving a lasting compromise between economic stability and development. We also count ourselves among those who believe that in practice stability corresponds to a concept of at least approximate equilibrium, that is to say, the absence of too many fluctuations. For the individual, this means that he can project present situations into the future, in the confident expectation of a higher level of well-being than the one he starts from. For the economy of a whole country, it means that the national income increases at the same rate as population and, in consequence, is able to buy, at the current level of prices, all the goods and services produced in the given period of time.

If that did not happen, if national expenditure were smaller or bigger than the supply of goods, foreign trade would tend to correct the deficiency or excess of national outlay. In the first case, surplus goods, having fallen in price, would be exported; in the second, goods would be imported from other countries where prices were lower. Foreign trade would have the function of propagating and thereby correcting the expenditure-income position in each country by linking it to the national incomes of other countries. The constancy of these relations, whether in real or in monetary terms, determines a zone of equilibrium, within which there is national and international stability. I quite realize that today the mechanism is much more complicated than this simplified exposition suggests. Nevertheless, it still seems valid in essence.

It is clear that, once established, equilibrium in any country remains exposed to the risk of being upset by a number of factors. Each country's search for the origin of disequilibrium suggests measures which can guarantee a certain degree of stability. It will consequently be seen that the measures undertaken by any one country are insufficient unless they are co-ordinated with the measures taken in other countries, at least in those which share this same goal of preserving a certain degree of stability. So, in the modern world, the very objective of maintaining stability in one country creates the concept of solidarity in the action both of individuals and of countries.

In proportion, as the idea of stability acquires a more and more definite shape, the idea of economic progress too gains in precision. Economic progress is closely tied to an increase in *per capita* income, which is a necessary, though not always a sufficient, condition for moving from one stable position to a higher one.

Now, this increase in real income per head occurs as the result of 'favourable events' which the international literature has analysed thoroughly. Cost-reducing inventions; the better organization of production by the use of methods tending to increase the yield of each productive process; the development of backward areas, which tends to establish the factor proportions demanded by current techniques and thereby to increase the return from each process of production used in these areas; the opening up of new markets; the discovery of sizable mineral deposits. These are the kind of events we have in mind, and their effects are spread by foreign trade. In each of them, the will of man remains an important ingredient, and by their effects we gauge how men, in each country, step by step ascend the slope, trying to cling to each conquered position and, when it seems secure, to go on to a higher one, there to consolidate a new stability.

Certainly, the discussions at this Congress will show whether, from the point of view of methodology, the theory of equilibrium is to be regarded as outmoded for the study of the right methods for safeguarding the positions of stability which are successively reached. On the other hand, they will show whether it should, instead, be combined with other theories, for example, the theory of economic planning on the individual as well as the government plane. The aim of all such plans is, first of all, to consolidate and maintain whatever stability has been attained; and second, to achieve stability at higher levels, whenever the present is stable enough to be projected into the future.

We await these discussions with an interest which can hardly be over-estimated. We are here in a University, free from the intrusion of thoughts other than the promotion of knowledge. I take great pleasure in expressing the wish that we may witness the beginning of a fruitful debate this very first morning, when we are to hear Sir Dennis Robertson — that forceful personality who has done so much to fashion more than one generation of economists. May this Congress, in terms of knowledge and in human terms, come to be regarded as a milestone on the not always easy road of international

5

collaboration. Collaboration amongst men of study, to be sure; but collaboration above all amongst men of good faith and good will, who are dedicated to the cause of scientific progress, mutual understanding and peace among all peoples who, through the centuries, have felt part of the comity of nations.

STABILITY AND PROGRESS:
THE RICHER COUNTRIES' PROBLEM

BY

PROFESSOR SIR DENNIS ROBERTSON

Chairman: SENATOR JANNACCONE (Italy)

THOSE who have planned this series of addresses have made a heroic attempt to divide the indivisible. To Professor Viner and myself has been allotted the general question — no small one — of Stability and Progress; to Professors Perroux, Haberler and Lundberg some of its particular aspects. Further, somewhat as Pope Alexander VI divided the New World between Spain and Portugal, so our officers have divided the *whole* world between Viner and myself. I yield to him Asia, Africa and South America more whole-heartedly than ever Octavian surrendered the gorgeous East to Antony, and I do not think I shall often be found trespassing in his orchard. But to my other three colleagues I offer my apologies if I find that I cannot discharge my task, even within the limits of my inadequate knowledge and understanding, without some mention of technology, of money, of international trade.

There is a further difficulty. Mine is a very wide and far-flung empire — 'realms and islands are as plates dropped from my pocket'.[1] What they have in common is to be richer rather than poorer; but they differ among themselves in many ways, and it is not easy to frame general propositions which apply to them all. It seems to me that for my purposes two of these causes of difference are outstanding. First, some of my countries are centrally ruled and planned to such a degree that their rulers may, for all I know, be in a position to achieve, at all events in the economic sphere, precisely what they want to achieve; but in others, while the visitor to them may hear a great deal about objectives, policies and even plans, it is of the essence of the matter that these projects are both partial and uncertain of fulfilment. Second, in some of my countries, policies and plans can be framed with very little regard to external influences; in others, these external influences are of dominant importance. Of this second

[1] *Antony and Cleopatra*, Act V, Scene 2.

7

dichotomy, which is a matter of degree, I shall try to take some account; but in the face of the first, even if it be also really a matter of degree, I shall take evasive action. In other words, I shall not attempt to extend my analysis beyond the border of what most of us, whether justifiably or not, are in the habit of labelling the free world. Within that limitation, then, here goes.

I

On looking up one of the recognized English authorities, I found, as I had expected, that the fundamental question about progress with which any country is faced had been posed long ago with exquisite simplicity.[1] 'The Caterpillar was the first to speak. "What size do you want to be?" it asked.' Alice's reply, 'Oh, I'm not particular as to size, only one doesn't like changing so often, you know', while natural enough in view of the trying experiences through which she had just passed, will not really do; and the Caterpillar's blunt retort, 'I *don't* know', was, in my opinion, fully justified. For it would seem that a country, richer or poorer, *ought* to try to form an idea what size it wants to be — more precisely, at what rate, if any, it desires to see its national income growing, and what proportion of its current income it should save and invest in order to achieve the desired result. Yet it is extremely hard to formulate any rational grounds for arriving at a decision. As is well known, another authority, Frank Ramsey,[2] some thirty years ago attempted to give, for a completely single-minded community constant in numbers, a solution framed in terms of the ordinary economic calculus of utilities and disutilities. If such a community is completely indifferent emotionally between the present and the future, the answer, you will remember, depends entirely on the function relating utility to consumption and on the maximum possible utility, conceived as finite, derivable from consumption. If, on the other hand, the community is not immune from feelings of time preference, then the solution depends also on the strength of this time preference, expressed as a rate of discount, and on the rate of return obtainable from the investment of savings. Professor Stone has shown recently[3] how the method can be adapted to the case of a growing population. But, as Ramsey warns us, these simplified solutions abstract from many difficulties rooted in the uncertainty of human affairs — in those possibilities of technological

[1] *Alice's Adventures in Wonderland* (Macmillan; People's Edition), p. 61.
[2] 'A Mathematical Theory of Saving', *Economic Journal*, Dec. 1928.
[3] 'Misery and Bliss', *Economia internazionale*, No. 1, 1955.

upheaval and of massed destruction of capital from which even the most totalitarian society is not exempt.

Further, not everyone, I think, will be convinced by Ramsey's idea of finite Bliss — a ceiling on the utility conceivably derivable from consumption. I have heard it argued that the ceiling is essentially a movable one, receding always as you think you have made an approach towards it. Further again, drastic revision of the solution seems to be required when we pass from the well-drilled, like-minded community to a society of ordinary men, each not only with his personal hopes and fears and myopias, but with his well-founded certainty of individual deterioration and demise. For the Ramseyan equation depends on the assumption that the economic operator whose utility function is involved realizes that its income and its consumption are going continually to increase. But the ordinary man is well aware that on retirement his individual income is going to fall with a bump, and that at death his individual consumption is going to cease ; and it seems to be not only inevitable but reasonable that his savings policy, while influenced also by regard for his heirs, should partly be governed by that knowledge.

One way and another, then, I am not sanguine about the possibility of determining the right rate of growth for a country by mathematical formulae. And the difficulty is increased when we remember, as Professor Devons has recently in a most penetrating paper [1] reminded us, that the sacrifices necessary to achieve growth consist not merely in passive abstinence from consumption, but in something which is much harder to evaluate mathematically, namely, consent to being disturbed in established routines of life and work. I do not find it possible to go further than attempting to list some of the considerations which a citizen of one of my countries — whether or not he be also a cabinet minister — might do well to bear in mind in attempting to arrive at a hunch whether the proportion of his country's income which is being set aside in the interests of growth is excessive or defective or just about right — it being then for further discussion whether the excess or defect is so great as to justify endeavours to reduce it by propaganda, by compulsion, by modifying the distribution of income, or in any other way.

(1) The first and most obvious consideration is the probable behaviour of population, in respect both of total numbers and of all the subsidiary complications of age distribution. Here, of course, we are in danger of going round in circles ; capital formation may be about right relatively to body formation, but is body formation itself on the right scale ? If I were dealing with Viner's half of the world,

[1] *Lloyd's Bank Review*, Oct. 1955.

I should have to say a great deal about this; and I am not saying that in my half too there should not be policies designed to influence the rate of growth of numbers. In Britain a Royal Commission assured us in 1949 that the existing size of the population was about right, and its members were fertile in devices for eliciting that missing one-seventh of a child per completed family which was needed to keep the population stable in the long run. Holland is anxious about her high birth-rate as a source of pressure on the standard of life; the United States, apparently, exultant about hers as a guarantee of the buoyancy of effective demand. Perhaps we should all agree that, if only we knew how to get it, what would really be most convenient is a population which is always growing but never getting any bigger. Meanwhile I do not venture beyond the platitude that our views on the right scale of capital formation must be greatly coloured by what is, in fact, happening, or thought likely to happen, to numbers.

(2) The second factor which I think might go towards the formation of our hunch — and here too I acknowledge a debt to Professor Devons — is consideration of the *kinds* of improvement in its standard of life which are open to a population which is already by hypothesis fairly well off. We talk glibly of doubling or trebling the standard of life in so many years, but what in detail do we conceive of that as implying? Throughout much of human history, two of the most important marks distinguishing the rich man from the poor man have been that he could occupy more *space* and that he could command more personal *service*. But these are precisely the two advantages which it is most difficult to generalize throughout large and urbanized populations. I am not arguing that they should be preserved for the few at the expense of the discomfort of the many, only cautioning that for societies which are already well fed, well clad and well amused, the quest for general higher standards is in certain important respects inevitably self-defeating, and that recognition of this fact should presumably colour their attempts to weigh up present sacrifices against attainable future benefit. In this respect their problem is a subtler one than that of Viner's countries, where some of the simplest and most straightforward improvements in well-being have yet to be achieved.

(3) Even, however, in most richer countries, there is clearly room for improvements of standard in more concrete and humdrum ways; and the next factor which should presumably affect our judgment of what is reasonable in the way of provision for the future is the available evidence on the relation under modern conditions between net capital formation and growth of output. Looking at the course of human history as a whole, and especially of the last two centuries

taken as a whole, there seems no reason to doubt the old view that an increase in the ratio of capital stock to output — in Hawtrey's phrase, a deepening of capital — has been not merely a symptom but a prime instrument of the enlargement of man's enjoyments and the lightening of his labours. But of recent years in the more advanced countries, we are now told, there has been a change. Invention and research are directed more and more towards the achievement of given results with an economy of material apparatus ; devices for the simultaneous transmission of half-a-dozen messages along a single wire may stand as typical of a great many of the triumphs of modern technology. Viner's countries may still be in the stage where they require the embottlement of large streams of thrift in the bulky basic instruments of power, transport and communication in order to launch themselves on an industrial career or even to rationalize their agriculture. But *my* countries, so it is said, provided they keep their wits about them, ought to be able to provide handsomely for their own futures with the aid of comparatively modest drafts on the net abstinence, voluntary or conscribed, of their citizens. For to the alleged change in technology to which I have just alluded we must add certain facts of a more book-keeping character. Not only, in a rapidly advancing economy, are the depreciation quotas being set aside at any moment always in excess of the sums being currently expended for replacement,[1] but further, when these sums do come to be spent, they will certainly in most cases be spent in ways which improve as well as merely replacing. During the inflation of recent years, it is agreed, there may have been forces acting in the opposite direction ; but taking a long look over the future, we can be confident that industry will contrive to make a great deal of material provision for growth which the statistician will not succeed in identifying as 'net investment' requiring to be balanced by 'net saving'.

I hope to hear much discussion of these topics by those in closer touch with the processes of industry in many lands than I am myself. Such discussion will no doubt attach due weight to those rather surprising calculations of Professor Kuznets [2] indicating that in the United States the ratio of reproducible capital to national output, after rising in the forty years following 1879 from the neighbourhood of 3 to the neighbourhood of 4, thereafter ceased to rise, and indeed by 1939 had lost half of the previous advance. It will no doubt endorse Kuznets' strongly emphasized view that in its expenditures on health, education and research, which are not ordinarily classified

---

[1] E. D. Domar, 'The Inter-relation between Capital and Output in the American Economy', *Economic Progress* (Papers and Proceedings of a Round Table, held by the International Economic Association, Louvain, 1955), pp. 258-61.

[2] 'Population, Income and Capital', *ibid.* pp. 36-9 and 46.

as 'saving', a modern country is making contributions towards its own future growth which are at least as important as the accumulation of physical instruments. But I hope too — if I may disclose my own bias — that the disputants will take heed of the possibility that inventions which at their first impact may seem to be 'capital-saving' may prove to be great eaters of capital in the end, just as those which seem to be 'labour-saving' may prove to be great employers of labour. Anyway, so far as the quest for higher standards can be satisfied at all by ampler flows of material goods, it would seem to me that, in at any rate the poorer of my richer countries, pretty massive embottlements of thrift in such things as strip-mills, oil-refineries, rejuvenated railway-systems are still likely to be required.

II

Well, having arrived somehow at our hunch — I will not go so far as to call it a judgment — about what we should like to see happening, I suppose the next thing is to set out in order the obstacles which may thwart the fulfilment of our wishes.

(1) First among these I place the danger that the citizens in our richer country will not spontaneously provide enough saving to supplement adequately that which is being done for them, for respectable motives and by respectable means, behind their backs. You will not fail to notice that I have phrased this proposition in somewhat provocative terms ; and it does, of course, cover up a whole string of controversial matters, some of them of so rabbinical a nature as to be unsuitable for exploration in a brief general address of this kind. But I must not run away from making some mention of the major issues involved.

First, what is to be the part played by government savings, that is, by budget surpluses ? I throw out, in order that they may be shot at in debate, some *ballons d'essai* — please remember carefully at this point that we are spending this morning in *my* orchard, not in Viner's. (i) A government can reasonably tax its citizens in order to repay at a reasonable rate debts incurred on their behalf for exceptional purposes such as war. (ii) It can reasonably tax them to defray expenditures on health, education and research which on a broad view contribute to the formation of capital ; but it should not as a normal settled policy aim at defraying out of taxation the cost of additional physical capital works except in very special cases. (iii) If the techniques of monetary control have broken down in an inflationary direction, it should accept the resultant windfall budgetary surplus, not give it away, and should even plan to repeat it until the situation is redressed; but it should recognize the situation as one of disease, to be brought to an end as soon as possible.

Next, what is to be the part played by saving done by company directors on behalf of their shareholders? Clearly, in my type of country this kind of saving has come to stay on a large scale, and so long as its dimensions are governed by the true needs and prospects of the enterprises concerned, as honestly judged by their responsible heads, it must, in my highly emotive language, be accounted entirely respectable. I suggest that it becomes unrespectable if its dimensions are unduly expanded by the inertia or the inordinate ambitions of particular persons, by the desire of governments to divert the savings to finance their own programmes, by popular pressures to constrict on distributional grounds the flow of money paid out in dividends. For the result of such policies is a distortion of the *character* of the country's capital equipment which may, to say the least of it, go a long way towards cancelling any merits which they may possess in facilitating the desired rate of global growth.

Next, what is to happen if, given 'respectable' savings policies on the part of governments and boards of directors, the spontaneous saving of individuals proves inadequate to implement the desired rate of growth? The first thing to be said in reply is that governments should not suppose that either they, or the company directors under their pressure, can, by making their tax or dividend policies *un*respectable, count on closing the gap. For a point may easily be reached when each extra £ of thrift so extorted means precious nearly £1 less of thrift spontaneously forthcoming. But it does not follow straightaway that the desired rate of growth need be abandoned. There remains a subtler way of extorting thrift so that it does not appear to be being extorted but to be coming forward spontaneously — a delusion which the magnificent labours of our national income statisticians in recent years have, I believe, done much to fortify in the public mind. The name of this device is inflation, and in case you have not heard of it, I must not filch from Professor Haberler the joy of telling you all about it. Many of us in the past, myself included, have had some words to say in its defence. But it is not such fun as it used to be, for too many people have learnt to dodge its consequences. I am not sure that in Britain the day when the Church of England climbed on to the bandwagon by entering the market for ordinary shares will not be seen in retrospect to have signalized the end of 'a little inflation' as a respectable policy. All I can say is that I should now have to desire a given rate of capital growth very strongly — more strongly than in my 'richer countries' I can see any reason for doing — to be willing to see it consummated with the aid of inflation.

In Britain a few years ago, there was a good deal of pessimism about the future of spontaneous individual saving, which appeared to have sunk virtually to zero. Since then there has undoubtedly been a change for the better. But there is now perhaps a tendency for the recorded figures to generate excessive optimism; for so large and varied is the company now assembled on the bandwagon of inflation that it is by no means safe to assume, as is sometimes done, that all the froth savings churned up by the wagon in its career are concentrated in the accounts of the joint stock companies and the government, and that the category labelled 'personal savings' can be regarded as virtually clean thereof. In most of my 'richer countries' the forces making for greater equality in the distribution of net income are extremely strong, and the provision made by the state in aid of personal misfortune (children being counted as misfortunes) very considerable. It seems likely, therefore, that, if we are resolved to reject the assistance of inflation, there will be need for a good deal of sustained and conscious effort — including the offer of appropriate interest rates — to break down schizophrenia, and ensure harmony between the rate at which the community thinks it would like to grow and the scale on which the individuals composing it are prepared to stoke the fires of growth.

Whether the United States constitutes an exception, of dominating and menacing importance, to this generalization, I must leave to the Conference to discuss. But I should like in this connection to revert for a moment to those Kuznets figures which I mentioned a short time ago. They can be cited as evidence of a decreasing need for thrift in consequence of the change in the character of technical innovation; but they can also be cited as evidence of a constraint placed upon the rate of growth by the limitation of the human propensity to abstinence. For the pendant to that stagnant or declining figure of the ratio of capital stock to output in the United States in recent decades is the figure of a stagnant or declining proportion of annual net income effectively saved. It is interesting that Kuznets' own thoughts seem to veer towards this ultimate explanation of his results: 'on a country-wide scale capital formation is identical *ex post facto* with savings; and limitation of the former proportion [that is, the proportion of capital to output] may in the final analysis be reducible to limitation on the savings proportion, in other words, to the spending habits of individuals'.[1]

[1] Proceedings of Columbia University Conference on National Policy for Economic Welfare at Home and Abroad (Doubleday & Co., New York, 1955), p. 41.

(2) I pass to another matter which has occasioned anxiety, the character (as distinct from the amount) of so much of the thrift nowadays forthcoming in a richer country — safety-seeking, risk-avoiding, and difficult therefore to transmute into industrial capital. This is, I confess, a senior bee in my own bonnet; it is many years since I began to harp on the risk lest in the Anglo-Saxon countries the attractions of the bank deposit, coupled with the strong preference of the banks in favour of lending for short-term working capital purposes, should exercise a chronically depressive influence on the course of fixed capital formation. In the United States in recent years the rise of the so-called term loan seems to signalize something like a revolution in this respect; in Britain it is perhaps regrettable, though inevitable, that the desire of the banks to raise the proportion borne by their riskier assets to the whole back to something like its pre-war level, and the consequent disposition which some of them showed on the morrow of the war to take a more adventurous view of their responsibilities, should have had to be damped down in the overriding interest of curbing inflation. Continental, especially German, banking has suffered from no such inhibitions about the character of its assets, and the lack of them has in the past plunged it into disaster; there the problem takes rather the form of how to create effective capital markets outside the banks, so as to relieve the latter of some of their traditional but perilous tasks.

For, of course, this is not simply a banking problem; its other facets include the investment policies of the great insurance companies and pension funds, and the excogitation of devices to interest the better-to-do worker in industrial investment without turning him into a reckless addict of the tape-ticker. I have neither the time nor the knowledge to plunge into a sea of institutional detail, and I am conscious of a tendency to split-mind in this matter. But I think what I am trying to suggest is that good may come out of evil; provided the dozen-year-old world-wide inflation itself is terminated and not resumed, the recent scramble for inflation-hedges may turn out to have led to a useful crumbling of certain institutional obstacles to the smooth progress of capital growth.

(3) 'The smooth progress of capital growth!' I have said more so far about the obstacles to growth than about the obstacles to smoothness. Perhaps I have been subconsciously funking to take the plunge, on an occasion of this kind, into the maelstrom of modern trade-cycle theory. And even now you will hear from me no stop-press news as to whether the matrix-multiplier does or does not oscillate; no confident judgment as to whether, when we rise from the floor, it is chiefly thanks to the heart-beats of Autonomous

Investment, pulsing away in the outhouse in happy oblivion of the world around him, or to Duesenberry Effects governing the consumption of the unemployed, or simply, as I am sometimes tempted to think, to the fortunate fact that with us, as with Dr. Johnson's friend who tried to become a philosopher, cheerfulness will keep breaking in. All I can do is to remind you briefly of some of the old snags and the new hopes — just three of each. Among the snags, I still put first, as I did forty years ago, the inevitable lumpiness of the process of investment, so that we cannot make provision for a manifest excess of Tuesday's over Monday's needs without making provision for a presumed excess of Wednesday's needs over Monday's, and possibly also for a conjectural excess of Wednesday's needs over Tuesday's. Next, the obvious dangers of loss of balance — vertical balance between the several stages of the productive process of a given type of final output, horizontal balance between the different types of final output. Next, and not to be neglected just because in the past some enquirers have failed to dig beneath them for *real* sources of trouble, the contagious forces of over-confidence and gloom.

What about the hopes? In mentioning them I feel obliged to mention also the doubts which make certain things seem to me to *be* causes for hope rather than for confidence or complacency. Avalanches of statistical information, including increasing quantities of that dis-aggregated type of information which is so relevant to the problems of inter-stage and inter-industrial balance, and used to be so difficult to come by. (But is there not, however cunning the devices of predigestion employed, some danger of the flair and judgment of executive persons being stunned and paralysed by this very abundance of riches?) Next, as we are told, the increased willingness of great industrial concerns to lay long-ranging plans of growth and stick to them without being dismayed by the threats of transitory recession of demand. (But may not long-run plans which go agley spread more havoc than short-run ones?) Next, the certainty that governments and Central Banks will be ready to take heroic action to prevent recession turning into slump. (But does anybody know for certain how much recession to accept before bringing up the big guns? In America, might not a little more tolerance of recession in 1927 have averted 1929 and therefore 1931–3? Did not Britain perhaps show a little too much alacrity in 1952, Canada in early 1955, to pump up the sagging tyres?)

One need not be a full-blown stagnationist to think it likely that the path of growth will continue to lead through patches of soggy ground — of temporary saturation and set-back. One may even perhaps feel that such periods of pause and readjustment are our

16

best protection — and in a humanely organized society a protection not too expensive in terms of individual welfare — against the strong social and political forces making for a continual eating away of the standard of value.

(4) Finally, for such small incursion as I propose to make into Professor Lundberg's domain. How far is each of my richer countries, in its efforts to achieve stable progress, likely to be affected, for good or evil, by the similar efforts of its neighbours? Some, as I started by pointing out, more than others — Britain, for instance, more than the United States. This greater sensitivity of ours to external influences is by no means, as in our more querulous moments we are apt to plead, an unmixed evil. It means that we are apt to be pulled up short in evil courses by balance of payments difficulties, immunity from which might tempt a more self-contained country to press on to the very brink of inflationary disaster. Further, if the penalties of neglecting the warnings of the foreign exchanges are in our case more severe, the rewards of paying them due heed may also be richer. In a self-contained country the risk that measures to check inflation may generate an uncontrollable spiral of deflation may well be greater than in a country whose level of activity depends largely on her foreign connections, and to whom therefore, provided she looks carefully to her costs, the buoyancy of world demand may render powerful assistance in setting a floor to any malign deflationary process. Exposure to all the winds that blow means exposure to fair winds as well as foul.

Nevertheless, the fact that, for whatever underlying reasons, the different richer countries are capable of different rates of growth is bound, in my view, to be a source of certain embarrassments. To dismiss these embarrassments as 'purely monetary' is not, I think, helpful : for, even if it were always true, the monetary measures needed to avert them may themselves be of such a kind as to contribute to instability. If productivity is increasing faster in A than in B, that may involve a choice between A taking her reward more largely in the form of rising money incomes and less largely in the form of falling prices than is healthy from the point of view of her own stability : or alternatively, of imposing on B a flexibility of exchange rates which, whatever the academic arguments in favour of such a régime, works out badly in its effects on the stability of B.

Moreover, it has been shown that these difficulties are *not* always 'purely monetary'. If the difference between national rates of productivity growth is itself differential between different branches of productive activity, strains may be imposed on the adaptive capacities of the weaker countries which impair their stability and inhibit their growth. I do not think there is any way to avoid these troubles except by a retreat into isolationism which would be worse than the disease. But they seem to make it all the more desirable that the richer richer countries should refrain from adding to the difficulties of the poorer richer countries by adhering tenaciously to lines of production in which the verdict of Lord Justice Comparative Cost has been decisively given against them. I have no doubt that Viner will wish to extend this reflection to cover his countries as well. When he has done so, we academic persons can have a pleasant time during the intervals of our debates inveighing against the misdeeds in this field of each other's Ministries of Agriculture and Commerce. We can but trust that their activities will not be so misguided as to hamper us too severely in our difficult task of growing at the right pace to the right size, and so, like Alice, finding ourselves 'at last in the beautiful garden, among the bright flower-beds and the cool fountains'.[1]

[1] *Op. cit.* p. 100.

THE DISCUSSION ON
SIR DENNIS ROBERTSON'S PAPER

Chairman : PROFESSOR JÖHR (Switzerland)

THE discussion was opened by *Professor Léon Dupriez* (*Belgium*). He said : As the first to speak, I think it may be useful if I explain the purpose of the two prepared interventions which will open each day's discussion. They have, it seems to me, the object of singling out from the main paper a few general ideas which are more especially suitable for discussion, and so preparing the ground for the later debate. In this spirit, I shall avoid disputing points of detail, and shall confine my attention to two main themes :

(1) the meaning of the word 'stability' in the context of our discussions
(2) the link between the rate of investment and the rate of progress.

I. THE MEANING OF THE WORD 'STABILITY'
IN THIS CONTEXT

It seems to me necessary to take up this point at the very outset of our discussion in order to avoid any confusion between 'policy' and 'abstraction'. The word 'progress' does not raise the same difficulty. Sir Dennis's lecture, and the later ones, show that objectives of policy concentrate on the promotion of progress, while 'stability' is 'to be maintained'. To link progress and stability is clearly a problem of policy which belongs to the art of organizing real life.

On this particular point, I feel that the philosophy of the Caterpillar in *Alice in Wonderland* is a little defective, acceptable enough for the 'wonderland' of mathematical constructions, but hard to translate into historical reality ; 'a country . . . *ought* to try to form an idea what size it wants to be — more precisely, at what rate, if any, it desires to see its national income growing, and what proportion of its current income it should save and invest in order to achieve the desired result'. Has not Sir Dennis taken a dangerous step in making the Caterpillar's reply his own, rather than supporting Alice's complaint ?

Is it really possible to start with an *a priori* definition of the objective as a desired rate of progress, which is the synthetic representation of a lasting combination of stability and progress? Can one take the existence of such a combination for granted and go on to study how the various contributory factors must submit to this overriding goal of the desired overall rate of progress?

Can one, moreover, assume *a priori* that any progress achieved at an *unchanged* overall rate (and unchanged for how long?) will necessarily be the best, except by pure definition of parameters, for avoiding serious accidents in the economy? Does such progress not rather represent a simplified picture of the current aspirations of the masses? Does it not imply its own contradictions, seeing that progress consists essentially in qualitative changes which underlie changes of dimension?

For my part, I am inclined to think that what is needed is a permanent watchdog policy to prevent the development of serious tensions, whatever their nature, in an historical evolution which encompasses numerous and diverse efforts to maximize the rate of progress. Such a policy should aim at reconciling this Schumpeterian form of economic activity with a concern for security and orderliness in economic life. Essentially, it takes different forms according to circumstances.

I believe that Sir Dennis would be fundamentally in agreement with me about the answer to give. The remainder of his lecture bears this out. It is simply because, at the outset, he found it difficult to disentangle himself from the 'wonderland' that I have looked for words to restate the case. The reconciliation of progress and stability, which cannot be summed up in any synthetic expression, comprises practically the whole of general economic policy. It raises the entire problem of economic fluctuations; how to achieve qualitative and quantitative development without serious setbacks. But the exact rate does not form part of the problem so defined.

This results from the fact that a policy for stability within growth is a general anti-cyclical policy. Giving free rein to the forces of expansion and *qualitative* change, it acts on the tensions and relaxations of the system to prevent expansion getting out of hand and leading to general depression. It is the function of policy to ensure that the social distribution in a changing society meets certain fundamental requirements, that it occurs and is directed in an orderly way in changing business conditions. It is a function which regulates the changes required by new economic equilibria but does not hold them back, for this could do nothing but harm.

It is consequently necessary to study the way in which an economy always tends towards equilibrium while labouring under *creative innovations.* In such a system, consumer demand changes under the impact of increased productivity, and prices are adapted to the new techniques. As Aftalion has shown very clearly, it is demand which is the ultimate determinant of what should be done in the economy, and more especially of the tools which it is opportune and possible to apply. It is more important to respect these fundamental conditions than to pursue some ideal rate of progress. Any politically acceptable rate is, moreover, in danger of coming to grief rapidly from economic contradictions and, in the longer run, from mathematical and technical contradictions.

In conclusion, I suggest that it would be wise to abandon any attempt to associate a desired rate of progress on the political plane with the safeguarding of a certain degree of security and orderliness in that progress.

II. The Rate of Investment and the Rate of Progress

In contemporary discussion, it is accepted, to the point of being taken for granted, that the rate of progress is linked to the rate of savings-investment, and indeed is in some way its result. The accumulation of capital is represented as determining the rate of development; it is considered the dominant variable to the extent that the others may be neglected in a macro-economic analysis. Sir Dennis's lecture associates him, by his context, with this point of view which I propose to dispute. Moreover, in a Keynesian perspective, the independent variable thus stressed, namely, net saving, is itself governed by individuals' propensities to save, that is to say, by the Paretian social constants. It would seem to me that this second aspect of current theory also needs some qualifications.

I should like to question these two relationships in the following sense. I do not consider them wrong or irrelevant, but would assign to them a more modest rôle in the explanation of the course of events, and so leave the field free for other decisive influences. In particular, I envisage relations of an economic order, which will enable us to avoid the acute embarrassment of blindly linking the fate of the economy to propensities which are sociological, autonomous and independent with respect to functioning of the economic system.

On the first point, I think that the economic problem is more closely connected with *gross* than with *net* investment, in all societies where technical progress is rapid. In fact, the sums set aside for depreciation are normally used to buy new machinery of the latest type, or are devoted to modernization schemes. Their reinvestment therefore implies a more or less marked improvement in production functions (*coefficients de fabrication*) and a reduction in costs. Schematically, at the end of an amortization cycle, all equipment which is not up to date should be eliminated.

Where progress is slow, this contribution from replacement is not big, and can, in the limiting case, be ignored in the analysis of a stationary state, as well as in the analysis of parametric progress, consisting in pure quantitative growth. But when qualitative progress is rapid, as at present, the rate of gross investment exerts a more decisive influence than that of net investment, and underlies any general spreading of better techniques.

Theoretically, one must even concede that progress need not imply any net investment at all, since new techniques allow the production of machinery which operates at lower real cost. The rate of such progress is inversely proportional to the time it takes to effect replacement ; in the limiting case, progress is immediate where production goods are consumed on their first use. These facts are not irrelevant to the spread of shift work with expensive machinery. It is not only a question of decapitalizing production, but equally, or even more so, one of allowing more rapid replacement.

Taken by itself, net saving does not have this same virtue of bringing progress. It only operates when new machines are being put to work. Even if these represent the last word, technically, this does not do away with the need to have recourse to old machines. Now, in an analysis concerned solely with the effects of net investment, these latter machines continue to work at the old level of costs. They remain intra-marginal and the market must take account of that. Net investment gives rise to producers' rent but does not inaugurate or impose any price change.

We can therefore precisely describe the part played by gross investment, either with or without net investment. In the case of major technical progress and rapid investment, a fall in costs is achieved in a not very long period with a volume of production which is sufficient to satisfy existing demand. Any cyclical recession, even moderate, quickly illustrates this feature of the economic system. It is by virtue of this process that machinery which is not renewed becomes sub-marginal ; equilibrium tends to be reached through a fall in price, as though the machines no longer existed.

It is true that this fall has a *de-stabilizing* effect, particularly if it becomes widespread ; but it is fundamentally linked to progress, and the function of stabilization policy is to allow such a fall to take place in an orderly fashion, not to thwart it.

My second point concerns the Paretian constants which are

involved in all Keynesian discussions as sociological determinants of net investment, but remain outside variables for the spontaneous working of the economic system. The distinctive feature of these constants is that they are extra-economic (if not outside economic policy) in the sense that they do not fit into economic analysis. They thus become the independent and inexorable variables of macro-economic evolution.

This latter form of explanation ingeniously relieves economists from giving a basic explanation of the economic chain of causation. Rates of progress and degrees of instability are linked by constraints to facts outside our field of action. Is this really satisfactory ? Does it not contradict our profound feeling that the economic system is endowed with a transcendent coherence, even when adaptations cause us so much trouble ?

I do not wish here to reintroduce elements of coherence which exert a re-equilibrating influence in the field of savings, by denying the reality of the Paretian constants. They are real enough, though no doubt less absolute in fact than in theory ; but they are not the only causative elements. Especially in our richer countries, it is not possible to accord them the exclusive rôle in net saving formation which theory usually accords them. The propensities and the net savings to which they lead cannot lay exclusive claim to being the 'villain of the piece' when there is a conflict between stability and progress.

Only a small proportion of saving in developed societies nowadays takes the form of individual net saving, with individuals responding to the Paretian constants. Savings are mainly institutional, and institutions are not subject to the same psychological propensities. I leave aside insurance, whose parameters of development badly need defining, and consider only the self-financing of firms, which is on a large scale and is decisive in many development decisions.

Direct saving, though self-financing, does not depend upon the Paretian sociological functions, but obeys other motives. It certainly depends upon financial results, but also upon the requirements of the firms' development — that is to say, on their economic needs for free capital. On the morrow of a war, for instance, when capital needs are enormous and the market short, self-financing increases, much to the detriment of the distribution of dividends. It is reduced when firms are equipped. It is strong in sectors which cannot find new capital on the market, and weaker in sectors which have ready access to the capital market. (For example, compare coal with electricity undertakings in this respect.)

The theoretical significance of these facts is considerable, for,

23

unlike the Paretian constants, the scale of self-financing depends on the particular size of the needs of different parts of the economy. Self-financing takes care of the needs of survival and development which cannot be satisfied at current rates of interest. Self-financing rests essentially on the needs of the economy and not on extrinsic social constants. Its scope is sufficient to complement private saving and to make total saving comply with the economy's own requirements — and thus to bring the analysis back within the economic system itself.

Professor Keirstead (Canada) made the following comments : For my point of departure I shall turn from the immortal Alice to a book with which I am sure Sir Dennis is equally familiar, the Book of Common Prayer. The passage I have in mind is that in which the penitent seeks forgiveness for the sins both of omission and commission. I hasten to add that I am not suggesting anything remotely resembling sin in anything Sir Dennis has said — or not said — but rather wish simply to fix our minds first on the points he has selected to make, and, second, on his choice of these problems for discussion.

It seems to me, if I properly follow him, that Professor Robertson assumes the question of stability in the richer nations to consist simply of freedom from cycles and excessive inflation and deflation. He regards this problem as pretty much solved and fixes his attention on the problems of progress — or orderly progress — in a well-regulated economy.

It is, I agree, beyond the scope of economics to determine *the* desirable or 'right' rate of growth for a country. This is essentially a political decision, and good politicians make the decision, I suspect, by their sense of what most people want and what they will not do without. It is possible, however, for economists to suggest the *practicable* range within which the political decision can be made. At least the Canadian government appears to believe this. We have in Canada today a Royal Commission which is charged with the duty of predicting the rates of growth of population, national income, resource development and capital formation for the next twenty-five years. Canadian economists have looked upon this Royal Commission with some scepticism, but its existence is evidence that the politician does seem to believe that there are certain causal and predictable variables, whose rates of growth will, along with policy, determine the growth of the economy as a whole. I realize that it is true that a violent change in Canadian immigration policy would affect the population figures of the future, but I think it makes a certain amount of sense to say that the probable rates of growth of population in Canada will affect both its rate of economic growth *and*

24

the political decisions which will be made in determining the 'right' rate of growth. The possession of undeveloped resources will have a similar effect. Capital formation also is likely to be more rapid in a country relatively short of capital and rich in undeveloped resources than in a country rich in accumulated capital but lacking new natural resources. And though national policy can affect these relative rates, it is unlikely to reverse the relationship.

On Professor Robertson's second point, as to the kinds of improvement which the richer countries may experience if they double or triple their standards of life, I should like to add this. Leisure is a third mark distinguishing the rich from the poor and already in North America it is apparent that the trade unions are thinking of increased leisure as perhaps the most important real gain they wish to achieve. (How that leisure will be used is an important and interesting cultural problem, which, however, is not germane to this discussion.) I should also like to suggest that, whereas in the older countries, such as Great Britain and Holland, the concept of an average standard of living has some meaning, it is a dubious concept to apply in regional, continental nations like those of North America. The average standard of living in the United States is the highest in the world, so it is said. But there are regions in the United States and in Canada where the conditions of life are so mean and so poor that they would not be tolerated in many of the western European nation states. Thus, before we come to speak of space, personal service and leisure, we of the North American countries must consider policies which, while avoiding the uneconomic allocation of resources, will at the same time provide certain minimum standards of health, education and housing for the distressed regions and will encourage some natural economic development in those areas.

While I am not sure that I agree that continuous inflationary pressure is a 'disease', as long as it does not become too powerful to be held in check by appropriate monetary and fiscal policies, I most heartily agree that the kind of forced saving inherent in the provision of excessive corporation 'reserve funds' distorts and misallocates the capital resources of the society. Appropriate tax remedies might be found for this. If, however, voluntary savings fall so short of what is needed to support the rate of capital growth desired by government and entrepreneurs, taken together, then, surely, in a free society, Sir Dennis is right. The rate of growth must accommodate itself to what the people want, and hidden methods of conscription of savings are not desirable. In some countries, of course — and I obviously have my own in mind — the capital formation will take place by heavy importations of capital. This solution may have some short-run inflationary effects, and there are long-run political dangers to be faced and a long-run account which must eventually be settled.

We have so far spoken of progress. Sir Dennis turns also to the factors governing stability. While I agree that there are certain 'built-in de-stabilizers', I think that we have two sources of confidence for 'better', that is, more stable, conditions in the future than in the past. One is that governments have more powerful stabilizing weapons to use and better knowledge as to how to use them than they used to have. (I admit they may sometimes be overprompt, as Sir Dennis suggests, to correct a slight slump and thereby pose themselves a problem of inflation, but on the whole, modern monetary and fiscal policy is likely to be effective in preventing a recession from turning into a depression.) The other cause for optimism is that the expectations of entrepreneurs are held with more confidence than in the past, the oscillation between extremes of confidence and gloom are much less marked, and long-term planning by great corporations (many of them, like steel and motor vehicles, indirect determinants of the general level of employment) is undertaken with disregard for the movements of the short-run cycle. There are, for example, pronounced short-run variations in the sale of commercial vehicles. Yet the motor companies, in Canada at any rate, plan their investment and procurement policies for ten years ahead.

I have one fear, which Sir Dennis does not voice and may not share, and that is that slight recessions in the United States may be exported and amplified by American tariff policy. When there was a decline of — was it 5 per cent — in sales of native cheeses, the United States promptly cut off the importation of cheese, thus affecting Canadian cheese sales by many times this amount. The dependence of all of us on the American market, in Canada's case for roughly 17 per cent of our total national income, and the inconsequentiality and discontinuity of American tariff policy, could mean that a slight recession in the United States could generate an almost uncontrollable depression in our country. And this really means that I share Sir Dennis's final hope that both the richest, the richer and the poorer countries will accept the verdict of the Lord Chief Justice to whom he appeals.

I now turn briefly, in conclusion, to those things Sir Dennis has chosen to omit. When we come to theorize in economics we unconsciously, I suspect, work from our experience of the day-to-day economic life we see about us, that is, the affairs of our own countries. Sir Dennis's richer country very strongly resembles England. Mine resembles Canada. Thus, if I were to take this title, *Stability and Progress*, and attempt to reflect upon it without Sir Dennis's firm guidance, I should have thought of the problems of a disorderly progress in a continent-wide state, where the progress was uneven, region by region, and where progress was often the enemy of stability of employment, of stability of the economic allocation of resources, of stability of relative factor prices, and also of political and cultural stability.

I have not the time, nor if I did would it here be appropriate, to treat in any detail these questions. I shall limit myself to a single illustration of the difference between Professor Robertson's 'English model' point of view and my own 'Canadian model'. In the Highlands of Scotland, as I understand, some of the streams have been developed for hydro-electric power, as part of a policy designed both for the orderly progress of the British industrial economy and to provide employment at improved wages for the chronically underemployed Highland cottar. The economic questions which arise are clearly those Sir Dennis has discussed. The St. Lawrence Waterway, by contrast, is a response to market demand for transport and power, presently inadequate, and for accessibility to new resources. In our case, the sudden and rapid development of new communities gives rise to the necessity for public works which yield external economies to industry. In passing, I suggest that we might have to take a quite different attitude from that of Sir Dennis on the question of providing for external economies (even when not directly income-yielding) from taxation. However that may be, my principal point is that the development of the Waterway in response to market forces is a constituent, and an important one, of Canadian economic progress, but that it is an enemy of economic and political stability in Canada. It does not provide employment for a chronically unemployed labour force. On the contrary, it displaces and reallocates the existing labour force in such a manner as to create the most difficult problems of public policy. It creates further problems of instability by its effects on capital obsolescence and on the allocation of domestic capital resources. There is finally the question of the potential instability, at some future date, in the Canadian balance of payments and the rate of exchange of the Canadian dollar in New York. Some, perhaps many, of these problems are for the future. I hope it will not be put down to a narrow nationalism that I think they should not be entirely ignored.

Professor Mossé (France) said that Sir Dennis had introduced the problem of 'whether the proportion of his country's income which is being set aside in the interests of growth is excessive or defective or just about right' (p. 9). He hoped he was correctly interpreting the meaning of this when he said that he wanted to rein in the champions of investment. In his own country, France, he was afraid that, for a dozen or so years, the country might have been over-investing. Had Frenchmen had the benefit of Sir Dennis's advice in 1945, they might perhaps have avoided some mistakes. Using French economic evolution since the end of the war as an illustration, he wanted to offer four comments on the difficulties of the 'always invest more' doctrine.

(1) The supporters of investment assumed implicitly that there was an automatic, causal link between a certain amount of net investment and an increase of output. Sir Dennis, however, had reminded us that a capital-saving device might represent an improvement. If one could do with one machine what one had previously done with two, efficiency had increased. But, when one did with two machines, one of these little utilized, what one previously did with one, one would have invested without advantage. Too often investment decisions were taken without sufficient economic calculation, and it might happen — and indeed it did — that the new equipment was more costly than the old. Whether the result of a given volume of net investment was calculated in physical output, in value added or in profit, this basic assumption had to be seriously questioned, particularly when one considered the institutional framework within which investment decisions were taken.

(2) Sir Dennis had reminded us of 'the danger that the citizens in our richer country will not spontaneously provide enough saving' (p. 12). Why should we assume that there was always enough saving and that one could force it into investment? What if investment should overtake saving? In France, this was the case until 1951, and the government had had to make up for the lack of private saving by fiscal and inflationary measures which might have offset the benefits of the investment. Some thinkers might approve of 'a little inflation' in order to facilitate investment, but French economists, who had had considerable experience of this phenomenon, should have known better than their Anglo-Saxon friends what inflation really meant.

(3) Sir Dennis had mentioned self-financing. In France, self-financing was a means of avoiding taxation and monetary depreciation. It therefore led to a systematic distortion in favour of too much investment, which led to business concentration and to a fossilization of the industrial structure. The importance of ploughed-back profits in the modern world certainly called for a sweeping reconsideration of the theory of interest and investment, starting with a realistic analysis of the true forces motivating decision-taking executives.

(4) Sir Dennis had also mentioned the need to 'ensure harmony between the rate at which the community thinks it would like to grow

and the scale on which the individuals composing it are prepared to stoke the fires of growth' (p. 14). That meant that an equilibrium must be reached, *ex post*, between global investment plans made by the government and the sum of individual saving decisions. But how could one plan *ex ante* for this equilibrium?

Professor Mossé was very concerned about the possible arbitrariness of government investment decisions, both in fixing the total volume of investment and in allocating this total among the various sectors. It was for economists to help governments to discover new methods (or rediscover old ones) by which they could find how to allocate the national product between present and future uses and between sectors.

In conclusion, Professor Mossé asserted that investment was not a matter of principle, but one of appropriate 'dosage'. Any motorist knew that he should sometimes use the brake and sometimes the accelerator. According to circumstances, we should, in the field of investment, sometimes gently apply the brake, and sometimes 'step on the gas'.

Dr. Krengel (Western Germany) said that he wanted to comment on Part I of Sir Dennis's paper, though he thought the discussion of the problem of differing rates of increase in productivity in countries A and B, and the alternative solutions put forward, was most interesting. For this was the problem of relations between Western Germany and other European countries. However, he would discuss only the first part of Sir Dennis's paper.

Professor Robertson had said that he was surprised about Kuznets' findings, that the ratio of capital to output in the U.S.A., after rising from 1879 to 1919, had stopped doing so afterwards, and by 1939 had lost half of its previous advance. Dr. Krengel said that on the capital-output ratio, he would like to make the following statements: (1) The capital-output ratio for the economy as a whole was the weighted total of the capital-output ratios for the different branches of the economy. (2) As these separate branches differed in their use of capital, the total (weighted) ratio might decline, though the ratio in every individual branch remained the same. (3) For example, there were large investment-needs in buildings, streets, houses, etc., but the contribution of housing and public buildings to gross national product was small. On the other hand, a large amount of value added came into the gross national product by way of industries with a low capital-output ratio. (4) Moreover, we had to think of the influence of crises or of a high level of production on the capital-output ratio. In the U.S.A., as well as in other countries, the capital-output ratio in 1931 was low because there was a great deal of reproducible capital lying idle in that year. (5) In view of all these facts, he did not think Kuznets' conclusions were as surprising as Sir Dennis seemed to find them. Nor did he agree that technical progress influenced the capital-output ratio — at least in the long run. With progress, one had better machines, but one used them to produce better and more complex products. In the long run, this represented a free gift to the consumer, and not to the producer.

Professor Hoffmann (Western Germany) said that Professor Robertson's paper contained an enormous amount of wisdom and that he would like to raise only a few questions on the first sentence of Sir Dennis's paper. Was it not necessary to divide indivisibles if one attempted to analyse a steady growth from poverty to opulence ? He doubted whether one could have a model which applied over the whole period during which a country was passing from being poor to being rich. Therefore he also doubted whether one could assume constant rates or constant ratios in a long-run model. So, for example, the poorer lands might have a limited capacity for saving. Yet an increase in income need not require a rise in the savings quota, since the richer a country was the more effective might be its capital — the smaller might be the so-called capital coefficient. One could not use models of a 'straight-line' character, but had to break down the continuous process into specific periods in each of which assumptions of constant rates or ratios might be made for simplicity. The structure of the capital stock might change from period to period.

If, on the other hand, rising or declining ratios were assumed, there arose the problem of how far such a process might go. If, for example, the capital-output ratio was high in the poor countries and low in the rich countries, what result did this give in a model including *all* phases of growth ? The savings quota was low in poor countries and high in rich countries, but how far could it rise ? This led to the conclusion that only for specific periods, with their own social and economic framework, could simplified assumptions about the constancy of some basic ratios be made. Therefore, to analyse the whole long-run process meant dividing the indivisible.

The practical result of this for the backward countries was that it would not be always in their interest to imitate the richer ones, and that specific models should be applied to their given conditions. For example, there were different forms of saving as well as of investment, and also different ways of increasing *per capita* income. This was a rejection of 'straight-line' growth models, but adjustment to the specific conditions of a country was important not only for stability and progress in the country in question, but also for the stability and progress of the world economy.

Professor Delivanis (Greece) thought Sir Dennis might be right in saying that economic progress implied annoying those people whom it forced to change their way of life. This was important when the advantages of economic progress were being stressed, but he disagreed with Sir Dennis about the difficulty of making further advances in cities. There was no more space available, it was true, but one could have more services. Rich countries differed, but even in those where there were already very many services, one could still increase their scope further. One could, for instance, make services more agreeable for the persons concerned, for example, the medical services.

There was also the question of capital for investment. Sir Dennis had said that, even in rich countries, big investments were needed, perhaps because of war or catastrophe. But with the kind of progress one had, say, in the Netherlands, no big investments were needed. In special conditions, like war, or destruction by an act of God, etc., one could not avoid investment out of a budget surplus, if this could be achieved. If there were any choice, one would not want inflation. But, normally, a big investment programme implied inevitably that some capital had to be supplied by the state.

Some factors had not been mentioned. Sir Dennis had spoken of a reduced willingness to assume risks. In traditional economic theory, those who took risks were assumed to get the resulting profits. In practice, especially nowadays, one had deliberate restrictions on the distribution of dividends. All such institutional interference with prices, dividends, etc., kept profits from the risk-takers. Similarly, progressive taxation reduced incentives, which was serious if one wanted to increase investment.

Professor C. Lowell Harriss (U.S.A.) said that the stability and progress of both richer and poorer countries would in future depend significantly on how much they spent on defence and on short-run changes in such spending. He could readily see why Sir Dennis's paper — and those to be heard in later sessions — made no explicit mention of military outlays. There was little to say except the obvious; yet that obvious was important. One had to remember that the costs of defence were large compared with national income in most countries. But they were much larger compared with what could be devoted to capital formation, and economic progress depended to a large extent upon capital formation. It was not wrong, therefore, to say that the tragic drain of military expenditure was large in comparison with the totals that could be made available for economic growth. It was unrealistic, of course, to assume that any money saved on defence would all be used to finance investment.

Some would certainly go for consumption. Yet it seemed probable that the resources available for capital formation would vary in an inverse relation with the amounts devoted to defence. The economist could offer little help in predicting what would or should be spent on defence in the years ahead. The governing factors were political, diplomatic and technical rather than economic. Consequently, economists were often justified in treating military outlays as 'given'. However, we should not ignore the possibility that conditions might become either much better or much worse; and in either case the implications for economic growth could be important.

Since the main cause of huge defence spending today was the threat of communism, the protection of most of the world now depended on the defence spending of a few countries. Several more carried burdens that were heavy in terms of their resources, and yet the real safeguards of the world West and South of the iron-bamboo curtain were paid for by a few richer countries. So, the amount the poorer countries would have available for capital formation and for current consumption — as well as their existence as free and in-dependent nations — depended on the amount and the effectiveness of defence spending by the richer countries.

Short-run stability was also tied up with defence spending. Events in the last few years had shown that changes in international relations could cause changes in military outlays which were big enough to influence significantly even the largest and most developed countries. In the United States, for example, the rise of about 10 per cent in the level of prices in the early 'fifties was directly caused by the Korean War. The recession of 1953–4, on the other hand, reflected to a substantial degree an adjustment to a lower level of military spending. Smaller and poorer countries had also felt the impact of changes in defence spending, perhaps relatively more in some cases than the richer countries. He would certainly not argue that any cyclical pattern had appeared, but there was no doubt that changes of the order of magnitude associated with business cycles of the past could now result from the sort of changes in military spending which were quite possible today. And these changes could occur even without a major war or a large reduction in international tension. Of course, it was not only the changes in spending but also the way they were financed that determined the result, though there was no time to go into these familiar aspects of the problem. It did, however, seem justifiable to suggest that any discussion of stability should give some attention to changes in military spending as sources of short-run disturbance.

Professor Haberler (U.S.A.) said he would make a comment in order to lighten his own paper. Professor Robertson had said that there was now less fun in inflation, and less joy in explaining this fun. The reason was that so many people knew how to beat inflation and the consequent danger was that a 'little' inflation could easily become a galloping one. He himself would like to offer one reservation to this. Almost any policy, however bad in an absolute sense, could be justified by applying the 'theory of the second best'. The only attainable alternative might be something even worse. Thus, inflation might be the lesser evil, for example, if one had aggressive trade unions which pushed up money wages by 8 per cent to 10 per cent per annum — faster than production could ever grow. One then faced a dilemma. If one prevented prices from rising, then there would be unemployment ; if one gave way, there would be inflation. Depending on conditions, inflation might be the lesser of the two evils. Some people took the optimistic view that trade unions were easily put in their place by correct monetary policies. He himself did not think it was really very easy, and this gave rise to the great dilemma.

Professor Haberler recalled that Sir Dennis had expressed the fear (on p. 13) that 'a point may easily be reached when each extra £ of thrift so extorted means precious nearly £1 less of thrift spontaneously forthcoming'. Was not this too pessimistic ? Had the £ sign some subtle relevance ? Had Britain gone farther in this direction than the U.S.A. ? Surely, Sir Dennis implied a change in the system rather than an increase in the percentage of income taken by tax in a given system. There would also be changes in government expenditure, and much could be done by fiscal policy. He was interested by the view (p. 12) that governments should not use their power to tax in order to defray the expense of capital construction. There were many value judgments here, and one should spend some time spelling them out.

Mr. Doyle (Ireland) commented on Professor Domar's view, quoted by Sir Dennis Robertson (p. 11) that, in a rapidly expanding economy, depreciation quotas were always in excess of replacements. With shipping, for example, replacement costs were five times the 1939 figure. In times of rapid inflation, depreciation reserves were invariably far too small. Nor could he see any significant drop in the pace of inflation in the United Kingdom. As Sir Dennis had said, the Church of England now bought equities. It had done this only with great reluctance when it had become clear to the Church's financial advisers that the buying and holding of gilt-edged securities had become a sure way of losing one's *real* capital. There was no excuse for inflation, and nothing more insidious than the delusion of a 'gentle' inflation — a delusion that persisted despite all the evidence to the contrary in Europe.

Mr. Doyle also commented on Sir Dennis Robertson's criticism (p. 15) of British banks' refusal to be adventurous. We had too many instances of the results of banks taking the adventurous view — for example, the disastrous failure of the City of Glasgow Bank in 1878, and the many German bank failures. He trusted that bankers would not listen to what Sir Dennis had advocated.

Professor Lerner (U.S.A.) said he thought that he was more in sympathy with Alice than with the Caterpillar. Having been for some years in one of the poorer countries, he felt the question of whether the rich countries should get still richer more or less quickly was not so urgent. If the question was only whether the rich countries should or should not save, in the light of their own marginal utilities, it seemed a narrow and selfish question to the poorer countries. However, an increase in saving by the richer countries could make resources available to the poorer ones.

Professor Lerner found it hard to get excited about the line between gross and net investments — a line far too much subject to the arbitrariness of definition. One could say that zero net investment was that level of investment which kept income stable. But if there were technical progress, and a falling volume of capital would sustain the previous level of income, what happened to one's definition?

Professor Lerner was not surprised that richer countries had lower capital-output ratios than poorer ones. Improvements in technique could have far wider application in the richer countries. For example, automation would enable richer countries to use their considerable stocks of capital much more efficiently, but would be of little help to poor countries with few machines. This was merely an illustration of the fact that it paid to be rich, and he was reminded of the story of the boy whose parents apprenticed him to the trade of being a millionaire.

Professor Lerner was interested in the problems arising where there were different rates of growth in two regions. Within a country, such differing rates of progress would have to be reflected by changes in the relative levels of incomes and prices in the different regions. Such adjustments could not be made easily. One piece of machinery which could make adjustment more simple was the existence of different currencies. One region could then adjust to another by altering the exchange rate instead of prices, wages, etc. He was therefore surprised to find that Sir Dennis seemed to object (p. 17) to solving the problem by changes in exchange rates. He was tempted to call this view 'sentimental internationalism'. This language was too strong to apply to Sir Dennis's careful statement, but there was a tendency to object to this kind of adjustment merely because different countries were concerned. Yet surely one ought to welcome the possibility of adjusting exchange rates, in order to make the world just a little less unhappy than it would otherwise be.

Professor Nakayama (Japan) said that as a representative of a poorer country, he was not qualified to discuss the richer countries' problems; we were all in the Wonderland of the scientists. He wanted to consider the problem of what constituted an optimum population. Sir Dennis had not really dealt with this question in his paper. On p. 10, he had managed to dodge the problem by hinting at a new optimum. He had said, 'What would really be most convenient is a population which is always growing but never getting any bigger'. Perhaps the language here was just a little too beautiful. Cannan, and more recently Meade, had considered this problem, and we now needed more definite ideas. Perhaps Professor Keirstead had been a little unfair on the concept; the need for discovering what was the optimum population was for Japan a practical problem and not just a theoretical exercise. For sixty or seventy years, saving had been as high as 20 per cent of real national income. Japan had benefited from the capital thereby created, but the increase of population had cancelled out much of the effect on *per capita* incomes. What would happen in the future?

Professor Rugina (U.S.A.) quoted Sir Dennis Robertson (on p. 7): 'Some of my countries are centrally ruled and planned to such a degree that their rulers may, for all I know, be in a position to achieve, at all events in the economic sphere, precisely what they want to achieve'. But was this really so? Professor Rugina doubted whether, either in Germany under Hitler or in Soviet Russia and her satellites, the leaders could always achieve precisely what they desired. Could State planning realize any project whatsoever in the economic sphere? Consider, for instance, the standard of living. Certainly, the Soviet or the Nazi planners did want their nations to reach a high standard of living, at least as high as that of the United States. Did they succeed completely and without great hardships for their nations?

Any economist with experience of the 'planned' systems knew how big were the discrepancies in such an economic order between planned and achieved goals. Any planned economy, socialistic or capitalistic, was very expensive to operate because the system itself was 'antihuman' and consequently needed a huge bureaucratic apparatus. That was why a planned economy could never really bring economic progress.

But this was not all, said Professor Rugina. Was a planned

35

economy stable? This was another question which puzzled many people. Even professional economists might be misled, because planned economies in action at times looked as if they were stable. The truth was that most of the time they were suffering from discrepancies and maladjustments, but it was usually forbidden to discuss such matters openly.

The term 'stability', unfortunately, had two meanings : (1) something fixed, which did not change by itself. We could call this 'fixed' or 'artificial stability', which at the same time might mean 'fixed instability', since both were of the same static nature. In this sense, a planned economy in action was carrying the burdens of a 'hidden instability' under the slogan (fixed) 'stability'. This had nothing to do with genuine economic stability and equilibrium.

The second meaning of stability was something which was not fixed, *i.e.* something flexible, elastic, and yet having in its structure a mechanism which would reduce fluctuations to a minimum and restore automatically any equilibrium which had been disturbed. This was what one might call normal or flexible stability, and was derived from the Walrasian equilibrium system.

The planned economy had nothing to do with this concept of stability and equilibrium. Turning from this standard concept to the capitalistic world, we must agree that the latter did not fit into a normal stability either. All that one could say would be that the capitalistic system had a peculiar kind of 'flexible' instability which we might designate as a 'shaking stability'.

The fundamental problem today was to have the courage and the wisdom to organize by democratic methods a number of consistent reforms in the economic, monetary, banking and financial fields in order to cleanse the present-day capitalistic system of all its inconsistent elements and institutions which produced contradictions and instability in the Western world.

Professor Rugina said that in Sir Dennis's paper there was no trace of such basic reforms. However, he finished his lecture with a reference to *Alice in Wonderland*, which might be interpreted as the model of a country with economic progress and normal stability.

Dr. Louise Sommer (U.S.A.) said that, according to classical economics, the only legitimate method of control over inflation was monetary policy. High interest rates, however, might slow down business activity, reduce business income, lead to more bankruptcies, and so on. What criteria gave monetary policy a selective character as a means of combating inflation? What were the scientific arguments justifying this special position imputed to monetary policy as a controlling organ? And what gave 'monetary interventionism' a higher dignity than other types of intervention, rejected in a liberal economy?

Professor Sir Dennis Robertson replied that he hoped the long question from Dr. Sommer would be answered on the fourth day. His own view was that he did not think that control of credit and interest rates was the only respectable or sensible instrument of economic policy. There was a need for fiscal and budgetary measures as well. He did not argue that there was no place for more direct controls, but he did feel that monetary measures had been too much neglected in the immediate post-war years, and was glad that one country after another had rediscovered these indispensable instruments of economic policy.

Sir Dennis said he was happy to feel that there was so little between Professor Keirstead and himself. He particularly liked the suggestion that leisure should be added to space and service as the commodities which those with a high standard of living had been able to acquire in large amounts; it would undoubtedly be possible and desirable for people to take a rising income, in part, in the form of more leisure. He wondered if, in some connections, one should distinguish between older and newer rich countries; in the latter, progress could be a very disrupting affair.

He had expected to be attacked for his arbitrary statement that a government should not seek to finance the construction of physical capital out of tax revenue. He admitted that there was no hard-and-fast justification for making this rule; even if it were a sensible rule in England, it might well not be correct for backward areas (the dichotomy of developed versus underdeveloped countries was somewhat misleading — the least developed areas in the world were perhaps Canada and the U.S.A.).

Sir Dennis felt that, to some extent, Professors Mossé and Delivanis had answered each other. Immediately after the war, inflation might have been a legitimate method of repairing damaged countries quickly. Nevertheless, even in such circumstances, countries might be wrong in trying to go too fast, and he was interested to hear that Professor Mossé thought France *was* going too fast. He was glad to find Professor Hoffmann, who was a master of historical and statistical measures of growth, somewhat sceptical about models of growth applicable to conditions in all times and places.

Professor Haberler, in the unusual rôle of defending 'a little inflation', and Mr. Doyle, had answered each other. But he wanted to make it clear that he did not blame the Church of England for investing in equities. The argument was rather that once institutions found this way out, as they hoped, it was a sign that the *effectiveness*

37

of a 'little' inflation was being impaired. Inflation depended on finding enough people to cheat. Now, in many countries, bitter past experience meant that there was no one left to cheat, and creeping inflation tended to become trotting and then galloping.

Sir Dennis said that speakers had been surprised that he was surprised at the falling capital-output ratio in the U.S.A. He did not want to enter into controversy on this point. The notion of a capital-output ratio was, in any case, a kind of hotch-potch, and it would take too long to discuss it fully ; it might be true that the ratio was *not* falling in the U.S.A. His point was that Professor Kuznets' own interpretation of his own figures suggested that there was no good reason for supposing that a richer country inevitably saved a higher proportion of its income than a poorer one.

Replying to Professor Lerner on foreign exchanges, Sir Dennis said he thought a case could be made for completely free foreign exchange rates, but he still felt that the prices of the world's major currencies should not float. He wanted to avoid this if it were at all possible.

SECOND DAY

STABILITY AND PROGRESS:
THE POORER COUNTRIES' PROBLEM

STABILITY AND PROGRESS:
THE POORER COUNTRIES' PROBLEM

BY

PROFESSOR JACOB VINER

Chairman : PROFESSOR AMZALAK (Portugal)

POVERTY'S HANDICAPS

THERE has been assigned to me the general topic of stability and progress as problems for the poorer countries. I hope I will be regarded as being responsive to my assignment if economic instability is dealt with only as it may be an obstacle to economic progress in the poorer countries, if progress is interpreted to mean improvement of the levels of *per capita* income, and if I make my main topic the causes of and the possible remedies for the poverty of the poorer countries.

Sir Dennis Robertson, who has carried out so brilliantly his corresponding assignment for the richer countries, has surrendered to me, with undisguised alacrity, all of Asia, Africa and South America. I will neither reject nor accept Sir Dennis's delineation of the boundaries of my territory, provided it is understood that peoples must be poor to fall within my jurisdiction. But did Sir Dennis intend to exclude from my orbit the Central American and Caribbean countries, which do not happen to be in Asia, or in Africa, or even in South America ? And did he unqualifiedly reject as outside his orbit all or any of those Communist countries which are not located in South America, Africa or Asia ?

In discussions of the problems of national poverty, the slightest gesture towards a general statement is liable to meet the objection that the poorer countries differ greatly among themselves in many relevant respects, and that what has just been said does not apply to some poor countries known to the objector. It would not be practicable for me, however, even if I had the qualifications to do so competently, to attempt to tailor my remarks to fit closely each of the fifty, or perhaps one hundred, countries with which I have been endowed. Of the making of generalizations, there will, nevertheless, be no end in this paper. I must therefore ask you in advance to interpret them as if they were believed by me to apply to most, or to many, but not necessarily to all the poorer countries.

The question why some countries are much poorer than others presents a challenge to the economist, to which he will respond in a great variety of ways, according to his methodological bent, his interests, skills, and insights, and the uses, if any, to which he expects his answer to be put. It is probable that there is scarcely any branch of human knowledge, useful or ornamental, which cannot be drawn upon for a contribution to the answer, and it is clear beyond dispute that political scientists, historians, sociologists, anthropologists, geographers, geologists and others can profitably be consulted by the economist in his search for an answer. I can speak only as an economist, however, and if I invoke non-economic causes of poverty as part of the picture, I concede in advance that I do so without claim to the necessary professional qualifications. Disciplines, however, usually prefer encroachment on their territories by outsiders to being ignored. On the other hand, there is almost no economic factor, no matter how important it may seem to most of us, which some economist will not ignore or minimize, either out of inadvertence or honest ignorance, or because recognition of it would get in the way of a desired conclusion, or mar a pretty theory, or complicate the analysis. I have done my best to avoid this danger, but my best may well be not good enough.

The concept of 'cause' has its own notorious difficulties. I will assume that we are all agreed that national poverty generally has many causes, and that if our interest is in how the poverty can be relieved, the proper procedure is to seek to identify those causes which are both major and strategic in the sense that their removal or moderation is not beyond the conceivable power of the relevant portion of mankind. But 'causes' all have their 'causes' in an infinite regress, and I will assume that the best procedure is to try to identify them and to understand their mode of operation at the critical stage at which there is most chance that they can be removed or moderated. In discussion in this area we are likely to hear much of the 'vicious circle' of poverty, with the implication sometimes drawn from it that, since poverty is self-perpetuating, the poverty of the poorer countries can be remedied only by the intervention of a *deus ex machina*, in the guise of aid from outside Asia, Latin America or Africa — or Europe, or Australasia. I do think, with many others, that there is an important element of the vicious circle in the problem of poverty, and that there is therefore good reason for invoking external aid to help break that circle and to help to undermine the defeatism on the part of the poor which recognition of the circle is liable to foster.

A part at least, however, of what gives rise to the vicious circle is the fact that some of the most important causes of national poverty reinforce each other by their simultaneous existence. Extreme poverty, for instance, is both caused by the absence of health and vigour and literacy and a barrier to their attainment, while lack of any of these leads almost inevitably to lack of the others. But this has its hopeful as well as its discouraging aspect, since it warrants the hope that the removal or weakening of any important barrier to economic progress will be of itself a contribution to the removal or weakening of other barriers. Economic progress is not completely indivisible, and its major elements seem to be at least moderately contagious. There may be as much of a beneficent circle in progress towards prosperity as there is a vicious circle in economic deterioration.

The Internal Handicaps

The most obvious cause of regional poverty is a regional scarcity of productive resources relative to population. But the meaning economists give to 'scarcity' in their value-theorizing is not an altogether appropriate one when what is in question is the economic status of a region and its people. For a resource to be 'wealth', to be 'scarce' in the sense of value theory, it must be appropriable and capable of being exchanged at a price in a market for some other 'scarce' good. But for institutional or other reasons, what is for the community a key resource, and scarce in the sense that the community would be better off if there were more of it, may be a free good to the individual, available to him for the taking so long, at least, as any of it is available at all. Sunlight is almost always, and water very often, in this status. Abundance of free goods, moreover, operates to increase the 'scarcity' of a given stock of non-free productive resources, by raising their productivity, and thus raising their market value per unit. Most resources, up to the point at which they begin to become nuisance-commodities because of their over-abundance, are 'rival' commodities with respect to the quality of 'scarcity' in the value-theory sense. As one resource becomes more abundant and therefore less 'scarce', most other resources, without change in their quantity, become more 'scarce' and therefore more valuable per unit. But from the point of view of national poverty and plenty, labour is the only resource whose 'scarcity' in the economist's sense is ever a favourable element — for labour 'scarcity' means high income per labourer, and labourers, including

43

the self-employed, with their dependants, comprise the great bulk of every population. From the point of view of community economic welfare, labour therefore is the only resource with respect to which 'scarcity' is an appropriate community goal for its own sake. But this is, of course, not necessarily true for specific kinds or qualities of labour.

The 'scarcity of resources' concept, moreover, has other complexities when used in community welfare analysis. Resources may be owned abroad, or owned at home but employed abroad, as in the case of capital. They may be imported from abroad, together with the persons who have claims to their imputed contribution to the national income, as in the case of the immigrant who brings with him his capital, his entrepreneurial or managerial skill, or his capacity for skilled or unskilled labour. They may be 'created', as in the case of domestic capital formation, through saving and productive investment, or, as in the case of labour, through induced natural growth of population or through transference, by education, rehabilitation and vocational training, of persons hitherto unproductive to the labour force. Technological discovery can convert a commodity from one which was a free good and useless, or even a nuisance-commodity, to a useful free good — as, for example, waste from lumbering, made newly useful as a raw material by some technological discovery, though so abundant that it has no market value. Technological discovery can similarly convert a 'free' good into a 'scarce' good in the value-theory sense — as, for example, the same residue from lumbering, after still more uses have been found for it. Changes in export possibilities and in domestic tastes can have the same effect as technological discovery in converting goods — in either direction — as between the categories of nuisance-commodities, of useless free goods, of useful free goods, and of 'scarce' goods.

For present purposes, the significance of what I have been saying lies in the corollary therefrom, that what is from a community point of view the scarcity or abundance of a resource is not to be measured by reference solely to its current market valuation, and that without changes in population or in physical supplies a country may become less well-endowed or better-endowed with productive resources as there occur changes in technology, in tastes, in export markets, in availability of complementary goods from abroad, or, in the case of labour, in the ratio of labour force to population.

There is also a 'quality' aspect to resources, which is likewise to some degree dependent on circumstances external to the resources themselves. A change in technology, or in tastes at home or abroad, may create a demand for a certain kind of skill and thus convert low-productivity into high-productivity labour, may upgrade minerals or other raw materials without any change in their physical characteristics, and may convert physically-unchanged land from the 'barren' to the 'fertile' status. Productive resources derive their economic value from their rôle as input items in production functions. Where government is important, whether for good or for bad, in the mode of operation of the national economy, which means almost everywhere today, the quality of the government, the wisdom of its policies, the adequacy or the excess of its activity, the integrity, skill, initiative and energy shown by its agents, help to determine how effective the productive resources of the country shall be in producing national income, or in other words, what the national productivity functions shall be.

For the purpose of our present enquiry, therefore, no resources, not even natural resources, can be taken as historically absolutely fixed or given in amount, or even as having given supply functions, since new discoveries, changes in tastes or in technology, changes in export markets, depletion, depreciation and obsolescence, may either increase or decrease their quantity in an economic sense.

In the poorer countries, labour is always abundant relative to capital, and for most of them labour is abundant relative to natural resources. If capital is scarce, if labour is inefficient, if managerial ability is scarce, if the quality of public administration is low, even a country rich in natural resources is likely to be poor in almost every other respect that is here relevant.

From an economic point of view, moreover, natural resources may be scanty even though the botanist or the geologist or the geographer waxes enthusiastic over their abundance. It is not mere square-mileage, but usable, economically productive acreage, suitably located with respect to markets for its products, which constitutes a satisfactory base for agricultural income. Tropical forests may be biologically fertile beyond comparison and yet may be, economically speaking, worthless if not a positive nuisance. Similarly with minerals ; they must meet some minimal criteria of quality, must be not too deep in the bowels of the earth, must be available in sufficiently large deposits, must be located suitably with respect to markets and to sources of supply of essential input items, to be valuable national assets. It is always important to remember that 'quality' may and ordinarily does have different criteria according to whether it is the natural scientist, the engineer, the business man or the economist who is doing the appraising. Poverty in natural resources is not fatal for a country actually or potentially rich in capital, in managerial talent and in skilled workers. But the accumulation of capital and of productive skills is a long-term phenomenon ; most

45

countries which have achieved it had, at an early stage of their development, a favourable ratio of natural resources to population.

Poor countries are generally poorly endowed, *per capita*, with capital, with natural resources, with managerial talent, with vigour and health in their labour force, and with efficient government. Even abundant capital and natural resources may not suffice to yield a *per capita* real income above the poverty level. Because of an unfavourable age-structure, the ratio of labour force to total population may be low. The labour force may not have the skills or the attitudes requisite for high productivity, and a rigid cultural pattern may be a formidable obstacle to their acquisition. Managerial ability may be deficient. In any case, since capital is a consequence as well as a cause of prosperity, abundance of capital will not be found in low-income countries.

In a changing world, adaptability is necessary — occupational mobility, technique flexibility, place mobility, product flexibility — if an economy is to move forward, or even to hold its own. The stagnant economy is, under modern conditions, certain to be a poor economy, or at least a deteriorating one, even if the same natural resources, methods of production and labour force once sufficed to bring prosperity.

Where natural resources are scanty relative to population, where the ratio of labour-force to population is low, where capital is scarce, where government is poor in quality, where the cake of custom preserves against change attitudes and patterns of behaviour which are unfavourable to economic progress, national poverty, therefore, is not a difficult phenomenon to explain, without recourse to additional factors. For many, though by no means all, of the poorer countries, all of these conditions are present, and sufficiently, if not completely, account for their poverty.

Were I to stop here, a critic might object that, while my details were unobjectionable, the overall picture of the causes of national poverty I had given was nevertheless seriously out of focus, because it does not go beyond what an economist in the classical tradition could have said fifty or a hundred years ago, and thus fails to utilize the insights which modern economic theory has provided, and that it over-emphasizes the internal causes of national poverty, to the neglect of the contribution which the richer countries — and especially the richest countries — have made to the poverty of the poorer countries. My procedure, however, has been deliberate, even if inexcusable, for I wished to discover — and to demonstrate — how far one could proceed by way of the traditional and the commonplace to throw light on the problem of national poverty. When James Mill, the father of the more distinguished John Stuart Mill, first took employment with the East India Company as a despatch writer, he asked a high officer of the Company what style he was expected to follow in drafting his despatches. 'The style we like', he was told, 'is the humdrum.' I have followed this procedure. Now I will examine what modifications need to be made in it when due account is taken of the fruits of the procedure currently fashionable among our modern theorists of seeking an escape from the humdrum, from platitude and commonplace, or from unwelcome conclusions, by resort to paradox.

The modern innovations of theory which have been applied to the explanation of national poverty are many. I cannot, therefore, deal with all of them, and I must deal briefly even with those I select for consideration. Since I am not unqualifiedly enthusiastic about some current trends of economic theorizing in this and in other areas, I am aware of the possibility that this selectivity and brevity will involve an unfairness which will be regrettable even if unintentional. Those who will discuss this paper, however, will have the opportunity, the motivation and the ability to redress the balance. It is also perhaps permissible for me to suggest the possibility that if I had time to cover more widely the range of new ideas and to deal with each at greater length, I could muster an even stronger case against them, especially by showing that to exalt the value of the new variables or the new methods of analysis they are expounding, the 'modern' school often tends to reject or neglect the old variables and the plural-causation aspects of the old explanations.

There are obstacles to economic improvement in the poorer countries which are wholly or mainly internal, but which I have so far neglected. These include some factors which writers of previous generations did not stress because they were inoperative in their time, as well as some which modern economists have newly discovered.

Let me take up first the question of the impact of inflation on poorer countries. Inflation is not a phenomenon peculiar to poorer countries, and if we compare today's price levels with those of 1930 or 1910 or 1890, France, Italy, Germany, and other countries within Sir Dennis's orbit, have at times surpassed, in their degree of inflation, much of Latin America and all of the past and surviving British colonial empire. There is probably not a single proposition of any consequence to which all economists would subscribe, and some economists are recommending deliberate inflation to the under-developed countries. Most of us will agree, however, that rapid inflation in any country does serious economic harm by making routine saving highly unprofitable to the saver, by distorting the allocation of investment, by creating a privately profitable but socially wasteful area of activity for middlemen of various species, and in other ways. It seems probable to me, however, that the greater importance of the market, as compared to subsistence-agriculture, in the richer countries, and the greater importance there also of long-term contracts and long-term debts stipulated in legal tender money terms, makes rapid inflation more damaging to the richer than to the poorer countries. Inflation in the richer countries, moreover, is, or used to be, intermittent rather than chronic, while in some of the poorer countries it has been very nearly continuous for a century, if not longer. Where inflation is chronic, the extent to which financial institutions, public finance, business and individual saving and investment patterns, and collective wage agreements or statutory wage legislation have been adapted at least to the usual degree of annual inflation seems to be fairly complete. In consequence, the chief injurious effect of inflation ceases to be the irregular and arbitrary dispersion of price trends, as in the case of intermittent inflation, and becomes instead the elimination as routine instruments of economic process of long-term fixed income securities, of long-term debt in any form, of long-term contracts formulated in terms of specific monetary units, and of types of economic organization requiring use of these instruments. I may well be wrong, but it seems to me that some at least of the evil sting of inflation is extracted when it occurs in a society in which the long-term bond and long-term contracts are unimportant, and in which by legislation or by collective bargaining the tendency of wages to lag behind a rising cost-of-living is substantially overcome. On the other hand, I fail to see much scope in poorer countries, as I have observed them, for the beneficial action of inflation as providing either an incentive to saving and investment or scope for forced saving. Inflation operates in that way when there are savings which can be borrowed to be repaid in depreciated currency, where there is labour which can be employed at wage rates not rapidly adjusted to changes in price levels, and where there are inflationary windfall gains which can be taxed away or borrowed away to finance public investment. These are possibilities which have been much more prevalent in the richer, more-advanced countries than in poorer countries with a long-established inflationary experience.

The distortions of investment and of the structure of relative prices, moreover, reach their peaks under 'suppressed inflation', but it is only the richer countries which have the administrative machinery and the populations sufficiently tied to the market and sufficiently submissive to complex regulations to make appreciable suppression of the price aspects of inflation feasible.

A low propensity to save is a barrier to economic progress wherever it chronically prevails, although I would try to come to terms with the more moderate of the Keynesians by conceding that in the richer countries it would not be a barrier to economic progress if it prevailed only during depression periods. In the poorer countries, especially when they are very poor, and especially if they have a tradition of chronic inflation, *ex ante* savings and *ex ante* and *ex post* investments are never far apart, and there is rarely, if ever, just ground for concern lest the disposition to save should lead to unemployment. Because the need for capital formation is especially urgent in poor countries, a low propensity to save would be for them a less equivocal handicap than for the richer countries.

It is commonly taken for granted that the peoples of the poorer countries have low propensities to save, and there has been extensive discussion of ways in which the propensity might be raised, as, for instance, by the development of savings institutions and of a domestic market for government securities, or the assumption of the saving function by the government. If, for present purposes, however, I may take the available international comparisons of income, savings and investment more seriously than perhaps they deserve, then the ratio of savings to income seems, for comparable *per capita* incomes, generally to be higher, not lower, in the poorer countries than in the richer countries. If capital formation is seriously inadequate in the poorer countries, therefore, it must ordinarily be because average incomes are low rather than because the propensity to save in relation to *per capita* income is exceptionally low. If 'capital' and 'investment', moreover, are given their usual meanings, 'spending' by individuals or by government for better nutrition, for health and for education may often be more productive in the long run than much of the investment which savings would make possible, and especially the investment in magnificent boulevards and public buildings in the capital cities, in uneconomic steel mills, in football stadia which the richest countries cannot equal, and in expensive housing for swarming bureaucracy engaged in planning for future economic development, and in obstructing current private development activities.

Overwhelmingly massive and wide-ranging as is the modern literature on 'economic development', the searching study of the influence of economic development on the pattern of income distribution and of the influence of the pattern of income distribution on economic development still remains apparently to be written. Such

questions, for instance, as whether highly unequal distribution of
wealth and income are favourable or unfavourable to rapid economic
development of poor countries, and as whether programmes of economic development should aim first at raising the income levels of
the poor masses or at promoting a larger middle class, seem frequently,
in the literature, either to be neglected or to be answered dogmatically
without the aid either of facts or of theoretical analysis.

Even in the countries where mass poverty is deepest and widest,
there are always enclaves or islands of wealth. Are these also sources
of leadership, of enterprise, of initiative, of saving and productive
investment? Must there be dependence on these islands for the
development of the new patterns of domestic life — including the
small family and the new standards of education which economic
progress requires — even if the persistence and growth of these
islands involves for a time the persistence or even growth in absolute
size of an ocean of poverty on which these happier islands can float?
We need new light on this difficult question, and it will probably not
be easily attained.

The rôle in economic development of the rich landlord is here
crucial. There is a long-established stereotype according to which
he is typically a spendthrift, a playboy, an inefficient or indifferent
economic manager of his estate, which he operates for display and
for play more than for production. It does not seem to me a fair
picture of the English or Scottish landlord prior to, and after, the
Industrial Revolution, although it may fit closely enough the Irish
landlord of the eighteenth and nineteenth centuries. I would not
take it for granted, in the absence of objective and competent study,
that it holds true for Asia, Africa and Latin America today, or that
'land reform' which involves chiefly the forcible breaking up of
the large estates is the appropriate remedy if the picture should
be true.

Economists have recently been making much of the so-called
'disguised unemployment' in countries where self-employed or
peasant farming prevails. I have elsewhere expressed my pronounced
scepticism as to the existence *on a large scale* anywhere of this phenomenon *if it is taken literally as usually defined*,[1] namely, the existence
of short-run and long-run zero or less than zero marginal productivity of labour where rural population is dense and farms are small.
The term in any case was an unhappy one for the idea it represented,
namely, unproductive employment, though I have no doubt the term

---

[1] I now italicize these words in my original text, because it seems obvious to
me that in some of the discussion of my paper the words now italicized were wholly
disregarded.

will be salvaged even if the idea should be irreparably ruined. But the prevalence of the phenomena of extremely low marginal productivity of labour and of low ratios of formally employed to total population is indisputable. If, as has been claimed for 'disguised unemployment', these phenomena and self-employment are causally associated, then there is available a new argument for plantation agriculture, for latifundia, provided the rich landlords are also 'improving' landlords. I deliver no verdict here. The little I have seen, and what I have read which is relevant, point inconclusively in both directions. This may be one of the instances where generalization without distinction of countries is especially dangerous. The question is important, however, and deserves systematic and, above all, objective investigation.

The prevalence of usurious rates of interest to farmers and artisans is often pointed to as a major obstacle to economic improvement. The real obstacle, however, may be the scarcity of capital, and the high rates of interest only a symptom, and conceivably even a healthy one at that, of this scarcity. It is also possible that the high rates of interest are not so much a reflection of either the scarcity of capital or the avarice of lenders as an inevitable consequence of the high cost of lending and of collection of principal and interest where borrowers are dispersed over a wide area, are poor, illiterate, improvident, and of high mortality, and borrow in small amounts and repay in driblets. In the literature on the rural moneylender in poor countries, we read much about the high *gross* rates of interest he charges, but we find no information on what the level is of the *net* rates that accrue to him, or, if these are assumed or alleged or observed also to be high, on why competition between moneylenders does not operate to lower them.

In the United States, capital is abundant and competition between lenders keen. Nevertheless, the effective rates charged to individual borrowers in connection with instalment purchases of automobiles and of other consumers' goods commonly exceed, and sometimes far exceed, 15 per cent per annum. Mere abundance of capital may not, therefore, be a sufficient remedy for high rates of interest to small farmers. In this respect also, plantation agriculture may have important advantages over either peasant farming or tenant farming. The only way of making moderate rates of interest in agriculture consistent with peasant or tenant farming may be the development of co-operative credit institutions which can enlist volunteer services for the handling of the otherwise costly details of conducting small-loan operations.

The External Handicaps

I turn now to consideration of obstacles to the economic progress of the poorer countries which may arise out of either the misbehaviour of Sir Dennis's part of the world or of the faulty handling by the poorer countries of such aspects of their economic relations with the richer countries as the poorer countries have it within their power to control.

I will disregard 'economic imperialism' and 'colonialism', if these are understood to mean resort by richer countries to their political or military power to impose on poorer countries an economic régime which is a barrier to their economic progress. However important these may have been in the past, and whatever contribution to the present poverty of the poorer countries' past 'imperialism' and 'colonialism' may have made, most of the countries within my orbit are today completely free from external political control over their economic policies. Even for those which are still in a 'colonial' status, it is in most cases at least a matter for reasonable argument whether complete independence would be to their economic advantage.

The commercial policy of the richer countries can most obviously be an important barrier to the economic improvement of the poorer countries when such policy includes severe barriers to the import of the staple products of the poorer countries. One example, chosen from the many available because it is a particularly glaring one, is the promotion, by import duties, import quotas, or subsidies, of domestic production of sugar by such countries as the United States, Britain and Canada. Another is the selection by the richer countries of staple products of the poorer countries, such as coffee, tea, tobacco, which have no close domestic competition, for specially heavy excise taxation, some of whose burden is undoubtedly shifted back to the foreign producers. These and other such measures are to be charged in the books, at least if the accountant is in principle an adherent of free trade, as debits against Sir Dennis's countries. Except on the principle, however, that in the economic relations between richer and poorer countries reciprocity should be on one side only, it is only fair to point out that the poorer countries are no longer novices themselves in carrying further than is even in their own interest, no matter how narrowly conceived, the attempt to attain prosperity for one's own people by the impoverishment, or the lessening of the prosperity, of other peoples. I leave the ethical question here to more qualified moral casuists, especially as my personal biases would lead me, with relatively minor qualifications, to invoke a plague on both sets of tariff-fostered hothouses. But spokesmen of and for the poorer countries would insist that this disregards the economic grounds on which what is sinful when practised by richer countries can be ethically justified when practised by the poorer countries, even if the richer countries should mend their own ways.

The poorer countries are largely exporters of primary commodities, and under universal free trade many of them would continue indefinitely to be so. It has been claimed that there is a historical law by virtue of which the prices of industrial products rise relative to the prices of raw materials and foodstuffs, and consequently the commodity or net barter terms of trade move against the poorer countries. The statistical record is appealed to in support of the existence of this law, although I would contend that the relevant statistical record has so far been only superficially and clumsily analysed, and that even the analysis so far made yields a clear or even plausible confirmation of the law only to those determined in advance to find such confirmation with the aid of judicious selection of base years and of terminal years. I have discussed this issue elsewhere. Here I will confine myself to calling attention to two generally neglected considerations. First, in using national price-index numbers in order to calculate terms of trade it needs to be remembered that such index numbers do not ordinarily, and cannot easily be made to, take into account changes in the quality of commodities over time and the introduction of new commodities. Over the past fifty or one hundred years, it has been the leading exports of the richer countries much more than of the poorer countries which have consisted of commodities improving greatly in quality over time or of commodities newly introduced into trade. Second, those who insist that there has been a secular trend of the commodity terms of trade adverse to the poorer countries should deal with the British economists who have, since early in this century, been contending that for Britain the secular trend of its commodity terms of trade was currently unfavourable, and promised, or rather threatened, for various reasons which they adduce, to continue to be so.

All other things equal, it is, of course, to the advantage of a country that its export prices should be high and should be moving still higher, relative to its import prices. As a rule, however, *caetera non sunt paria*. If the real costs per unit of producing a country's exports have been falling, it may be getting more in return per unit of factor-input devoted to production for export, even if the prices of its imports are rising compared to its export prices, that is, its 'single-factoral terms of trade' may be improving even when its

53

commodity terms of trade are deteriorating. No one terms-of-trade concept can suffice to catch all the subtleties and escape all the ambiguities of the 'gain-from-trade' idea. But I believe that the single-factoral terms-of-trade index, though inconclusive, is clearly and unquestionably superior to the net barter or commodity terms of trade index as representing the trend of national gain from trade.

It has been objected that the factoral terms-of-trade concept is not useful because it is not susceptible of statistical measurement. I am not even yet, at this late date, prepared to accept statistical measurability as a crucial test of the relevance or usefulness of concepts for economic thinking. In any case, one should not underestimate the ingenuity of the quantifiers. In a recent publication of that hive of statistical innovation, the National Bureau of Economic Research, of New York, series of labour-input and property-input, per unit of output, and weighted combinations of these, are presented. Construct such a factoral-cost index for a country's export commodities and multiply its reciprocal by the index of that country's commodity terms of trade, and you have its single-factoral terms of trade.

It has been claimed, however, that the prevalence in the richer countries of entrepreneurial and trade union monopoly enables them to withhold from the poorer countries any share in the benefits of technological improvement in the production of the richer countries' export commodities. Perhaps so, although it should not be accepted without more statistical or other testing than it has so far received. The effects, such as they are, of the cartels and monopolies of the richer countries on price levels and price trends may be less marked for export prices than for domestic prices, because of dumping and of competition between national monopolies. In appraising the effect of monopoly on the level and on the trend of the terms of trade between rich and poor countries, there need also to be taken into account the valorization schemes and the export taxes which the poorer countries use, perhaps unsuccessfully, to raise *their* export prices. In any case, I am wholly unconvinced by any arguments I have so far encountered that in the process of trade bargaining, richness is always, or even generally, an advantage and poverty a handicap. Britain, India and the United States are all exporters of cotton textiles, and I cannot see how their relative *per capita* national incomes affect the commodity terms on which they exchange these cottons for imports. Nor can I see why Canada has a bargaining advantage in buying oranges from the poor West Indies rather than from rich California or Florida. Effectiveness in trade bargaining for a country depends on bargaining skill, on the will to bargain, and on the availability of alternatives. In all these respects, there seems to me to be no presumption, and assuredly no certainty, that the advantage will lie with the country with the higher *per capita* income.

It has been argued recently that the attractiveness of the products of the richer countries to poorer peoples may be obstacles to the economic improvement of the poorer countries, not only by involving them in balance of payments difficulties, but also by lowering their propensities to save. Having in recent years found myself frantically avoiding being run down by American Cadillacs on the thoroughfares of three not-so-poor Latin American countries, I see some point to this extension of Duesenberry's 'demonstration effect' to the relations of poorer with richer countries. Some difficulties, however, remain to bother me about just what is the significance of the argument.

In the past, economists and others often attributed the lack of economic ambition they thought they could observe in some at least of the poorer peoples to lack of sufficient attractiveness to them of the things they were acquainted with which money could buy. Aside from the question of incentives to work hard, to acquire skills and to embark on new enterprises, may not the first consequence of a new relish for radios, bicycles and refrigerators be, not the impulse to spend more (especially if all was already being spent which was available for spending), but to save more in order eventually to be able to buy these attractive novelties now beyond their reach? In the case of the Cadillacs, moreover, it is conceivable that they do not result in net additions to spending but are substitutes for older and obsolescing forms of luxurious spending — trips to Paris or large retinues of servants, for example.

The new lures to spending, at least in the Latin American countries, seem to take the form, aside from the case of automobiles, of such things as radios, fountain pens, refrigerators, soft drinks, and monumental office buildings and apartment houses — all of them, apparently, suitable products for the early stages of industrialization. Without the home demand for these products, there would be no scope for the development of facilities for their domestic production.

The same lures to spending also operate, of course, in the countries in which these commodities originated. It is not clear to me why they should be more of a depressant of the propensity to save in the poorer than in the richer countries. The point may be that when the richer countries first began to emerge from *their* poverty, these temptations not to save did not yet exist, or perhaps the point is that, if there is to be any saving at all in the countries in which almost everyone is poor, the temptation to spend must be less for persons of a given level of income in the poorer countries than in the richer countries. I could support this by appeal to American statistics, which purport to show that, with the aid of instalment purchasing, there is net dissaving in the United States up to levels of income much higher than the average levels prevailing in many poorer countries. But it may still be true that in the long run the incentives to increase earning capacity which attractive commodities stimulate into being contribute more to economic progress than the incentives to current spending on these commodities subtract from it.

It is becoming increasingly fashionable to invoke the concept of external economies as providing a fresh argument for protection of new industries against foreign competition in underdeveloped, that is to say, poor countries. Alfred Marshall coined the term 'external economies' primarily to signify the cost reductions, technical and pecuniary, which result to the firms comprising a single industry when the industry expands its output through an expansion of the number of firms within it. It has been extended to include the reductions in cost which accrue to a particular industry from the expansion of other industries in the same country or region, and it is these economies — which might be called the economies of complementarity of industries — which are relevant here. They can be used to support a broadened version of the old infant industry argument, as justification for protection to a whole range of new industries where protection to a single one of these industries might be ineffective or uneconomic.

External economies to industry A from the expansion of industry B can be technical, that is, may consist of reductions in A's technical coefficients of production or units of input required to produce a unit of output. Or they may be pecuniary, that is, reductions in the prices industry A has to pay for its input units. Conceivable instances of technical economies to industry A from the expansion of industry B would be: the availability to A, as a result of the proximity of industry B, of services of a kind which could not otherwise be obtained or which A would have otherwise to provide for itself at greater cost or with less efficiency; the elimination or reduction for industry A of transportation costs and the prompter availability with respect to certain input items when they are produced by a near-by industry B; the general inter-industry diffusion of know-how and skills, both at the managerial level and in the rank and file of the labour force, resulting from the proximity to each other of many industries.

Pecuniary economies to industry A from the expansion of industry B are also national or social economies only if they are the result

56

either of internal economies of scale of plant or firm within industry B or of intra-industry external economies within industry B.

These external economies of complementarity of industries are distinct from, but can reinforce, the advantages which Nurkse has suggested as associated with simultaneous or 'balanced' investment in a range of industries, as compared to investment in one industry at a time. According to Nurkse, investment in a single industry may be unprofitable because of the absence of an adequate market for its product, whereas if a number of industries are simultaneously established, each industry by its payroll and other expenditures will help to create a market for the products of the other industries.

All of this seems to me to have unquestionable theoretical validity, but needs careful interpretation for even theoretical purposes, and may call for major qualification if it is presented as having much practical significance.

First, as to the external economies. It is always net, not gross, external economies which are relevant, net external economies being the amount of gross external economies minus the amount of external diseconomies. Examples of pecuniary external diseconomies to industry A from the expansion of industry B would be prices to A, for input items which it purchases elsewhere than from industry B, that are higher as a result of competition between the two industries for a common supply of labour, or power, or transportation services, or other input items. There could also be technical external diseconomies for industry A from the expansion of industry B, as, for example, if internal costs of production in industry A were increased because of air or water pollution, or traffic congestion, or depletion of water supply, as the result of the establishment or expansion of industry B. The pecuniary external diseconomies to industry A resulting from expansion of industry B can, moreover, result, at a second stage, in technical diseconomies to industry A — and to third industries. This can happen when adaptation by A to increased prices of its inputs — these increases constituting the pecuniary diseconomies to A — takes the form of a forced alteration of the proportions in which it uses the various input items and thus brings into play the law of diminishing returns in its variation of the proportions of the factors sense.

Even if the external economies are net economies, for the industries directly involved and for the national economy, this is not sufficient to establish a case for the new industry or industries, since the net economies resulting from this investment have to be compared with the net economies which would result from alternative investments. If it is a question of subsidy or of tariff protection, it

57

should especially be borne in mind that there is no presumption that an investment which would be unprofitable without subsidy or tariff protection to its owner would yield a larger flow of external economies to other industries — or to the community at large — than one which could maintain itself without subsidy or protection.

Other qualifications are applicable to the argument for balanced investment, where the advantage claimed is the mutual provision of a market for the products of the respective industries instead of external economies in the form of reductions in each other's unit costs of production. The argument of an inadequate market for the product of a single new or expanded industry will have no, or less, weight if the investment under consideration : (*a*) is cost-reducing instead of output-expanding ; (*b*) is import-substituting ; (*c*) is for production for export ; or (*d*) is some combination of these. A great deal of the investment in poor countries falls into one or the other of these categories.

It needs further to be pointed out that the economic advantages of spatial proximity between plants are subject also to exaggeration, that foreign trade does not necessarily mean distant trade, and that external economies are not by their nature confined to industries close to each other geographically but can flow across national boundaries.

I apologize for the detailed argument which I have imposed upon you. It seemed to me potentially useful to do so, however, if it served to reduce to reasonable proportions the current enthusiasm for the new arguments for protection of industries yielding external economies and for 'balanced' investment at the cost of profitable investment in the private sense.

THE ECONOMIC STABILITY OF THE POORER COUNTRIES

I have so far had nothing to say about the problem of economic instability for poorer countries. As far as volume of employment is concerned, instability is less of a problem for them than for richer countries, or at least than it used to be for richer countries when the major business cycle still seemed to be a law of nature. The usual explanation of this seems satisfactory to me. The poorer countries, because of their lower *per capita* incomes, have investment cycles of smaller amplitude, and these cycles involve smaller fractions of total national income. The export staples of the poorer countries have greater cyclical flexibility of prices than the major exports of the richer countries, and therefore have smaller cyclical variations in volume and in the employment they afford. In many of the poorer economies, a good deal of subsistence-farming survives, and the urban population still has important family links with the rural population. When depression comes, therefore, there is a reflux of population from the towns to the farms, which act as a safety valve for urban unemployment. In times of depression, the governments of the poorer countries also resort more readily and more freely to exchange depreciation and to the printing-press than do the governments of richer countries, and their national stocks of money are less dependent on the volume of loans made by commercial banks. The poorer countries, therefore, suffer less in depression periods from the conjunction of falling domestic price levels, rigid wage scales and shrinking supplies of loan funds, than do the richer countries. For these reasons, and no doubt for other reasons as well, cyclical unemployment is not a major problem for the poorer countries.

The situation of the poorer countries with respect to the stability of national income, or at least of that part of national income which passes through the market, is not so favourable, however. Receipts from exports play an especially large rôle in the national incomes of the poorer countries, and, because these exports consist primarily of agricultural commodities and raw materials, their prices, at least in terms of hard currencies, have an amplitude of cyclical swing far exceeding that of the prices of their major imports, of freight costs, and of external debt charges. Where the imports consist largely either of luxuries or of machinery and other supplies associated with investment in durable production facilities, the demand for imports has high income elasticity, and the decline in export receipts during depression therefore does not result in severe pressure on their international balances of payments. But in all the poorer countries the decline in real national income during a world depression presses hard on already low levels of consumption and of capital formation.

The wider the range of primary commodities exported by a country, the greater is the probability that the average cyclical fluctuations in their prices in terms of hard currencies will not greatly exceed the average cyclical fluctuations in the prices of primary commodities, in general, in world markets. The less dependent the country is on exports, the more stable also is its real national income likely to be cyclically — although it should be noted that this has not been the experience of the United States. The desire for economic stability has therefore led poorer countries to seek for a widening of the range of their staple export products, and for diversification of their economies by increased domestic production of manufactured commodities largely obtained by import. However, this may not be a wise procedure, for the reduction in cyclical instability thus obtained may be purchasable only at the cost of a substantial reduction in the national real income for the cycle as a whole.

The poorer countries press hard in ECSOC and through diplomatic channels for assumption by the richer countries of major responsibility for the artificial stabilization of the prices of primary commodities, so far with little or no success except with respect to primary commodities such as wheat and sugar, of which the richer countries are also important producers. Such stabilization, judging from the historical record, is difficult to negotiate and to administer, and the extent to which it is beneficial is at least open to debate. When the countries which are exporters of primary commodities ask for the stabilization, on a world market basis, of their prices, they often mean stabilization at or near the cyclical peaks, rather than at the mean prices of the cycle as a whole, or than at the price levels which would stabilize the *ratio* of these prices for the cycle as a whole to the average prices of their import commodities. The problem, moreover, of how to stabilize cyclically the prices of particular commodities without interfering with their long-run trends, may be technically and administratively an insuperable one and, in any case, still awaits a tolerable solution. The experience with wheat stabilization presents a clear-cut illustration of this.

The instability of the prices of primary commodities is largely, though not wholly, the result of the cyclical instability of the richer countries and of their tendency to intensify their import barriers during depression. If the problem of the major business cycle really has been largely solved by the richer countries, then the problem of the instability of the prices of primary products on world markets will not be nearly so serious in the future as it has been in the past. If to general maintenance of economic stability the richer countries were to add stabilization — or still better, reformation in the direction of free trade — of their import policies, I think the poorer countries would have obtained about all that was practicable in the way of international co-operation to stabilize the prices of primary commodities. I once ventured to propose an additional measure in the form of an international investment fund which would operate counter-cyclically. While I still think this in abstract principle has its attractions, I see no practical future for it in a world split by the cold war, and in a world in which the potential major lenders would not be much more than one, and the potential borrowers would be more numerous than one, could easily count.

60

'LORD JUSTICE COMPARATIVE COST'

Sir Dennis, having made an appropriate appeal to the richer countries to follow the dictates of 'Lord Justice Comparative Cost', presumably both in their own national interests and in the interests of the poorer countries, went on to express confidence that I would extend similar advice to the poorer countries as well. I appreciate his trust in me, and I hope I have already in large part justified it, even if I have not so far been brave enough to use the precise term which so many modern economists find so distasteful, without always making quite clear whether it is its triteness or its error which they dislike.

The doctrine of comparative costs, properly phrased and properly interpreted, would seem to me to go little beyond common sense, were it not that men of intelligence and intellectual integrity have for generations fought it tooth and nail. To some, it has unfortunate associations with a 'real cost' theory of value which they do not believe in, and is defective in its implication that either it is 'costs' alone, in whatever sense of the term, that need to be compared when guidance is sought as to appropriate allocation of resources, or that 'costs' are important above all other considerations. But I, for one, am just as content with the term 'comparative advantage' as the label for the doctrine, and would not object strongly to the substitution for both of these terms of the term 'comparative income'. In any case, what need to be compared are the national real benefits to be derived from alternative patterns of economic behaviour ; and *all* the benefits — and worsements — that are involved are relevant to a judicious verdict. When private money costs are not closely representative of social real costs, the doctrine ceases to be a doctrine of allocation of resources according to comparative private money costs. External economies and diseconomies need to be explored and accounted for, and allowance made for monopoly elements in prices and for the effects on relative prices of such things as subsidies and discriminatory taxes. But Ricardo himself not only would have conceded all of this, but insisted repeatedly on some of it. I am not salvaging a doctrine by changing its meaning, but restating it in its original form.

It is today often objected against the traditional doctrine of comparative cost that it is a static doctrine and thus affords poor guidance for a dynamic world. Perhaps so, but I am not at all convinced that when the classical economists stated the doctrine, as they did, in long-run terms, they did not intend to include in their 'long-run' all

61

the dynamic factors which could reasonably be foreseen or provided for in advance. It was always costs as they could be presumed to be in the long run, and not costs as they might prevail fortuitously at the moment, which they regarded as the crucial factors to be measured and compared. Their acceptance in principle of the 'infant industry' argument cannot otherwise be explained. In any case, this is the only kind of doctrine of comparative cost I can support. I may add that it calls unqualifiedly for free trade only in a world in which market prices can be accepted as as close measures of the real long-run social costs of production and social worth of the commodities in issue as are available. When better measures are available, market price should be made to surrender its judicial robe — but not to promiscuous protectionism.

THE POPULATION PROBLEM

I have not yet liquidated my indebtedness to Sir Dennis for sound advice as to what to include in my paper. He commented that if he were dealing with my part of the world, he would have to say a great deal about population. Unfortunately, I do not have time or capacity to say a great deal about population, but I will substitute emphasis for quantity.

First, I want to emphasize that the population 'problem' arises not only from an excessive rate of increase of population, but also, even in the absence of any increase, from an excessive ratio of present population to natural and other resources, and from a high ratio of present population to labour force, or a high ratio of dependants to total population.

Second, confidence in rising prospective levels of income as sufficing to solve the problem of excess population by operating in some unspecified way to reduce birth-rates seems to me unwarranted. If this has worked in the richer countries, it has worked for them, despite the more favourable position from which they started, only at a pace too slow to satisfy the poorer countries of today, and too slow to meet their urgent needs. The first essential ingredient in this recipe, moreover, is to catch the hare, or to attain the rise in *per capita* income of the masses. It took England, as best I can determine, a full two centuries before technological progress brought an unambiguous rise in *per capita* income for the working-classes.

Modern public health activities, moreover, even if welcome on some other humanitarian grounds, can operate in a new way to intensify the population problem. They can, at extraordinarily low costs *per capita*, and therefore without being dependent on prior economic improvement, reduce mortality-rates, while not appreciably reducing, and even while increasing, age-specific fertility rates. The net result may therefore be : an increase in overall population above what it otherwise would have been ; an increase, for a generation or longer, in the ratio of dependants to workers ; and an adult population unimproved in health and vigour.

It is often taken too much for granted that industrialization means urbanization, that urbanization means higher *per capita* income levels, and that both the higher *per capita* income levels and the urbanization *per se* mean lower fertility. On the basis of these assumptions or affirmations, it has recently been argued that population needs to be introduced into the comparative cost doctrine as an additional variable, and that it then becomes, or can be made, evident that investment in industry is preferable to investment in agriculture, even if the latter yields a higher return to the investor. I do not deny the possible validity of this argument, but I will not concede its general or even probable validity until more supporting evidence or argument is supplied.

Aside from the effects on population growth, the most rewarding investment is often in the countryside and in the villages, not only in agriculture proper, but also in such non-agricultural undertakings as hydro-electric plants, cement plants, mining, tile and brick kilns, cotton gins, seed-crushing plants, bridges and roads and railroads. Second, the public health activities which reduce mortality-rates may be concentrated in the cities, partly because the governments of the poor countries often favour the cities in their expenditures, and partly because the *per capita* costs of given public health activities are much lower in the cities than in the countryside. Third, the higher *per capita* money incomes in the cities may be subsidized or parasitic incomes at the expense of the rural population, and may not be higher real incomes after allowance for the higher cost of living. I wonder if the population experts are still so sure that in poor countries the natural rate of increase of population is slower in the cities than in the rural areas, and I venture to suggest that the reasons I have given suffice to remove warrant for such assurance.

Even if it were true that industrialization and urbanization of themselves would eventually check the rate of increase of population, can they be relied upon to do it soon enough ? If the serpent of excess of population will have bitten before the urbanization charm put on it can work its effect, then there is no advantage in the charm (see Ecclesiastes x. 11). 'The house is crazy', Adam Smith reported a weary traveller as saying to himself, 'and it will not stand very long; but it is a chance if it falls tonight, and I will venture, therefore, to sleep in it tonight.' For many of the poorer countries, tonight is already dangerously late, as far as facing up to the population question is concerned.

THE PROMISE OF BETTER THINGS TO COME

My emphasis, so far, has been on the obstacles to economic improvement, and on the need for self-discipline, for temporary sacrifice, for the prudent husbanding of scarce resources, if these obstacles are not to prove decisive. This, I fear, has given my paper an excessively pessimistic and austere tone. Let me, therefore, redress the balance somewhat by devoting the conclusion of my paper to the more cheerful side of the picture.

The poorer countries have today one great advantage which the richer countries did not have when they began to emerge from deep and pervasive poverty, and which the richer countries do not have today despite their prosperity. There is available today to the poorer countries a great stock of scientific and technical knowledge which they have not yet exploited for the purposes of economic progress. The richer countries must in the main rely for further economic improvement, aside from further accumulation of capital, on new scientific and technical discovery, whereas the poorer countries have in large measure still available for borrowing the existing stock of knowledge. This knowledge will not flow to them automatically, and it may not be precisely what they need. Progress in education, immigration of skilled personnel, foreign capital and technical aid, the travelling merchant and the foreign entrepreneur in search of profit, all of these, however, promote the international sharing of knowledge and its adaptation to local needs.

The poorer countries also can reasonably count on some supplement from outside to their own capital formation, even if they must reconcile themselves to the prospect that they will have themselves to finance most of the facilities, the tools and the implements necessary for increased productivity, out of savings from their own meagre earnings.

Some of the poorer countries have favourable prospects of the discovery of new mineral resources, and others still have empty or sparsely settled areas which in time there will be the capital to open up to profitable settlement. The growth in income and in population of the richer countries, and the progressive depletion of their own mineral resources, are operating to make them better markets for the export staples of the poorer countries, and it is conceivable also that more liberal commercial policy on the part of the richer countries will make an important contribution here.

If population increase is checked, the improvements in public health techniques will have their major effect in improving the health and vigour of the population as a whole, and in providing the incentives and the financial resources for making what is for most of them the most productive in the long run of all investments, investment in education for modern production and for good citizenship.

I do not regard this as merely ceremonial balancing of utopian aspirations for the future against wholly grim realities of the present. Some of the poorer countries are today outpacing many of the richer countries in their annual rates of increase of *per capita* income. I have recently visited three underdeveloped countries where, superficially at least, there is all the evidence of economic progress proceeding at a spectacular rate. I am sure that if only they seek and find a solution of their population problem, most of the poorer countries of the world can have good prospects of substantial and sustained improvement in their levels of living, without need of recourse to forced labour, to forced saving, or to subjection to dictatorship, whether personal or collective.

THE DISCUSSION ON
PROFESSOR VINER'S PAPER

Chairman: PROFESSOR IVERSEN (Denmark)

THE first to comment on Professor Viner's paper was *Professor C. N. Vakil* (India). He said: We should congratulate ourselves on having received such a masterly exposition of the problems of the poorer countries from Professor Viner. One may not agree with all that he has said, but I am sure we shall agree that he has rendered signal service by drawing attention to so many problems in so short a space and in a manner which will provoke thought and stimulate discussion.

I shall take up at the point where he left off, namely, the importance of the population problem. There is common agreement that, to the extent to which it is possible to reduce the rate of growth of population, the problem will be eased, and the time when the standard of life of the people in poorer countries can be raised brought nearer. Whereas methods of population control may be tried towards this end, let us accept the fact that this is bound to be a long-drawn-out process, so long that dependence on it may prove economically disastrous. Is it not possible for us to suggest methods by which the rate of economic growth can be made faster than the rate of population growth in poorer countries? Have not the richer countries passed through some such stages in their history? I shall have to refer to a few basic considerations peculiar to underdeveloped countries in order to bring out my point, and I crave your indulgence while I do this.

In the first place, I should like to emphasize the co-existence of modern and primitive organizations in poorer countries. In the former, most of the features of the modern monetary economy as in the West are present; in the latter they are not. The former is the smaller sector; the unorganized sector accounts for the larger portion of the economy. To the extent to which the two can be integrated, the problem of economic development will be eased.

The smaller degree of economic integration between the different sectors in such an economy is a reflection of the low ratio of marketable surplus to output. The level of wage rates is low, and most of the wages of the workers are spent on food grains, cloth and other necessities. These ultimately depend upon the agricultural sector in one way or another. So it is the ratio of the marketable surplus of

66

agricultural commodities to output that determines the extent of non-farm employment. Other things being equal, unless this ratio rises, it is not possible to establish modern forms of economic organization in such countries.

Let us contrast normal economic conditions in an underdeveloped economy with those of a developed economy in a state of depression. There is unemployment in both, but the genesis and the implications of such unemployment are radically different. In an underdeveloped economy, there will be a substantial amount of unemployment, mostly of the disguised type. It is possible to produce the amount of current output with a lesser volume of employment, provided the methods of production are improved. Disguised unemployment is a ubiquitous phenomenon in all sectors of the economy and is very conspicuous in agriculture. The volume of this type of unemployment goes on increasing, the rate of this increase depending on the pace of population growth and the rate of growth of capital stock. Under conditions in which technical change is rapid in the non-agricultural sector, or in certain branches of agriculture itself, unless the rate of capital formation is raised by a sufficient magnitude with a view to reabsorbing the unemployed, the pressure of disguised unemployment will tend to increase. Thus population growth plus technological changes, in the context of a slow rate of accumulation, would tend to lead to the emergence of the phenomenon of continuously rising disguised unemployment.

This term, disguised unemployment, was originally evolved in connection with the description of low-income categories of occupations, under conditions of depression in a developed economy. The phenomenon of disguised unemployment in an underdeveloped economy is different. The disguised unemployment is normally a drag on the system. It tends to reduce the volume of investment below what would have been the case otherwise. The consumption of the unemployable does not enable the level of activity to be higher. On the contrary, it presses it down.

The increased population pressure is absorbed through a reduction in the average unit size of farms and through various other inferior forms of organization. Thus it is through a deterioration in the forms of organization that the additional population pressure is absorbed. The direct effect of such a process is a reduction in the magnitude of the surplus available for investment.

The trouble with the economy is that the total volume of unemployment exceeds the total of employable units. The surplus of wage-goods available is, therefore, less than the amount necessary to provide employment for all the 'disguised unemployed' at the ruling wage rate. This deficiency is the critical wage-goods gap. Unemployment in an underdeveloped economy is, therefore, caused by the existence of this gap. The solution lies in filling it.

The problem of disguised unemployment arises because, under normal conditions, the economy does not step up the rate of investment above that of population growth. At best the two rates are equal; hence the disguised unemployed remain untouched. The central problem of economic growth in India and other underdeveloped countries is the creation of conditions under which the rate of investment can be increased above that of population growth. The disguised unemployed in agriculture and other sectors would thus be productively absorbed in the economy. A substantial proportion of the work force is unproductively engaged in consumption activities. The only difficulty in the way of their transformation into productive workers in investment activities is the prevalence of the wage-goods gap.

If we assume that investment increases at the same rate as population grows, the initiation of the cumulative process becomes a possibility. For any increase in the supply of wage-goods, it is possible to step up employment in investment to a greater extent. Thus, any given increase in the supply of wage-goods made available through forced savings will start an upward cumulative process. This process comes into play as soon as both investment and population are made to keep in step, and additional quantities of wage-goods are made available for investment purposes. The secret of the cumulative process consists in the possibility of a higher rate of transformation of unproductive workers into productive workers. The emphasis has of necessity to be laid upon a quick increase in the output of wage-goods. The strategy in this approach is to bring about a more than proportionate rate of expansion in the wage-goods output as compared to population growth in the immediate stages. If those in charge of economic planning in these countries embarked upon special measures to bring about this change, even at some sacrifice, their problem would soon be on the way to solution.

While this process of development is going on, the existence of attractive foreign commodities leading to luxurious spending by the few is not likely to stimulate economic progress. A reduction in luxury consumption would release labour and wage-goods for employment in investment, and for the expansion of wage-goods output, which is most desirable in such countries.

Similarly, the impact of inflation is most undesirable on developing economies. In the process of attaining a higher rate of growth, they would have a higher degree of monetization, reflecting a rise in the ratio of marketable surplus to agricultural output. Our experience has been that the very process of growth would be hampered if there were a rapid rise in the price level. This is so because it would lead to a reduction in the willingness of the agricultural sector to trade with the non-agricultural sector. The ratio of marketable surplus to output would generally be adversely affected, and the economy would relapse into habits of hoarding or unproductive saving. Besides, the middle classes would be hit most, and in such countries they form the backbone of the development process.

It is often taken for granted in discussions connected with international relations that it is through a speeding up of the process of capital migration that the growth rates in underdeveloped countries can be raised. The world as it is today consists of considerable areas in which the rate of economic growth is slower than would have otherwise been the case, because these areas are short of labour. Underdeveloped countries would welcome even temporary migration of population, as such migration would be twice blessed. The overpopulated, underdeveloped countries would obtain relief inasmuch as their capacity to save and invest would be raised. The countries receiving the population would be benefited inasmuch as their growth-rates would be raised. Migration in such cases has to be looked upon from points of view other than those of charity and sympathy. Even enlightened self-interest will, perhaps, favour such a course. It should be possible for international agencies to take up this problem and make selective experiments, in the interests of the stability and progress of the world as a whole. So, in course of time, the distinction between richer and poorer countries might disappear.

Professor Ragnar Nurkse (U.S.A.) made these comments: We have listened to a fascinating address, full of wisdom as well as brilliance. It covered a vast range of topics; but it was mainly devoted to a critique of 'currently fashionable' theories. Professor Viner thinks that his own positive statement might be criticized as not going beyond 'what an economist . . . could have said fifty or a hundred years ago'. Modern economists, as he sees them, are a restless lot, always looking for something new to amuse them. But has the world not changed in the last hundred years?

I. Excess Population

One big change has been the growth of population. World population has doubled between 1850 and 1950. About two-thirds of the increase has taken place in the poorer countries, chiefly in

Asia, largely through a fall in death-rates. As Viner has put it, the population problem consists not merely in an excessive rate of increase, but actually in a present state of excess population in relation to capital and natural resources.

Now, in the poorer countries, as a rule, the great bulk of the population works in agriculture to start with, for basic and obvious reasons. In such countries, therefore, rapid population growth naturally leads, and in some of them has already led, to excess population on the land, or surplus farm labour. A number of writers, including myself, have called it 'disguised unemployment', but we need not use this label at all. Viner rejects not only the label, but the idea itself. He has not dealt with it here at any great length, but the subject is so important that I feel bound to poke a little into this hornets' nest. The idea whose irreparable ruin Viner predicts earlier in his paper emerges triumphant at the end: the idea of excess population. In my view the two ideas are substantially the same.[1]

Consider for a moment the effects of excessive population growth in a peasant community. Numbers are increasing while land, capital and techniques remain unchanged. Alternative employment opportunities may be lacking because of the rigid social structure, and may, in fact, be decreasing because of the decline of traditional handicrafts. With the growing pressure of people on the land, farms become smaller and smaller. Moreover, they are divided and sub-divided into tiny strips and plots. This increasing fragmentation absorbs labour-time merely because of the need to move from the homestead to the scattered plots and from one plot to another. It is wasteful not only of labour but also of land, because of the paths and boundary strips which can take up as much as one-fifth of the surface. This is far from being the whole story, but at least to some extent fragmentation is a direct outcome and reflection of excess population on the land. The labour surplus 'concealed' in this way in subsistence farming cannot be withdrawn without bad effects on output, unless the fragmentation is reversed and the holdings are consolidated. Over a certain range, the marginal productivity of labour may conceivably be zero even without any such reorganization. It may be zero over a much wider range if the remaining factors are appropriately reorganized, which means, for one thing, consolidation of plots.

There are a number of empirical studies that tend to confirm

[1] Note added after delivery, relating to last two sentences: 'This was a regrettably loose and rhetorical statement. What I had in mind was the proposition, developed later in this comment, that "disguised unemployment", in the sense of zero marginal productivity of labour, is a special case of "excess population".'

this picture. Of course, the evidence may not be altogether satisfactory. But I doubt whether any evidence can be wholly satisfactory in a matter such as this, where some things — including the weather — must be held constant and others subjected to an 'appropriate reorganization', which may require a revolutionary change in rural life, bringing inevitably other changes with it. Besides, I agree with Viner when, in another connection, he refuses to accept statistical measurability as a crucial test of the usefulness of concepts for economics. Conceptually, excess population can surely be so great in relation to land and capital that the marginal productivity of labour is reduced to zero.

There are two reasons why this idea may be difficult to accept. First, anyone trained in Western economics would have to ask: who would employ these people if their product is zero? Or else one might ask: how can these marginal people live? What do they eat, if they really produce nothing?

The answer to the first question is that in many countries the wage-labour system, which we are apt to take for granted, hardly exists. The prevailing condition in subsistence farming is one of peasant family labour.

The answer to the second question — how can they live? — is that they live by sharing more or less equally in the total product of the farm, which includes the product of intra-marginal labour, and of any land and capital goods the peasants may own. The product from these factors goes into the same pot and the members of the household eat out of the same pot. These institutional arrangements are foreign to the economics of business enterprise, and so the conditions which they make possible appear paradoxical.

If we consider this sharing of food a little further we can see the ultimate limit to the multiplication of people on the farms. If the average total product per person falls below the physical level of subsistence, we reach the Malthusian state of starvation cutting down numbers, or at least checking their further increase. At the point where this average product equals the physical subsistence level, the marginal product of labour may well be zero or even negative. (Professor Meade has shown this very clearly in his *Trade and Welfare*, Chapter 6 and Appendix 1.) Still, it need not be as low as zero. Conversely, if and when labour's marginal product is zero, the average product need not be as low as the physical subsistence level; it may be a little above that level. In any case, let us remember that a state of excess population *implies* that the marginal product is less than the average. And if the average product is as low as we know it to be, is it so far-fetched to suppose that in some cases the marginal product of labour may be zero ? The upshot of the argument does not, of course, depend on its being *exactly* zero, although this is a convenient, and, I think, not unrealistic case on which to concentrate. However, the question might still be asked : why this obsession with the margin ? Why not stress the obvious fact of a low *general* level of productivity ? The answer is that the marginal approach is useful here precisely because of the need to *take away* some labour from current production for work in capital construction.

The low general level of productivity has many causes, some of them cultural, on which economists do not have much to say. But there is one cause on which economists in the classical tradition do have a lot to say, and that is the shortage of capital. Spare time is the basic source of capital accumulation. In overcrowded peasant communities spare time already exists in the form of surplus labour. The transfer of this labour from current to capital work need not involve an intolerable sacrifice of already low living standards. In such communities, as Professor Ellis has said, 'a large amount of "saving" is being done to support the surplus labour. The State, by appropriating this saving, can command vast amounts of potential capital.'[1] No one, least of all Professor Ellis, under-estimates the practical difficulties of realizing this potential. It could be done by everybody on the land devoting part of his time to capital work. But division of labour is the more effective principle, here as elsewhere. It means that the community's spare time is segregated into a separate labour force devoted entirely to capital work.

Let me turn back to the general population problem. Professor Viner distinguished between two things : an excessive rate of population increase over time and a state of excess population at a point of time, in relation to existing natural and other resources. 'Slow down the rate of increase' is the advice given by those concerned with the first aspect of the problem. The advice is sound in the light of past experience and present population structure. But what of the state of excess population that has actually been reached in some of the poorer countries as a result of the population explosion of the past hundred years ? This would exist even if there were no further increase. A remedy here would require not merely checking the rate of increase, but actually *reducing* the number of people. You can tell them, for instance, to stop having children altogether for ten years or so. But it would be a rather academic suggestion to make.

A solution must be sought elsewhere. Population is excessive in relation to capital and natural resources. If you cannot reduce population, you can still reduce its excessiveness by increasing the

[1] *Indian Economic Journal*, Jan. 1956.

stock of these other factors of production. Even land can be created through river dams and irrigation. Yet, in general, nothing much can be done about natural resources except, as Viner very rightly says, that the amount of useful natural resources is never a fixed quantity but always a function of people's knowledge and know-how. But something can be done about capital. Excess labour can be put to work producing additional real capital. This is the one practicable way of relieving the problem of excess population.

Some writers argue very simply that since the problem is *agricultural* overpopulation, the cure is to transfer labour from agriculture to industry. Although I agree that industrialization is a normal consequence of development, this view is, in my opinion, superficial. The effect of overpopulation is low productivity, for which capital formation, not industrialization as such, is the basic economic remedy. In what particular fields the capital is applied depends on domestic income elasticities and foreign trade opportunities. Often it is the category of public overhead facilities, such as transport and electric power, that claims the biggest share in a poor country's investment programme. Often it is here also that surplus farm labour can best be used.

Not all the poorer countries suffer from the trouble of excess population. Some suffer from it not at all, others only in a mild degree. The trouble is acute in a group of countries to be found mostly in the area from South-East Europe to South-East Asia.

Apart from this geographical limitation, the excess-population model is subject to all the other limitations of any simplified outline. I may be quite wrong, but I cannot see why it should be an unreasonable or unrealistic outline. To some of us it is probably a tedious platitude rather than a paradox.

II. DEMONSTRATION EFFECTS

Let us move on briefly to another point : the 'demonstration effect'. This, as Duesenberry formulated and I applied it, concerns the choice between consumption and saving out of a given income. Professor Viner is right in pointing out that this is not all ; there may be effects on income. Aside from that, his main query is why the attraction of advanced living standards should depress the propensity to save in the poor more than in the rich countries. I should like to remind him that the original purpose of the Duesenberry theory was precisely to explain why 75 per cent of American families save nothing, and why all the personal saving in the United States comes from the 25 per cent in the higher income groups. It is quite possible that the consumption pattern of these top 25 per cent stirs up the desire to spend among the people with lower incomes in America even more than among people with comparable incomes in other countries. This is perfectly consistent with the original theory. Americans are even more exposed to temptations to spend. But for America this handicap, if it is one, is more than offset by the advantage of having within its borders the top 25 per cent who do save a great deal. Similarly, as Viner suggests, when the richer countries first began to develop, it was an advantage for them to have no superior consumption patterns to imitate. It is the same point; saving comes more easily to people who have above them no Joneses to keep up with.

In some of the poorer countries the behaviour of the local entrepreneurial classes especially is influenced by the demonstration effect, which leads them to spend their profits rather than save them. Where this is the case, inflation as a means of development finance becomes ineffective. As an instrument of forced saving, inflation is supposed to work, and has often worked in richer countries, by shifting the distribution of income from people with a low to people with a high propensity to save. Viner did not even mention this point in favour of inflation, and perhaps he was right to leave it out, because in most of his countries it does not always work. A shift to profits does not increase total saving where the profits go at once into luxury spending rather than business saving.

Against this gloomy aspect, Viner stressed the favourable effect which attractive novelties can have in creating an incentive to work harder and produce more. This is another demonstration effect; it concerns the choice between leisure and work. It is undoubtedly a useful reaction in some circumstances, for instance, when natives in Africa, where labour is scarce, are drawn into the money economy. But does it make the American work longer or even harder? He seems to prefer a shorter working week. And in the rest of the world today the imitation of American living standards may partly take the form of increased demands for leisure. Demonstration effect No. 1 may block demonstration effect No. 2.

Moreover, one can raise the fundamental question whether increased production through longer working hours, even if achieved, could be counted as progress at all. It can be argued that true economic progress means greater efficiency of labour, not a greater quantity of inefficient labour. We want a higher output per man hour rather than more hours worked. To the extent that output per man hour depends on capital, it still seems to me possible that demonstration effect No. 1 makes progress harder in the poorer countries.

There is a demonstration effect in a broader sense that is worth considering. Comparison of material welfare is meaningless when tastes are altogether different. Today tastes are becoming more uniform, the desired patterns of consumption more similar. Such statistical measures as we have indicate a growing gap in real income between the richer and the poorer countries. Because of the increasing similarity of tastes and desires, this gap is acquiring a more real psychic significance. The question which Viner stated at the outset, 'why some countries are much poorer than others', must be answered in part, because they now accept the same standards of economic welfare. They therefore *feel* poorer than others, and that is what matters.

The distinction between richer and poorer countries, so prominent on the programme of this Conference, reflects a state of affairs that hardly existed a hundred years ago. At that time the familiar distinction was between the old countries, in Europe, and the new countries, in temperate latitudes overseas, not poor by contemporary standards, not backward, but growing rapidly with the aid of migration and capital from Europe. And then there were the exotic countries, in Asia and elsewhere, but these were countries to which Western economics did not apply; countries which felt indifferent or even antagonistic to Western material standards. Since then, these standards have conquered the world. All this may make the poorer countries more ready to suffer disturbances in their established ways of life for the sake of economic development. But it can also lead to disturbances harmful to their progress.

III. EXTERNAL PROSPECTS

Speaking of the promise of better things to come, Professor Viner held out a prospect of better markets for export staples. He rejected the view that the terms of trade of the poorer countries have persistently deteriorated. I wonder whether his criticism of statistical efforts in this field covers also Kindleberger's recent study. Kindleberger is not specially concerned with the poor countries, but he has calculated Europe's terms of trade separately for various parts of the world, including in particular two groups of countries overseas: the areas of recent settlement (not including the United States) and the poorer countries (*i.e.* the 'rest of the world' in his grouping). Viner's point about quality changes applies to both cases; the new countries and the poor countries alike are exporters of primary products. With the new countries, Europe's terms of trade have remained about the same. With the poorer countries, however, Europe's terms of trade show a significant improvement since 1870. The contrast is even greater in the factoral terms of trade, for which Kindleberger has also given some numerical indications. The poorer countries' terms of trade, at least in their transactions with industrial Europe, have definitely got worse.

Other recent studies show that world demand for the poorer countries' export products has tended to rise much less than in proportion to the richer countries' incomes and production. It is chiefly among the richer countries that international trade has been expanding in the recent past. The richer countries themselves are efficient primary producers, especially of food. Their demand for exotic raw materials, like crude rubber, silk, nitrates, jute and vege-table oils, has been affected, and will certainly continue to be affected, by the growth of the chemical industry in the twentieth century. I believe this to be one explanation of Kindleberger's findings. Only for minerals is the prospect favourable.

Therefore, it seems that the poorer countries, even if they are only to keep pace with the richer (to say nothing of catching up) must expand production for their own internal markets. On the question of what lines to push in home production Viner has, among other good things, a nod of qualified approval in the direction of 'balanced growth' and a restatement of the comparative cost doctrine in dynamic terms. To the student of international trade theory this restatement will have been the most sensational part of the whole paper. He told us that the classics intended the doctrine to be a long-run one, 'including all the dynamic factors that could be foreseen or provided for in advance', and that this was the only kind of doctrine that he himself supported. In this form, it seems to me, the doctrine ceases to be a matter of market mechanism, ceases to have any claim to explain the existing trade pattern, and becomes in effect a principle of economic planning. But the real trouble is that it still does not give us any very useful tools with which to foresee or provide for the dynamic factors to which Viner refers. I hope I am wrong, but my feeling is that until we have developed a more adequate view of economic growth, comparative advantage as a planning principle will remain a rather empty formula.

Finally, there is the question : where is the capital to come from, for the structural changes which the poorer countries want to bring about in their domestic economies ? Viner assures them that they can count on 'some supplement from the outside to their own capital formation', but stresses in the same sentence the major need for domestic saving. This emphasis is surely right. We can probably all agree that the poorer countries cannot count on receiving private foreign capital in anything like the same proportions as the new countries did in the nineteenth century. For one thing, the international trading position of the poor countries today is hardly comparable with that of the new countries which received most of the capital flow in the nineteenth century and, in return, supplied the great mass of food and fibres for which there was such a strong demand from the rising industrial nations. Quite apart from other difficulties, the commercial incentives for a large-scale movement of private capital to the poor countries today are probably non-existent. If this is so, a part of the external supplement may have to come, year in, year out, through governmental channels. But the long-term outlook for unilateral income transfers from rich to poor countries is not bright. We need not exclude the possibility of a continuance of such experiments as are now going on, not only under national — chiefly American — auspices, but also in the form of international technical assistance programmes. The arguments against them are often reminiscent of the objections levied against the growth of highly progressive taxation in the first half of the twentieth century in the United States and other rich countries. A very simple but crucial difference between internal and international transfer payments is that the poorer countries do not command any votes in the United States. So long as this is the case, such transfers will probably remain only a small and precarious source of financing economic development.

What I have said has served to supplement rather than contradict Professor Viner's distinguished paper. The upshot is that large-scale foreign aid had better not be relied upon ; countries should use their own resources to the utmost. This conclusion again is a platitude, and it leads back to my first point about the use of excess population, if and where it exists. Domestic effort is the first prerequisite. Without it even the most lavish outside aid could not ensure progress.

Professor Viner opened the general discussion by offering his thanks for the forbearance of his critics. He was now sure that it had been a mistake to mention disguised unemployment in his lecture. Past correspondence had shown that it was hard to find two users of the term who agreed on its meaning, or any user of the term who adhered to his own definition. He had not said disguised unemployment was inconceivable. He said that speculatively it was quite conceivable, because economists were very good at thinking of conceivable things which were highly unlikely to be significant.

Professor Nurkse had accused him of starting with no excess

population and ending up with emphasis on it. Yet economists had been discussing excess population for very many years before they had discovered the concept of disguised unemployment. Excess population seemed capable of a perfectly simple definition, namely, that one had more population than was consistent with maximum attainable *per capita* income. There was no need to marry this simple idea to a term that was completely far-fetched, and in any case it was not he who had been guilty of it. The only concept of disguised unemployment that he referred to — and it was Professor Nurkse's concept as well as that of many other economists — was that which defined itself as the phenomenon of zero (or less) marginal productivity of employed labour. Professor Nurkse had said that the marginal productivity of labour in backward areas could be zero. He himself had agreed that this could conceivably be the case. The question was rather whether zero marginal productivity went far to explain the failure of the hopes and aspirations of backward peoples.

Professor Viner said he would give an illustration of disguised unemployment as usually defined. People were often claimed to be non-productive, though these people were nevertheless not unemployed. He had been told, for example, that in India there were very rigid institutional patterns of tasks to be done. If the family was small, these tasks were done by a few people ; if the family was large, they were done by many. Yet the aggregate total of tasks remained the same in both cases, except in very unusual circumstances like times of flood. So some of the people performing these tasks were not really needed. If this kind of thing really was important in India, then he would yield.

Professor Nurkse had, of course, said that there was empirical evidence of the widespread existence of disguised unemployment ; he himself would like to see this. During the war the American army in Trinidad had taken labour off the land. As a consequence, agricultural output fell. Again, Theodore Schultz had recently been seeking evidence showing the existence of disguised unemployment in Latin America. So far he had not found any case where agricultural output would rise, or even remain constant, if labour were taken away from the land. The concept of disguised unemployment was new and bright, and attractive to economists because of its paradoxical note. But a paradox, he contended, was merely a surprising statement, not necessarily the statement of a fallacy.

When Professor Vakil had spoken of disguised unemployment, he had brought in, as a change in data, a radical improvement in methods of production. In other words, he was working with two independent variables, not one. The action of one of these variables was diminishing productivity; the other was increasing it. This was not the concept of disguised unemployment as it was usually defined. Professor Viner wished it could be shown that Professor Vakil was wrong when he said that the population problem in India was so intractable. Immediately after his reading of his own paper, it had been suggested to him that he had not sufficiently stressed the problem of population. In fact, he did feel that the problem looked very serious, and unless one could find new resources, it was unlikely that the backward countries could win out if they did not get population under control.

On the Duesenberry effect, he was still puzzled. In the poorer of the poor countries, it seemed, everyone was too poor to save; in the richer poor ones, it appeared, everybody spent their money copying America and had nothing left for saving. Consequently, none of the poor countries was able to save at all. In fact, the percentage of income saved in these poor countries was generally higher than for comparable income classes in the developed countries, and in some of them very substantially higher.

Professor Baudin (France) thought it was unwise to define poverty as a relation between resources and population, for this seemed to dehumanize the problem. Important aspects would be excluded if objective criteria alone were considered. The essence of the matter, he felt, was subjective. Anyone might be regarded as being poor whose desires grew faster than his means for satisfying them. He wished to stress the extent to which the craving for riches had been over-estimated in some parts of the world. There were peoples who were not concerned with raising their standard of living. They realized that, in order to do so, they would have to work, to save, or possibly to mortgage their national independence by accepting foreign aid.

Professor Baudin wondered whether the so-called demonstration effect, which, in fact, was identical with imitation, deserved any prominence, since it was neither universal nor continuous. It did not occur everywhere, and even where it did occur, it only did so beyond a certain 'psychological threshold' which was hard to determine. The spectacle provided by the rich peoples was certainly not always of such a nature as to incite other peoples to follow their example. He also felt that Western scholars were far too apt to conceive of other nations as created in their own image. The underlying differences were frequently neglected, and there was a tendency to rush to the aid of certain countries before any appeal for help had been sent out, in order to help them to adopt given standards towards which they were completely indifferent. It was essential

79

for economic analysis to adopt a relative point of view and to take account of national psychology.

Professor Qureshi (Pakistan) said that most of the poorer countries which were in the process of economic development had no well-developed local facilities for making capital equipment, so that it was mostly imported. Such imports used up foreign exchange over and above what was needed to pay for consumer goods and other ordinary imports. This brought the poor countries face to face with balance-of-payments problems. Their exports consisted mainly of primary products, often agricultural produce subject to weather conditions, so that dependence on the weather was a factor making for instability in export earnings. This was unavoidable, but superimposed on it were acts of men, the acts of richer countries.

As was well known, the world demand for primary products was subject to very wide fluctuations, and this led to big fluctuations in the export earnings of poorer countries. These variations could be as big as 50 per cent from one year to another, as figures for the export earnings of, say, the countries of the ECAFE region during the last few decades showed.

Such wide fluctuations in export earnings exposed the development programmes of the poorer countries to big jolts, and prevented them from maintaining a stable rate of growth. Many countries in Asia and the Far East, like Burma, Thailand, Ceylon, Malaya and Pakistan, depended upon a limited number of exports, such as rice, timber, tea, coconuts, rubber, tin, cotton and jute. In addition to the widely fluctuating world demand for these exports, technological developments were adversely affecting the economies of such countries. For example, the production of synthetic rubber was a potential threat to some of them, as were technical developments leading to the more economical use of tin. Developments in bulk handling and in the production of substitutes for jute gave rise to a similar threat. So, if these poorer countries tried to diversify their economies and reduce their dependence on uncertain export markets, 'Lord Justice Comparative Cost' had no reason to be angry. These countries simply had to produce import substitutes, even if this meant a loss of efficiency in terms of the international division of labour. It was essential for their stability and the stability of their rate of growth. The richer countries could help by stabilizing their demand for primary products and by not pushing technological changes so far as to make them completely independent of some important exports of the poorer countries.

The shortage of foreign exchange imposed other limitations on the poorer countries. Whether Cadillacs and other luxury goods were desirable or undesirable as incentives for increased production was beside the point. The poorer countries just could not afford them. One more Cadillac meant so much less foreign exchange for importing capital goods.

One of the favourable factors referred to by Professor Viner had been that the poorer countries could draw upon the enormous heritage of technical knowledge which the richer countries had acquired in the course of their development. This was certainly a great advantage. But its adaptation and reorientation might well present difficult problems. In particular, most of these techniques were labour-saving and capital-intensive. The poorer countries, with their enormous pressure of population, probably required a different approach. They wanted techniques which were labour-intensive and capital-saving. This required research. One wanted to discover how production would have been carried out in richer countries in the early stages of their development if they had been faced not with a shortage of labour but with abundant labour and a shortage of capital. The techniques which the poorer countries required could not be obtained, so to speak, off the shelf.

There was also, said Professor Qureshi, a large non-monetary sector in the poorer countries, where a subsistence economy prevailed. Its monetization was highly desirable, for the commercialization of this sector would certainly result in increased production. However, till such monetization took place, an attempt should be made to mobilize the savings of this sector for capital formation. This sector usually had a good deal of leisure, having a large number of people who were at least underemployed, if not unemployed. Such an underemployed labour force might be mobilized for capital formation — for the construction of facilities for the local communities. Such community development programmes held out a great prospect for capital formation and progress without the generation of inflationary pressures.

Professor Rubinstein (U.S.S.R.) said that one of the major problems of the modern world was that of stimulating economic development in the underdeveloped countries, and eliminating as quickly as possible the gulf which separated them, economically, from the small number of developed industrial nations.

According to a study by the United Nations,[1] underdeveloped countries now accounted for some two-thirds of the population of the globe. Yet their relative importance in world industrial production was quite insignificant. For instance, they produced only 4 per

---

[1] *Processes and Problems of Industrialisation in Underdeveloped Countries* (New York, 1955).

cent of the world's steel, and only 6 per cent of its electrical power. Economic advance and social progress in the underdeveloped countries required first, and as rapidly as possible, the complete elimination of colonialism in all shapes and forms. Although several Eastern countries had now achieved political freedom and entered on the path of independent development, colonialism still existed, mostly in the economic sphere. It still hampered economic growth and hindered the progressive development of peoples in a number of the underdeveloped countries of Asia, Africa and Latin America.

Professor Rubinstein said he could not agree on this point with Professor Viner, who had discarded colonialism, at least on paper. He himself agreed more with Mr. Sukarno, the President of the Republic of Indonesia, speaking in Washington, D.C., in May 1956, when he said, 'They tell us that colonialism is dead and that we are whipping a dead horse. Our answer to that is simple. Go to Asia and take a look at everything yourselves. Go to Africa and take a look at everything yourselves. Colonialism, even in its classical form, will not die as long as there is one country that is not free, as long as in any territory the ideals of the United Nations Charter are not applied. There is no such thing as beneficent colonialism, just as there is no such thing as beneficent disease.'

In the economic sphere, went on Professor Rubinstein, colonialism manifested itself first of all in a systematic opposition, by influential circles in certain industrial countries, to the development of indigenous industries in underdeveloped countries. Typical of this attitude was the report of an American Congressional Committee headed by Herbert Hoover, presented to the U.S. Congress in June 1955. Among the Committee's recommendations was one which said that 'in the "Asian-African arc", with the possible exception of Japan, no large industrial plants be constructed, except for production of strategic materials; otherwise all industrial aid be confined to small industries'.[1] These recommendations had received full ideological elaboration in American economic literature.[2]

It was self-evident that views like these were fundamentally opposed to the aspirations of underdeveloped countries and the desire to foster the rapid development of their economies and attain higher living standards for the broad masses of their peoples. The governments of India, Burma, Indonesia, Egypt and a number of other underdeveloped countries, which possessed sufficient resources in the form of raw materials and labour, had made clear their determination to plan their economic development and to industrialize as

[1] *U.S. News and World Report*, 10th June 1955, p. 108.
[2] Cf., for example, the well-known book *Economics of American Foreign Policy*.

rapidly as possible, while at the same time raising the production of agriculture, transport and other branches of their economies. So the world was changing, and not only in the growth of population, as Professor Viner had said. It was changing in many other respects, and Professor Rubinstein believed that economic thinking which did not want to see these changes was doomed. For the proof of the pudding was in the eating, and the truth of economic theory lay in economic practice.

Professor Rubinstein then outlined the position of the Soviet Union so far as economic collaboration with underdeveloped countries was concerned. In 1917, at the time of its birth, the Soviet Union had been a very backward agrarian country, with an industry that was both insufficiently developed and dependent on foreign capital. Now the U.S.S.R. occupied the second place in the world in industrial production. The Soviet Union knew from its own experience what a decisive rôle was played by industry, and particularly by industries making capital goods, in securing the independence of a country and in achieving growth in all the lines of economic development. The Soviet Union had also largely removed the great differences in living standards between the industrial and the underdeveloped districts within that country. Hence, the Soviet Union felt great sympathy with the efforts of the peoples in underdeveloped countries to achieve the all-round development of their national economies and particularly to create their own industry — the strong foundation for national independence.

On the basis of the high level of industrial, scientific and technical development now achieved, the Soviet Union had already begun to give assistance in the general economic development and the industrialization of such countries, by supplying equipment — including that for large enterprises — by drawing up plans, by handing on scientific and technical information — including that obtained in the use of atomic energy for peaceful purposes — as well as information about economic planning, and by training specialists. Soviet help was now playing an important rôle in the process of industrializing China, a process that was of world-wide significance. The Soviet Union was also helping the economic development of Burma, Afghanistan, Egypt and several other underdeveloped countries.

For the Soviet Union regarded the broadening and strengthening of trade relations on a basis of equality and mutual advantage, without any military and political conditions attached, as a most important means of aiding the economic advance in underdeveloped countries. The best form of aid to underdeveloped countries was 'aid through trade'.

Nor was the spreading economic collaboration between the U.S.S.R. and the underdeveloped countries confined to the expansion of trade only. Other forms of collaboration were constantly growing in importance, for example, technical help in building factories, in training specialists, in studying and developing natural resources, in organizing scientific research work and so on. It would be difficult to over-estimate the importance of these first steps in giving planned help in the industrialization of underdeveloped countries. They represented new methods of peaceful economic competition between two systems. Professor Rubinstein felt that the United Nations and all its specialized organizations, as well as the economists of all countries, should co-operate in every way with the mighty and irresistible urge of the peoples of underdeveloped countries for economic development. This would be beneficial not only for them but for the whole world economy.

Dr. Nasr (Egypt) thanked Professor Viner for having paid so much attention to the problems of the poorer countries. He wished to say, first, that he was sceptical about the rôle which Professor Viner seemed to assign to the small 'islands' of wealth in an ocean of poverty. In a poor country, these 'islands' belonged mainly either to the business class or to the land-owning class. In both cases, the savings of those concerned tended to find such unproductive outlets as buying up stocks, or land, and the building of houses. They might even be deposited abroad. So one could only direct these savings into more productive channels by making life difficult for their owners. This, incidentally, was one of the objectives of Egypt's agrarian reform.

It was a pleasant experience to hear Professor Viner explode the somewhat pretentious theory which tried to apply the demonstration effect to the poorer countries. According to that view, these countries were poor because they tried to ape the Western world. The theory implied that millions of poor, undernourished and badly dressed people spent their time buying radios, refrigerators and washing machines, or having holidays in Paris !

Dr. Nasr also wondered whether the version which the speaker gave of the theory of comparative costs had not demolished that theory. Professor Viner's 'common-sense version' left everyone somewhat embarrassed, and Dr. Nasr hoped that Professor Viner would one day explain what he meant by 'real social costs'. Would he also take into account the two types of instance where this theory was suspect in the eyes of the poorer countries, namely, when one was considering the problems of primary products and of long-term economic development ? Dr. Nasr asked to be allowed to express his doubts on the value of the 'Malthusian myth'. Excess population seemed to him to be meaningful only in relation to a given volume of employment, or a given economic structure. Increase this volume, change this structure and the excess would be absorbed — population pressure would disappear. Again, Dr. Singer had shown admirably that one must not mix up an analytical explanation of poverty (whether right or wrong) with the problem of development policy. Excess population was not necessarily an obstacle to development, even if it provided the explanation for poverty. Similarly, the idea that the best form of long-term investment was technical and civic education seemed rather unrealistic. Unemployment among intellectuals and underemployment of skilled technicians was characteristic in poor countries.

Finally, Dr. Nasr would have liked to hear Professor Viner discuss the number of years (Professor Lewis could say whether it was 100 or 150) necessary for a poor country to double its meagre *per capita* income. This would convince economists in the rich countries that the problems of the poor countries were perhaps, after all, also those of their better-off neighbour, whoever he might be.

Dr. Browne (U.S.A.) thought that one of the many important contributions in Professor Viner's paper was his emphasis on the 'quality' aspect of 'resources' (p. 44). In discussing the poorer countries' problems, it was most important to underline the fundamental changes in the value of resources brought about by the use of new sources of energy and by the development of new methods for using conventional sources of energy. Economists had unfortunately left much of this kind of discussion to engineers.

Even in the United States, where coal deposits could last for centuries, and where future petroleum production was expected to exceed all present projections, the use of nuclear fuels would be essential if, despite the pace of population growth, the living standard of 1975 were to be as high or higher than the living standard of 1950. For the poor countries, however, the better use of existing energy resources and the tapping of new ones was crucial. And even in many of the richer countries, costs of producing and transporting conventional fuels had risen so sharply that their living standards were endangered unless they used new sources of energy.

Most of the countries now called poor were those where energy resources were scarce or badly located. Especially in parts of Asia and Africa, but also in many Latin American countries, the development of hydro-electricity would foster new industries. A much more radical change in standards of living had to be expected when the complex problems of using nuclear energy for peace-time purposes were solved — which might happen within the next ten or twenty years, even for the poorer countries.

Miss Browne was in complete agreement with Professor Viner that once there was a substantial increase in average incomes in the poorer countries, there would be less reason to worry about their low propensity to save.

Professor Barkay (Israel) said that he wished to add to Professor Viner's paper. First, there was the question of the length of time which would need to elapse, in any poor country, before *per capita* income rose above the subsistence level. In recent years, poor countries had begun to feel that they should no longer tolerate sickness, hunger and disease, and we therefore faced a revolution against secular apathy. Some of the reasons were the fact that the war had increased the rate of economic development, and that technical change was now rapid. The desire to change the existing international distribution of incomes was clearly gaining in momentum and velocity. The poor countries did not want to wait for ever for a marked improvement in their relative position. Lord Justice Comparative Cost might well be right; but the poor countries would not wait long enough to discover.

Second, Professor Barkay discussed the rôle of the public sector. It was obvious that no government of a backward country could remain neutral; the public sector was the driving force of the economy. As a result the percentage of development expenditure financed by the government was out of all proportion to that in richer countries. In Israel, for example, the government financed some 75 per cent of all development. Much was spent on health and education as well as on transfer payments. Much also went on roads and harbours. Once this initial government expenditure had been undertaken, private outlay could follow, but at present, the public sector was developing the economy.

Professor Gudin (Brazil) said that he agreed with almost everything Professor Viner had said, so he would content himself with variations on the same theme. He shared Professor Viner's views on disguised unemployment; he, too, could not understand what the term meant. Except when land was scarce, why should such a thing exist? There was low productivity, it was true, but that was something quite different. For example, agricultural productivity was very low in most parts of Brazil; but if five men were hoeing in a field and one was taken away, output fell 20 per cent. It was low productivity which was the great problem.

The root of Manoilesco's theory, in that connection, was that if one transferred a man from agriculture to industry, output rose. But what the theory ought really to say was that if one took away from agriculture a man with a hoe, and put him in a factory with 10 kilowatts of power and $1,000 of capital behind him, national output rose. One might as well say that if one took a man from a local industry like hand-loom weaving, and put him on to the land working with modern tractors, knowledge and fertilizers, national output would rise too.

Professor Gudin also agreed with Professor Viner that there was no theoretical reason why the terms of trade should always turn to the disadvantage of the primary producers. The trouble with primary-producing countries was of a different kind. Business cycles, for example, were not generated by them, but by the actions of developed countries. The underdeveloped countries were not strong enough to create cycles. During depressions, it was Sir Dennis's countries which suffered from unemployment, while the primary-producing countries suffered from low prices. Industry could reduce output, but, for well-known reasons, agriculture could not; hence prices fell. Inelasticity of demand, Engel's Law, and inelasticity of supply were responsible for this price fall. The price of Brazilian coffee (with the volume of exports exactly the same) had fallen from 23 cents per pound in 1929 to 7 cents in 1931.

This kind of experience led the poorer country to seek structural and economic changes to get away from inelastic demands and supplies. Hence the schemes for buffer stocks and commodity agreements which, at Bretton Woods, both Keynes and White had recommended and considered essential in any attempt to redress the failings of the world economy.

Professor Gudin said he was interested in Professor Viner's remarks (p. 60) on the misbehaviour of Sir Dennis's part of the world so far as foreign aid was concerned. He himself had said at Istanbul in 1955 that the World Bank needed less banking and more statesmanship. The Bank demanded from underdeveloped countries standards of behaviour that were not easily found even in the well-developed countries. There had been a great change in the financing of underdeveloped countries since the days when Britain was the world's creditor. Before 1914, Britain often lent 50 per cent of her savings abroad — something like $1\frac{1}{2}$ per cent of her national income. Now, the U.S.A. was receiving and absorbing interest and amortization payments much in excess of the amount of new loans. The U.S.A. was much better at giving than at lending. Furthermore, when Britain was the lender, the money was provided both for foreign goods and for local expenditure, because poor countries had not enough savings. Under present conditions, only the resources for buying imported equipment were provided.

Professor Lipinski (Poland) said that Poland had been a member of the IEA for only a few days. With Jugoslavia, there were now two representatives of the socialist economies, but he hoped the list would grow, as the presence of Russian economists suggested it might. The absence of sufficient representatives from these countries probably explained the lack of discussion of socialist economies in past meetings of this Association — and indeed in the papers of Professors Robertson and Viner. Yet socialist economies experienced some particular problems that were of great interest to economists in any country, and he himself hoped that these problems would soon find their place in the discussions of the IEA, so aiding the development of economic science. This development was of great interest to economists of the socialist group, because, whilst some of these countries were richer than others, they had the common characteristic of being centrally planned.

In Poland, stability was not a problem in the planned economy; nor did unemployment exist in the usual sense. Yet the Polish economy did have its own problems of growth and progress. It was possible largely to determine the rate of growth, through control over the volume of investment, but there were certain economic and political factors which had to be respected in deciding on the optimum rate of growth.

Professor Lipinski said that economic progress was now inseparable from political change. Planning was recognized as the only way to end backwardness and poverty in individual countries and whole continents. Here was a great opportunity for peaceful coexistence. For there were many interesting common problems in the development of socialist and capitalist economies. There was no doubt that central planning was gaining ground in capitalist countries. On the other hand, in Poland decentralization was being discussed on a nation-wide scale, and the efficiency of the economy was being improved by giving more scope to the managers of individual state enterprises, thereby increasing the initiative of firms and individuals. In the course of this present discussion in their country, Polish economists hoped to lay the foundations of a theory of the socialist planned economy. This theory would help Poland, but it would also contribute to the progress of economic science throughout the world.

Professor Tabah (France) stressed the importance of high birth-rates and declining death-rates in most underdeveloped countries. The birth-rate was usually about 45 per 1,000, which, owing to a high marriage-rate at a very early age, led to a greater population increase than a corresponding rate in Europe in the middle of the eighteenth century. The death-rate was about 20 per 1,000, which was comparable with the figure for European countries after 150 years of almost uninterrupted development.

While the improvement in Europe was largely due to better economic conditions, the fall in the death-rate in the poorer countries was at present mainly the result of medical progress, which had been introduced from abroad. In Europe, on the contrary, it was internal in origin, and had consequently followed the pattern created by economic progress. To make matters worse, the giving of medical assistance on an international scale was now regarded by the advanced nations as a duty, particularly as it was less expensive than giving economic help. Any reduction in the birth-rate, on the other hand, depended on cultural patterns, and so attempts to lower it would often be ineffective and evoke a certain amount of resistance. Any deliberate attempt to reduce birth-rates might weaken the social fabric.

Although it was difficult to predict when the demographic trend in underdeveloped countries would become similar to that in Europe, the general view was that the change-over would be as slow as the analogous process in the Western world had been since the middle or the end of the nineteenth century. For the cultural and economic factors making for the change were more favourable in the West. It was therefore almost certain that, for the next generation at least, the momentum acquired would lead to an increase in the rate of population growth. Whereas the population of Egypt had more or less doubled in the fifty years between 1897 and 1947, it would take only half as long for a further increase of 100 per cent — irrespective of the policy followed by the government of the country. The annual rate of population increase in Algeria was at present 2·5 per cent, which was twice as high as in pre-Malthusian Europe in the first half of the nineteenth century. The underdeveloped countries as a whole (*i.e.* those where average annual income was less than 100 dollars) would double their population in twenty-five years and more than quadruple it in fifty years, a rate of growth unparalleled in human history. Developed countries, on the contrary, would take between fifty and sixty years to double their populations.

While the growth of population in nineteenth-century Europe had stimulated economic progress, it was clear that it would be extremely difficult even to maintain the standard of living in the poorer countries. It was essential, however, to try to increase that standard and at the same time to prepare people's minds for a birth-control policy, even though this policy could only be adopted if the impetus came from within the country itself. Tentative studies already showed that, within the next twenty-five years, population growth would cancel out any rise in output per head. For the period beyond that, progress would depend almost entirely on whether there was a decline in birth-rates. A calculation showed that, where any population was increasing at the rate of 2·5 per cent per year, 10 per cent of its net revenue would need to be invested to maintain the present standard of living, and a further 10 per cent if that standard were to be doubled in thirty-five years. The gap between the rich and the poor countries was clearly bound to widen under present conditions.

There appeared to be three ways out of this impasse. First, the birth-rate might fall fairly fast, as had been the case in Brazil and other Latin American countries. This would permit economic and social progress. Sociologists and demographers, however, were sceptical about the possibility of a rapid spread of birth control, even if governments concerned were favourably disposed. Second, abortion could be legalized, as had been the case in Japan since 1948; but it was unlikely that similar measures would secure adoption in many other countries because of religious, cultural or governmental opposition. Third, the maintenance of a high birth-rate might lead to a decline in standards of health. A decline in the rate of population growth and some degree of equilibrium would then be gradually achieved.

Professor Sauvy (France) thought the discussion had shown that the problem of the poor or underdeveloped countries could not be studied on a purely economic plane. The collaboration of economists, sociologists and demographers was essential, as had indeed been recognized by the Population Conference held in Rome two years earlier. This view was reflected by the Institut National d'Études Démographiques in Paris.

He did not deny that the poorer nations faced vital economic problems, but these could not be tackled without the basic demographic data. The heart of the matter was that, in the nineteenth century, European medicine could only keep pace with economic resources for two reasons. First, because that medicine was mostly based on commercial preparations, and second, because both its development and the concomitant economic development stemmed from the same scientific source. At present, on the other hand, the techniques for lowering the death-rate were much less expensive than those for ensuring the prosperity of the people thus saved. In the underdeveloped countries, it was clear that the death-rate would continue to decline, and the consequent increase in population would be two and a half times more rapid than in Western Europe. It was therefore pointless to study the economic problems of the poorer countries without taking this into full account.

Professor Sauvy was in complete disagreement with Professor Viner's proposals for economic progress in these countries. Very briefly, his own view was that every country should work out its own salvation in accordance with its own traditions. If, as would no doubt be the case, drastic changes had to be made, it was all the more essential that the relevant decisions should be taken on their own initiative by the countries concerned. This precept was particularly true in the field of birth control, as experience in Japan and China showed.

Cultural factors should be given an important place when economic doctrines and policies were being formulated. Development was achieved less by discovering new techniques than by spreading existing ones. In other words, progress was a problem of culture and education. The lack of engineers and skilled workers was more important in holding back economic development than lack of capital. For, given the former, machines imported on credit could be paid for in a few years. The human factor, though not capable of measurement, and hence not explicitly reflected in current models, was still the dominant factor. The whole problem of the underdeveloped countries was extremely urgent and it was impossible for the more advanced countries to ignore it, since, in the modern world, all nations were linked together like mountaineers on a rope. Only complete realism and frankness could prevent diasaster.

Professor Leduc (France) wished to offer a few comments, on the basis of his fairly wide experience abroad, on Professor Viner's paper. He agreed with the view that the economic problems of the poor countries were different from those of the richer ones, but thought that this proposition applied with greater force to Asia than to Africa. He also agreed that inflation was a danger to both rich and poor countries. Indeed, nowadays, the latter tended to suffer more acutely from the consequences of inflation. As Professor Viner had pointed out, savings were quite large in underdeveloped countries. The trouble was that these savings were badly used. In particular, they were often hoarded, and the main problem was how to channel them into sound investments.

Professor Leduc felt, however, that Professor Viner might well have paid a little more attention to some sociological aspects of economic progress in the poor countries. More specifically, he wished to draw attention to the need for a fuller survey of the geography and resources of certain areas. It was not yet known, for example, what the capacity of the South Sahara region was. The surveys necessary to obtain this type of information were expensive, and the cost obviously could not be borne by the countries of Africa. Yet, such surveys would show how tropical climate affected economic progress.

He was in broad agreement with Professor Tabah and Professor Sauvy on population, and emphasized that religious, legal and political considerations were of the greatest importance.

Professor von Hofmannsthal (U.S.A.) regretted that Professor Viner's paper contained no reference to the influence of legal security on economic problems. Yet, security was surely an important factor in economic life. Unless they were guaranteed a sufficient reward, workers would lower their output and capital would not come forward. Unfortunately, however, that security was lacking today in underdeveloped countries, for there had been widespread confiscation of foreign capital.

Some time before, he had calculated that in an average of fifteen years, all foreign investments would be confiscated. It was accordingly necessary for investors to demand an extra 7 per cent of yield annually in order to offset the cost of this insecurity. Recent events had shown that this period must now have been shortened to ten years, or even eight. Accordingly, the 'insecurity rate' of additional yield which ought to be demanded might be as high as 10 per cent or even 12 per cent. It could thus be calculated that the peoples of underdeveloped countries had to pay from two to three or even three and a half billion (thousand million) dollars annually for the insecurity created by their governments.

No responsible manager of entrusted capital, no economically minded government, could now reasonably invest its funds abroad. If the underdeveloped countries wished to encourage the influx of foreign capital, it was essential that the present tendency towards confiscation should be reversed.

Professor Kitagawa (Japan) returned to the question of comparative costs. He was interested to hear that the theory admitted some modifications to deal with external economies, subsidies and employment. Perhaps Professors Ellis, Fellner and Scitovsky should be quoted in this connection. But he wondered how external economies could be measured, so that one could allow for them convincingly in practice, or at least in a modified theoretical formulation of the doctrine of comparative costs. If one considered a very long period, one might have new industries or changes in productivity or cost and demand conditions. The classical model, conventionally formulated, should surely be timeless rather than deal with any given period.

The balance of payments was also an important problem. Underdeveloped countries depended on exports of primary produce to acquire those imports which were not always income-elastic, since they were somewhat inflexibly related to their economic plans to create social capital. But Professor Viner was optimistic in thinking that the balance-of-payments problem in backward countries was not very serious. Even in England, savings were said to be short. This might well mean that the underdeveloped countries would find it hard to borrow abroad unless there were some international mechanism like the one Professor Viner mentioned in his report.

Japan could be quoted as an instance of a poorer country which had developed. The absolute number of agricultural workers in Japan had not declined over the past seventy years, but the natural increase had gone into other sectors. Japan had used labour-intensive methods in either agriculture or small-scale industries. There was a wide gap in wage levels as between modernized big firms and the small ones just mentioned. And yet Japan was being forced to transform her economy, following the pattern of the chemical and engineering industries. If she were to be taken as a model by Asian countries, the same trouble might be experienced. Her past development, moreover, had been helped by the presence of good markets in near-by countries; this might be a unique circumstance, and might not be repeated by other Asian countries.

Professor Resta (Italy) called the attention of the Congress to the fact that, even among developed countries, there were rich and poor ones. Therefore, the chances of growth for poor but developed countries were affected by any scarcity of economic resources owned by these countries, assuming that growth did not succeed in freeing such economies completely from this scarcity. To simplify his exposition, Professor Resta set out the following definitions:

(*a*) The concept of a developed economic system with a given space.
(*b*) The concept of available productive resources in the given economic system, grouped in the three categories of land resources, capital resources and labour resources.
(*c*) The notion of the number, M, of such resources.
(*d*) The notion of the quantity, r_i, of such resources.
(*e*) The notion of the number, n, of the uses of the resources.
(*f*) The notion of the collective product which might be obtained by a macro-economic productive combination of certain quantities, r_i, of the available resources.
(*g*) The notion of a technical production coefficient — the quantity of a certain resource used for the production of x_j units of a good.
(*h*) The notion of the total quantity of product demanded, according to certain demand functions.

Professor Resta said he would denote the economic system covering a given space by the quantity of the factors r_i, available in that economic system in a certain period. Since these quantities varied over time, the expression

$$P(t) = F^{(t)} \; [r_1 (t) \ldots \ldots \ldots r_m (t)]$$

could be regarded as the most general form of the equation of the economic structure of the system.

If one considered a period of time long enough to allow the causes of stability and development in the economic system to be discovered, four variables could be used:

(1) The quantities of the factors of production available, as in (*b*) above, with their variations.
(2) The collective product and its changes over time according to certain values of F in the structural equation.
(3) The demand functions with their variations over time.
(4) The technical coefficients, as in (*g*) above, which altered with changes in technique.

An analysis of stability and growth in the structure of the system showed the possible relations between these four variables. The fact that the volume of resources available changed over time led to corresponding changes in the collective product. Hence, in the long run, the growth of national output was a function of the structure of the system.

Nevertheless, if the area in which the system operated was assumed to be given and constant over time, what did *not* vary was the tendency of a certain type of factor, for example capital, to increase more or less quickly than other groups of factors. In other words, with the passage of time, there was a tendency for some factors to be in excess supply compared with others, despite international migration.

This constant long-term tendency (analytically nothing more than the form of production function), Professor Resta called 'type of structure'. It was this unchanging type of structure in a given system which mainly determined whether the national product over time tended to grow at increasing or decreasing rates.

Thus, if, in a particular country, capital was relatively more abundant than labour, and if capital could, to some extent, take the place of labour, the laws of productivity would lead to full employment and then automation, so that the national income might well increase at increasing rates. In other words, this would be a rich country, or one with a 'strong type of structure'.

On the other hand, if one had a country where (because of a high birth-rate, restricted space or infertile land) labour was more abundant than natural and capital resources, and if labour could not readily be substituted for capital, the national income would grow at a decreasing rate. One then had the well-known phenomenon of a long-term fall in *per capita* income, or a poor country with a 'weak type of structure'.

As the rate of economic growth in a system depended, in Professor Resta's opinion, on the type of economic structure, it followed that the stability of an economic system also depended on its type of economic structure. So progress and stability in any economic system were long-term phenomena and should not be treated, as was usually the case, in a Keynesian manner or on a short-term basis. Nor should they be linked to the savings-investment dichotomy, especially since savings and investment ultimately depended on the flow of income over time and so were also linked to the type of structure possessed by an economic system. In consequence, Professor Resta understood the term 'stability of an economic system' to mean its capacity to produce a flow of national income to cover constantly total production expenses, allowing for changes in the volume, and trend of growth, of resources and for changes in demand functions over time.

On the ability of the economic structure and of demand conditions to change over time would depend the degree of employment of factors, and whether, with a given increase in population, the economic structure of a country could produce a rate of increase of social output which would guarantee both full employment and a rising *per capita* income.

Political plans must therefore take as their starting-point, and operate in accordance with, conditions in their own given economic structure. More specifically, in any model of general dynamic equilibrium, the economic structure was to be regarded as holding a position prior to all the relationships linking the variables in the system.

Professor P. L. Reynaud (France) expressed his agreement with Professor Baudin. He said he would discuss qualitative demography, which dealt with the potential and actual ability of people, and in particular with methods such as tests for singling out those who were able to absorb modern techniques most rapidly. One of the greatest shortages in underdeveloped countries was that of capable specialists. If a fraction of the money invested in searching for raw materials were applied to human material, hundreds of capable technicians could quickly be found. There had been frequent talk of unemployment among workers in underdeveloped countries, but experience had shown that a good technician was more likely to provide work there than a large capital investment, which might be squandered.

The second point on which he wished to insist, as a result of the work of the Research Centre at Strasbourg, was the importance of 'thresholds', which he defined as critical points indicating the discontinuity of economic phenomena. The income/population 'threshold' was of particular importance in the present context. There was considerable evidence for the belief that, at a point above an annual income of 300 to 400 dollars, fertility decreased. Below that figure it increased. Another 'threshold' occurred with profits. Beneath a certain point productivity collapsed. In the same way there was the 'threshold' of wages, beneath which strikes and labour discontent became endemic. The trouble was that at present far too little was known of these 'thresholds', and too little of modern economists' time was being devoted to their study. In conclusion, Professor Reynaud asserted that only a reversal of this situation, leading to a conscious search for an *élite*, could ensure growing prosperity in the underdeveloped countries.

Professor Pitigliani (Italy) said he had been faced by two problems: one geographical and the other conceptual. First, he had wondered whether Italy was a poorer or a richer country. The fact that he was now speaking on Professor Viner's paper proved that he thought Italy was among the poorer countries. Perhaps he had followed Caesar's maxim that it was better to be first among poor countries than last among rich ones. However, to judge from p. 41 of his paper, Professor Viner did not agree that Italy was one of the countries allotted to him.

Professor Pitigliani said his second problem was that he thought the idea of stability needed clarification when applied to underdeveloped areas. Studies carried out both in Italy and in the U.S.A. suggested that the main differences between developed and underdeveloped areas lay in a combination of five factors, namely, natural resources, entrepreneurial ability, confidence in the future, social action to promote welfare and a favourable demand/population relationship. Other factors, such as favourable economic trends, acted as 'accelerators' in the process of expansion.

Professor Pitigliani believed that capital formation, often thought of as a primary element in progress, was itself the result of entrepreneurial ability and social action. Yet improvements were often most rapid in less-advanced countries. In Russia, for thirty years, and more recently, in Israel, and even in southern Italy, new machinery and other methods of farming had been introduced with remarkable success.

Professor Pitigliani stressed the importance of foreign aid, which should be regarded as a fundamental element in bridging the gap between present poverty and future wealth. But this kind of help had political implications, since loans could often be used to gain political influence. He also wanted to stress the extent to which bureaucracy could hold back progress in backward areas. It was consequently essential to discourage dependence on the public authority for every productive activity.

Mr. Leonard Rist (France/World Bank) said he had looked in the discussion for something which would make his own job easier. He was economic adviser to the World Bank in Washington, and his main job was to suggest or criticize proposals for development and investment in poor countries. But the solutions, however well meant, must not lead to results opposed to progress. They must ensure the most efficient use of these countries' resources. He was constantly faced with the problem of linking economic theory to economic policy, and it was comforting to know that Professor Viner and other members of the Congress were asking themselves the same questions as he was. He hoped these experts would continue their research and give the World Bank the benefit of their work.

Mr. Rist asked for more certain facts and fewer hypotheses on macro-economic relationships. He had long been asking himself whether there was a more or less fixed long-term relation between increased investment and increased income. A few years ago it was generally held that a poor country without social capital equipment, such as electric power or transport, had to resign itself to investing more, during a number of years, to obtain a smaller increase in income than the same investment would yield in rich countries. Yet today, in South-East Asia and in South America, there were a number of cases where rapid growth was accompanied by relatively small investments. The importance of agriculture, where capital investment was often less crucial than improved techniques, the minor rôle of housing, and the high profitability of capital in countries where capital was scarce, were perhaps reasons for this. But we needed to find out more about the problem.

Mr. Rist said he did not believe that savings in a poor country were necessarily low, and he was pleased to hear Professor Viner confirm not only that the income-savings ratio did not fit into any *a priori* scheme, but also that very often this ratio was not dissimilar in size to that found in more advanced countries. He had repeatedly been surprised at the flexibility of the marginal propensity to effect

H 97

savings. We needed to be better informed about it and to know more about the human motives underlying it.

Another problem which the World Bank found difficult was how to measure the average yield of capital. There could be no hesitation in approving an investment which was expected to yield more than the average return on capital in the country in question. If it brought in less, however, should it be rejected ? This seemed, *a priori*, to be the case, but what choice did it open up ? And what reservations did it call for ? How could one calculate social yield ?

Mr. Rist said he could not insist too strongly on the importance of this problem of social yield. It affected the whole field of investment, loans and investment programming, and might sometimes drastically modify them. Professor Viner had talked about social costs ; what he himself was anxiously looking for was a really satisfactory method of calculating them.

He further wondered whether, in the overpopulated countries, one should encourage, in principle, investment using abundant labour supplies, as against that which was capital-intensive. Should we not encourage industries which needed a great deal of capital if there was some hope that they might set off a chain reaction, bringing a whole series of related or ancillary undertakings. To take a picturesque example, full justice had never been done to the rôle of the brewing industry. This was a capital-intensive industry *par excellence*, which in more than one South American town had brought about the creation of scores of enterprises making glass or metal containers, packing machinery and so on. This process of 'triggering off' deserved to be analysed, for Professor Nurkse's 'balanced investments' did not need to be simultaneous. These were but a few of the many urgent practical situations where theory should enlighten policy.

Mr. Rist concluded by saying that he would like to ask Professor Viner to be indulgent towards bureaucrats drawing up investment programmes in poor countries. They were acquiring an insight into the relationship between economic phenomena which was useful for their countries as well as for theory. But still more important, they were studying development problems in their own *milieu*. That was a contribution to science, which foreigners could not make.

Professor Weiller (France) said that quarrels over terminology were disturbing because they held back one's attention at an initial stage, always far removed from one's ultimate objective. In order to understand problems more fully, we studied them, beginning from Ricardo, Keynes or List, without wishing to remain Ricardians, Keynesians or disciples of List. What mattered was the way these men had reached, revised or even refuted the proofs which, for lack of anything better, we thought it useful to study.

It was useless to discover whether we had been faithful to Ricardo when we had insisted on the legitimacy of long-term expectations on a national scale, for instance as a result of population pressures or migratory movements; or when we had allowed for the play of what we called expansionist pressures (whose importance Hicks had now stressed very successfully when speaking of differential rates of growth). In that context, the concept of structural disequilibrium was simply linked, in the immediate post-war period, to discontinuities of a historical nature, with interruptions of growth and even the threat of decline towards secular depression.

Had we, on the other hand, been good Keynesians? Through the need for a common language we had been happy enough to talk of levels of activity in the terms of an underemployment analysis. But the present dispute over 'disguised unemployment' threatened to shift the emphasis of the debate, which had always taken place in the context of historical development, combining questions of employment, productivity and changing structure.

For another reason, we were now in a situation where it was essential to reinterpret our theories. The problem of 'reconstruction' had presupposed, above all, an interruption of growth — some collapse in Professor Dahmen's 'blocks of development'. We were now faced with other problems. The big change came from the underdeveloped, and often overpopulated, countries, where rapid increase of population concentrated their efforts in investment policies and programmes of internal development. The 'Listian argument' had to be considered as a starting-point. On the other hand, the law of comparative advantage would doubtless continue to hold in a strict sense, since exports of staple commodities like cotton, tin and rubber would continue to be the main ones. But this consideration would take second place. It was therefore necessary, whilst no doubt the traditional concepts were quite capable of dealing with the problem on a short-term basis, to rally round the new concepts and methods of analysis and of expression which would be needed for a long-run analysis.

Professor Delivanis (Greece) said he would like, very briefly, to give three extra reasons for the poverty of underdeveloped countries. First, there was the desire of their inhabitants to work as little as possible. Second, there was the low average ability of entrepreneurs. Finally, there was the fact that administration in these countries was slow and not very efficient.

Professor Viner replied to the discussion, which he thought had

99

been stimulating and fresh. Professor Baudin had called for a relative and subjective approach to welfare, and he agreed wholeheartedly. International comparisons of income and welfare, for instance, were often statistical parades which hid as much as they revealed of the true nature of welfare. An initial obligation was to respect the free choice of free people as to what constituted welfare for them. There should be no pressure, and not even much effort at persuasion, to adopt particular avenues of development.

Professor Viner said that there had been much discussion over his statements on comparative costs, and he had been asked how external economies could be 'measured' so as to be taken into account. If participants wanted him to produce a mathematical formula, they would have to be disappointed. His notion was such that it could not be put into any simple formulation readily subject to quantification. But that did not mean that it was not of great significance.

Professor Viner said he had been much gratified by the novel experience of listening to Professors Rubinstein and Lipinski. This was the first time he had ever heard communist economists, and he did not want to mar the event by engaging in controversy. He would, however, like to tell Professor Rubinstein that in references in Russian journals, he himself had been called, in the usual manner, the 'servant of the capitalists'. Now, however, he found that Professor Rubinstein and he cherished the same slogan — Aid through Trade. Professor Viner said that he felt that if economists from East and West could be true scientific economists, they could make a real contribution to understanding and open up a common area for fruitful discussion. He welcomed their coming together for this purpose.

Professor Viner was not sure how far he agreed with Professor Nasr. He was certainly not an advocate of a society consisting permanently of islands of luxury resting on a sea of misery. When he had stressed spending on education for health, vocational training, etc., he had been taking a humanitarian approach. But he would never lightly abandon the belief that war on the sickness and disease which afflicted half mankind might be one way of achieving economic progress.

Professor Viner pointed out that he was not a demographer, but he was not surprised to hear that the idea of limitation of population was distasteful to some people. There were very many people, nevertheless, who were most anxious to know *how* to limit their families. Again, population growth might have been a positive causal factor of economic development in the nineteenth century. But why did the industrial revolution proceed for one hundred years, after 1750, before there was an increase in income per head? There had been an increase in middle class incomes, but not in the incomes of the mass of the population.

The terms of trade were important. Seventy-five per cent of England's exports were textiles in the early 1800s. The world had been flooded with English textiles to the benefit (*a*) of the profits of the English middle classes, and (*b*) consumers in undeveloped areas. The growth in the size of the English labour-force had kept real wages constant and had transferred the benefits of technological progress to the middle classes and to foreign consumers; and it did so by lowering Britain's terms of trade. He suggested that we needed to consider the effects of rising population on exports, on the terms of trade and thus on *per capita* income.

Professor Viner said he was prepared to abandon the term comparative cost, and to substitute one with fewer historical associations and implications. But he warned against abandoning the term merely to get freedom to advocate, without losing respectability as an economist, national allocation of resources without regard to comparative economic advantage, rationally interpreted.

Professor Viner concluded by saying that in his paper he had ignored what some economists seemed to think the crucial point: was the gap between rich and poor countries widening? Two recent publications seemed to suggest a new neo-Marxian law: the poor countries are getting poorer and the rich countries richer, and the poverty of the poor countries is the result of the richness of rich countries; the only way out, therefore, is through international sharing. The suggestion was that what mattered most was not how high incomes were today as compared with yesterday, but as compared with Smith in England today, Hans in Germany today and so on. Yet merely to impoverish the rich countries without bothering to transfer income to the poor countries would equalize incomes internationally, and if relative incomes were all, or nearly all, that mattered, this could be brought about much more easily than international sharing. Relative incomes were certainly important chiefly because they were regarded as such. But there were many millions of people who just would not know what international income differences were, were they not fed with international income comparisons whose reliability was much to be questioned. Professor Viner concluded that most economists appeared to want to equalize incomes internationally. His aim was not this. He wanted poor countries to be richer; but he had no particular longing that the American number of Cadillacs per thousand of population should become universal.

THE THIRD DAY

THE QUEST FOR STABILITY:
THE REAL FACTORS

THE QUEST FOR STABILITY:
THE REAL FACTORS[1]

BY

PROFESSOR FRANÇOIS PERROUX

Chairman : PROFESSOR ROBBINS (United Kingdom)

ON THE DIFFERENCE BETWEEN CONTRA-CYCLICAL POLICIES AND POLICIES AIMING AT BALANCED GROWTH

A SOVEREIGN authority with a quasi-pontifical gesture — to whom Professor Robertson so aptly alluded — has set down for us the limits of this world, demarcated it into empires and also stated our objective.

Growth there must be, and it must proceed in as stable a fashion as possible. This is not easy, we are told. The certainty that difficulties will be encountered springs, amongst other things, from the presence of the enigmatic real factors.

Could these be aggregate flows and stocks in money terms divided by some index ? One would then be exclusively confined to macro-economic models, mainly concerned with national economies. Or are they factors which are unresponsive to monetary strategy, namely population, innovations and institutions ? These are traditionally, and not without justification, considered de-stabilizing.[2]

The enigma might well take the form of a provocation — in the Latin sense of that word ! *Pro-vocare* : to summon out. Out of

---

[1] Professor Perroux's lecture differed very greatly from the two texts (English and French) originally circulated in Rome to members of the Congress. It was therefore agreed that the discussion of Professor Perroux's lecture should be based on these *original* French and English texts, rather than on the version published here.

[2] Every theory of the cycle is simultaneously real and monetary. Even the so-called 'real' models of the cycle, which proceed in terms of global flows, inconceivable without the existence of money, are in no way intended to eliminate monetary phenomena. Their object is rather to show that the cycle can be constructed without recourse to monetary phenomena and that forces largely independent of them are at work in observable cycles.

In analysing trends and fluctuations, it is best to treat the real factors (population, innovations, institutions) as autonomous. This does not mean considering them as altogether beyond economic analysis, nor that changes in them are completely uninfluenced by the cycle ; it means that neither general equilibrium theory nor pure cycle theories alone are capable of explaining such regular patterns as they follow.

A change in any one of these factors (population, innovations, institutions), taken in isolation, alters investment and consumption. Regarding the processes what ? Out of orthodoxy. Nothing of the sort, however. The tutelary and near-pontifical authority already extolled has presented us with a complex though inescapable task — that of explicitly allowing for the relation between innovations in their contemporary forms on the one hand and population and institutions on the other, as a basis for framing policy.[1]

In our century this problem has acquired a content all its own, which can be set out under three headings.

which, for the past ten years, I have declared to be characteristic of the dynamics of economic growth ; cf. R. Barre's excellent book *Économie politique* (P.U.F., 1956).

Analysis of growth with fluctuations will have to select a certain number of variables from amongst these three major groups and establish a logical connection between them.

Population growth at an increasing or decreasing rate clearly does not influence only overall supply and demand, investment and consumption ; we also need more specific information about demographic structure (by age, occupation, branches of activity) if we are to analyse particular supplies and demands, and also the ease and speed with which the available labour-force adjusts to the structural changes of a growing economy. But we often have to be content with much more summary indications.

Institutions are sets of compelling conditions for economic subjects, whose field of choice is limited thereby. They represent 'armistices' in the struggle between social groups and as such are always subject to pressure which modifies their content, even if the 'legal framework' remains unchanged. The analysis of economic growth with fluctuations has, in general, kept rather aloof from minor, or major, institutional changes, but they simply cannot be overlooked when it comes to policy proposals.

Innovations are changes in the production functions within an economic system. They create new goods or reduce the cost of production of existing goods, and are, moreover, specified by the nature of the additional investment which they often occasion. The most important, for our purposes, are overlapping innovations (the effects of one are not yet exhausted when another occurs), innovations likely to call forth a large number of further innovations (nuclear energy and automation, for example), and innovations which take effect by means of indivisible investments of real and money capital. We shall call an innovation 'efficient' if it increases real average productivity in a well-defined economic whole.

In the analysis of balanced growth, innovations are often neglected (perfect competition, compensation between innovations with an overall 'neutral' effect, uncertainties over the precise extent of technical progress and the comparison of its effects over successive periods, serve as a pretext for simplifying the models).

Since our subject is economic policy, the main real factor to be considered is innovation. Any concrete policy must necessarily assume the existence of innovations, and indeed today possesses powerful methods of influencing the emergence and the propagation of innovations. Innovation obliges us to reconsider our models and modern innovations force us to take account of precisely those difficulties which we used to set aside : public innovation and investment, major indivisibilities, and highly imperfect competition.

[1] Unless otherwise qualified, growth is defined as a lasting increase in the size of a — simple or complex — economic unit, accomplished through changes in structures and eventually in systems, and accompanied by varying degrees of economic progress.

This concept inseparably links an increase in size with structural changes, and excludes the identification of growth with progress.

It comprises four groups of phenomena :

(*a*) Increases in the size of a unit which, in themselves, have no economic meaning at all. They can be measured by several indicators of size, including gross national product.

(*b*) Changes in structure (the proportions and relationships which characterize

In the first place, the emergence of new industries can no longer be regarded as the outcome of great innovations in the Schumpeterian sense ; nor is it a 'cluster' phenomenon which, as will be recalled, Schumpeter in any case left unexplained. New industry emerges today, for some of the most representative types of technology, through the application of vast resources of indivisible capital of a monetary and technical kind ; such capital is indivisible for technical units, for firms and for the industries constituted by such firms. The case of automation at once springs to mind. One could equally have quoted coke-ovens, power stations, oil-refineries, iron and steel mills, whether these be newly constructed or modernized by the addition of indivisible units. It frequently happens that the flows, prices and expectations of the free market and perfect competition are not the only links connecting the firms in an industry. These are also joined by such non-classical linkages as financial participation, common management, long-term contracts and official or semi-official government regulations. Often firms constitute oligopolies or enter into loosely knit associations behaving oligopolistically. Furthermore, such arrangements are not necessarily private, whatever their official or ostensible status.

The strategic nature of innovation, its far-reaching effects, and its impact upon the whole economic structure of a country provoke widespread government control and supervision over these new or modernized industries, some of which may, even if their status does not clearly show it, be regarded as of semi-public or public character.

an economic system, or these same elements taken as constant for the purpose of some specific analysis). They are measurable chiefly by structural coefficients,

$$\frac{\text{Industrial product}}{\text{Total product}}, \quad \frac{\text{Profit}}{\text{Total product}}, \quad \frac{\text{Total product}}{\text{Total capital}}, \quad \text{etc. etc.}$$

(*c*) Changes in systems. A system is a body of institutions which, by their mutual relationships, influence the achievement of fundamental economic functions. Thus, if an output of a particular quantity and quality is useful to or necessary to the consumer, it is desirable that its cost should be reduced. The system of private enterprise and of the market influences the achievement of this fundamental economic function differently from the system of centralized planning. The logic of a system is the set of sequences, either hypothetical or proven, which link the institutions to the functions. In all cases, the logic postulated by the beneficiaries or supporters of a system differs from its observable logic.

(*d*) Progress consists in the advance of an economy, or of one of its parts, towards an end which is considered desirable. It is measured by indicators of average quantities (for example, average real income), structural indicators, and groups of several simple indicators. These operational concepts of economic progress are in no way sufficient for defining an economically progressive society. An economy is progressive when the effects of innovation spread most rapidly and at least social cost, within a network of economic institutions in the widest sense. (For more detail, see François Perroux, 'Les Mesures statistiques du progrès et la notion de société économiquement progressive' (fasc. 1) n° 47, 1956 ; I. Les Composants, 1. La Création (fasc. 2) n° 59, 1957 ; I. Les Composants, 2. La Propagation, A. Modèles micréoconomiques (fasc. 3) n° 60, 1957, *Cahiers de l'I.S.É.A.*)

The features outlined will, I fear, raise difficulties for the admirable analyses of traditional pattern upon which all of us have been reared, since I seem to recall that indivisibilities, conjectural relations, oligopolistic agreements and, finally, state intervention, defy incorporation into models aspiring to reflect perfect competition and complete determinacy. To suggest that these phenomena are quantitatively unimportant is no solution. In any case, this would not be true of the new forms of energy or of numerous other industries fitting our description. Moreover, the de-stabilizing effect within an economic organism cannot be appropriately measured by the quantitative extent of a given investment in the short period.

A further factor renders the problem at once more precise and more complex. Among modern innovations must be included those of an organizational character, and one may safely claim that these are not confined purely to the private sector. Despite counsels of excessive prudence and occasional somewhat agitated protest, many contemporary governments do make use of decision models, national economic forecasts, five-year programmes of expansion and modernization and even venture to set themselves very long-term objectives. These are facts; I state them without attempting to justify them.[1]

These various estimates and blueprints — resented by those who, like Bastiat, put their faith in natural economic harmonies — embody desired rates of growth of real product for the economy as a whole, as well as for its component parts, together with extrapolations of levels of productivity both in the aggregate and by sectors. These rates owe little to the perspicacity of the authorities, but much more to a reasonably democratic mechanism of consultation through committees wherein the aims and requirements of entrepreneurs, unions, government departments and even ministers are expressed and discussed. This process of collective groping enables fundamental incompatibilities to be eliminated from the outset and corrections to be made as time goes on. In the more discreet countries, nameless plans or programmes take the place of official blueprints. In such countries I see no single flexible plan but, what amounts to the same thing, co-ordinated programmes of internal and external investment, programmes for carrying out innovation in the public sector and detailed periodic study of the results, with the aid of national accounts.

By reason of such practices, the distinction between what is clearly private and what is clearly public has become blurred. Aggregate demand and supply, prices and technical coefficients, in the

---

[1] On the pure theory of planning and the economic and financial activities of the State, G. U. Papi's work is well known. Of his numerous writings, I would here mention only the latest, *Teoria della condotta economica dello stato* (Milan 1956).

aggregate and by sectors, are functions of two sets of variables: those expressing spontaneous reactions and those expressing hierarchical decisions.

There is a further complicating factor : the periods do not coincide. We all have our theories of the short, medium and long period ; these cannot be used here. Schumpeter's [1] long cycle, which is of particular interest to me since I have to deal with innovation, has recently come somewhat under fire and it would not teach me very much to be told that we are, in fact, in the midst of a Kondratieff-Schumpeter recovery. Much more useful is Keirstead's analysis of the non-cyclical succession of various overlapping innovations, provided it is used in conjunction with Levi-Strauss's concept of the 'cumulative historical period' and briefly defined with reference to a period of growth.[2]

In this paper I propose to devote my main attention to the case

[1] The major Kondratieff-Schumpeter cycle has not been confirmed by the data collected on aggregate flows (W. Hoffmann, *British Industry* (Oxford, 1955)) ; A. Gayer, W. W. Rostow, A. J. Schwartz, *The Growth and the Fluctuations of the British Economy, 1790–1850*. What remains of the process formed by the linked phases of the achievement of major innovations and the subsequent 'harvest'? The comparatively greater increase in the production of consumer goods during the 'harvest' is not borne out in the case of Great Britain (1787–1842 ; 1843–97). In any case, the fall in the prices of some consumer goods and the spread of their current consumption does not necessarily imply that all the investments have completed their period of maturing.

The need to give it the benefit of the doubt, as one must in view of the near-impossibility of separating statistically monetary from other factors, should not blind us to the logical weakness of the interpretation. Certain innovations (textiles) send down the prices and increase the output of consumer goods. Others (transport) reduce the prices of both consumer and producer goods. The appearance of clusters of innovations frees Schumpeter from the need to define a structure of innovations which alone could help to date, within the selected focus, the strongest period of the inflationary or deflationary effect caused by the initial innovation and then the 'harvest' of consumer goods.

The third Kondratieff-Schumpeter, which interests us directly, occasions some scepticism ; it will be recalled that in the Schumpeter-Kuznets chronology, as recorded in S. Kuznets, *Economic Change* (New York, 1953), p. 109, the first (Industrial Revolution) is from 1787 to 1842 and the second (the so-called 'bourgeois' cycle) from 1843 to 1897. If a fourteen-year recovery period is added to the third phase of the third Kondratieff-Schumpeter (the depression of 1925–39), this would take us up to 1953 (through many 'exogenous' factors !). Since then, we should have the intellectual satisfaction, at least, of knowing that we have entered the prosperity phase of a long cycle, for which it only remains to find a suitable institutional adjective.

[2] The long period, theoretically conceived as a period of total adaptation following an initial disequilibrium, or as a period during which particular variables are assumed given and constant, is of little value for the study of growth with fluctuations.

Ultimately it is periods of growth alone which interest us.

When trying to identify them by statistical and historical investigation, or to characterize them conceptually, it is usual to speak of 'a period containing several cycles'. This may be defined either by reference to the Kondratieff-Schumpeter long waves (about 60 years, 1787–1842 = 55 years, 1842–97 = 55 years), or else as a period of increase or decrease in the rate of increase of real product, identifiable by means of structural characteristics and fundamental coefficients (investment, consumption).

where population is growing,[1] but at a decreasing rate, with a growing burden of maintaining the older groups, and where the coefficients of investment and consumption are tending [2] to become stable. This general framework could be made a good deal more specific for a detailed analysis: it distinguishes growth in an old economy from the initial phases of growth which are characterized by a rising investment coefficient, and by an increase in the share of aggregate profits in national income at the expense of aggregate wages. The general conditions assumed have the merit of throwing into relief the specific rôle of innovation.

Thus the situation which economic policy has to resolve is the following: we have a combination of counter-cyclical policies relating to the cyclical period, which we know is difficult to define with any precision, to five-year expansion and modernization plans, and longer-range plans and programmes — these plans being tested and corrected as best they can by reference to national accounts and short-period targets. One cannot, of course, overlook a number of supplementary periods, such as the production-period of capital goods, their maturation period, and, above all, the period elapsing between invention and innovation.

The problem of achieving stability, whatever meaning may be attached to that term, would seem insoluble.

But, as I have pointed out, this problem cannot be circumvented. For theories or models which ignore any or all of the three difficulties outlined have most assuredly no bearing whatever on the concrete tasks of a policy of stable growth (real factors).

The way I have chosen to set out the problem has the advantage of revealing quite plainly, even brutally, the limits of our present theoretical knowledge; it has the additional merit of acquainting us with the types of policies actually practised,[3] even though to the exasperation of the purists, with the object of mitigating instabilities in the growth process and rendering them bearable.[4]

[1] Alfred Sauvy, *Théorie générale de la population*, vol. I and II (P.U.F., 1952 and 1954); Buquet, *l'Optimum de population*, Collection Pragma (P.U.F., 1955).

[2] Lasting forces are at work to maintain the coefficients at a fairly constant level.

[3] There is more than one way of getting rid of the things one does not wish to talk about: the whole discussion is begun from a postulate (perfect competition) which slides over the difficulties; later it is said, generally without detailed or rigorous proof, that things 'happen more or less' as in the initial model — or else, anything that cannot be explained in terms of a market of small competitive units is declared not to be 'economic', and thereby relegated to politicians and their wisdom.

[4] G. Blardone, in his 'Avantages et coûts sociaux de la croissance économique', *Semaine sociale de Marseille*, July 1956, has used very felicitously the idea and concepts of bearable disequilibria. Concerning the idea of bearable disequilibrium, cf. François Perroux, 'Les Trois Analyses de l'évolution et la recherche d'une dynamique totale chez Josef Schumpeter', *Economie appliquée*, n⁰ 2, 1951, p. 311.

This major change seems to me a distinguishing feature of twentieth-century policy, whose aim it is to influence the dynamism of growth and simultaneously to reduce cyclical fluctuations.

I shall explain why this is so by means of an analysis of the differences between counter-cyclical policy and a policy of balanced growth, and shall show that they are not merely verbal differences but differences of substance.

I shall further proceed to define the content and limitations — and these are severe — of a policy aiming at balanced growth on a national scale. I shall finally extend the analysis by considering the relations between a number of different economies. In the latter sphere I hope to dispel some illusions, or to put it more bluntly, pretences, concerning international stability under conditions of short-term expansion and long-term growth.

Paul Valéry was wont to say that 'A writer should be judged by the difficulties he has chosen to face'. My choice was made for me by that quasi-pontifical authority mentioned earlier, and it was made with a perception, sagacity and feeling for present-day problems that deserves every praise : for the difficulties in question are not only inescapable but very 'real'. They inject into economic dogma the amount of doubt necessary to keep faith alive, while preserving sufficient inventive confidence to save the highest values.

I. The Differences between a Contra-cyclical Policy and a Policy of Balanced Growth

It would be gratifying to be able to claim that, in the case of balanced growth, theory preceded practice. This would, however, be inaccurate. It would, at this juncture, clearly be irrelevant for us to discuss Cassel's regular progressive growth, or Schumpeter's expanded circular flow in the absence of major innovations, or the paths of equilibrium growth in recent models, which are purely imaginary constructions, if in real life the prevailing conditions are those of imperfect competition. Our task is to determine what conscious and systematic measures can and must be applied if the effect of real instabilities is to be lessened.

To begin with, just as we have grown accustomed to look into the store-room of 'data' in our attempts to discover how such data may be modified appropriately, so we view processes of economic growth as taking place according to trends that are influenced by deliberate policy.

(1) Since the price mechanism clearly does not operate under

conditions of perfect competition, even approximately so, and simply heterogeneous, we have not only refrained from attempts to adapt the static system of optimum allocation of resources to a dynamic context, but we have even called into question more complex systems of workable competition. We have focused attention on the dynamic influences of super-normal profits accruing in particular sectors and industries; on the differing degrees of imperfection of competition in the various economic groupings; on the unequal ability of firms or groups of firms to shift towards the right, through selling expenditure and modification of the structure of their business rivals, their long-period demand curves which are supposed to be more elastic than their short-period demand curves. Thus the state seems to have intervened in the sphere of price determination with the firmest of theoretical justification.

At the same time, doubt has been thrown on the beneficial value of cyclical contraction. The firms most capable of withstanding depressions, by virtue of their financial strength, selling costs and ability to secure emergency credit, are not necessarily those which serve the best interests either of the consumer or of long-term national productive capacity. It is therefore perfectly reasonable for the state to refuse to accept the verdict of depressions and to adhere, as best it may despite them, to its choice for the long-term structure of the economy.

(2) Moreover, for purely technical reasons, and also because of wars, public research in both pure and applied science has been greatly extended. Simultaneously, the way in which information is spread has changed, as large firms, complex units, organized industries and economic groups have come into being. The time which elapses between the conception of a new idea and the construction of the first machine, its experimental application and its general use, which we know used to be considerable, now tends to be deliberately reduced in an environment which is itself consciously regulated by the intervention of the state and of industrial groups.[1]

(3) One should add that none of the characteristic structural population features are any longer considered spontaneous. The conservation of natural resources is a confession as well as a corrective step: it is, in effect, a condemnation of blind liberalism. Over and above the effect of innovations, the volume of resources available is also affected by institutional changes. As for investment in human beings (health, education, general economic training), as opposed to

---

[1] I study in the general theory of progress the three 'moments' of creation, propagation and meaning. So far as the second is concerned, I take pleasure in citing Giovanni Demaria: 'Su due modi di diffusione delle conoscenze tecniche', *Giornale degli Economisti*, Nov.-Dec. 1955, pp. 589-602.

investment in things, it shows every sign of becoming a *leitmotiv* after having been a subsidiary or forgotten theme.

An awareness of these kinds of intervention, acting upon real factors contained in trends of which neither the rhythm nor the conditions are purely cyclical, suffices to locate the problem of monetary and fiscal policy in an 'environmental dynamics'. By this we mean tendencies imposing constraints upon the cycle, rather than being engendered and determined by it, wherein modifications of the real factors are no longer seen as unconnected operations but are closely linked together in the form of typical sequences. Moreover, the policy of balanced growth is the complete antithesis of the haphazard piling up and incoherent juxtaposition of measures of intervention ; its aim is to act simultaneously upon the real factors in the trend and the real factors in the cycle in order to secure from the economy, in its concrete and historical setting, the maximum product of a socially optimum structure.

This concept of balanced growth has been studied in France for over a decade.[1] It is also to be found in the work of Ragnar Nurkse on underdeveloped countries, in that of Tibor Scitovsky on European integration, and W. W. Rostow's work on structural and dynamic equilibrium. As is the case with any idea, for example, its predecessor, counter-cyclical policy, it becomes progressively conceptualized. That is to say, it arms itself with intellectual tools which we construct in order to understand and to act—in terms which are as quantitative as possible, of course.

The first concept is that of maximizing the aggregate real product and of keeping its fluctuations to a minimum.

This may sound paradoxical.[2] But our discipline abounds in resolved paradoxes : for instance, those of utility and value, of saving, and a host of others of a statistical and economic character. In this, economics resembles other sciences whose advances have all, at various times, been regarded as paradoxical. I trust you will grant that for more than forty years it has been realized that investment is neither marginal nor continuous. As for incoherence, this is another and complex story. People who deal competently with technical problems are usually critical of Schumpeter and sceptical of his dynamic entrepreneurs — those rather individualistic heroes — and their 'clusters'. They believe there are broad, foreseeable technical

[1] Very many writings bear this out, more especially those concerned with regional economic policies.

[2] The concept is measurable econometrically but requires a working definition of the *amplitude* and the *duration* of the product movement. The morphological characteristics of the *severity* of the contraction are not the same thing as these two factors.

trends which call forth investment, the total quantity or relative effectiveness of which cannot, of course, be known in advance. One should note, however, that even in its early and unsophisticated forms anti-cyclical policy aimed at reducing the severity, amplitude and duration of the contraction; such policy sets itself the twin and insoluble task of choosing the timing and extent of intervention just as it is plunged in uncertainty when a clear distinction needs, in practice, to be drawn between the primary and secondary content of expansion and contraction. What is important today is that our policy concentrates on real output instead of on the price level, or even employment. The relative abandonment of full employment implied by this change is a recognition of the modification of technical coefficients, a possibility that was ruled out in short-period models based on the General Theory. The selection of a rate of growth that is capable of being maintained is the first task of those programmes and plans which, however low the esteem in which they are held, are more or less openly or covertly used by most countries. The rate of growth is expressed as an increase in the rate of productivity deemed desirable for the economy and for its constituent sectors. Measures of productivity in physical or value terms have serious shortcomings, and only take on meaning through economic analyses which can be initiated in a decision-model or plan. An overall view of this type will pinpoint the methods as well as the results of discretionary and automatic counter-cyclical policies.

The second concept is that of reducing distortions between the main constituent sectors of the economy.[1] It would not be helpful to suggest that this choice is implicit in macro-economic policy; for the very problem of the government, whose task is to select and act, is to make the choice explicit. The government has at its disposal an ever-changing stock of potential innovations and aims at maintaining a given rate of growth. It tries to see which are the 'impulse industries' which will set in motion complementary and induced effects. The government is forced into a difficult choice between their expansion, which implies specialization, and the preservation and stimulation of regional growth, the claims of which stem from the very structure of the national state and the various incompatible demands put forward by local electorates. Thus, even in the most liberal countries, we see options for new structures influenced by the objectives of the state with regard to the direction of expansion.

---

[1] This second concept does lend itself to econometrical measurement, at least through comparison of the absolute magnitudes and the rates of increase which are intended and achieved.

The perspicacity of the governing groups was perhaps neither better nor worse in 1860 than it is today; reliable historians tell me that it was even then quite common for big industrialists to confer with ministers; from which I am inclined to conclude that commissions planning for modernization and for general equilibrium are not inventions of the devil, presaging the end of the world.

The third concept is probably the most important, since it divests equilibrium of its 'mechanical'[1] aspects and shows clearly that compatibility between rates of growth of investment, saving, productive capacity and the labour-force is basically the compatibility of projects conceived by very real persons and groups. The spate of mutual vetoes that would ensue if oligopolies were informed of each other's investment plans has been conjured up suggestively enough by Domar. Everyone now realizes that workers are no longer taken in by the Keynesian trick of reducing real wages through 'intelligent' inflation. Everyone also knows that self-financing, investment based on long-term programmes, and the sterilization of part of savings through capital issues by public or semi-public bodies create conditions which are not propitious for market regulation of innovations, given the representative long-term rate of interest. It is also clear that the grossest incompatibilities are discussed, and as far as possible ironed out in programmes and in plans, and are kept under close observation during the execution of such plans. It is a fact that permanent unemployment is no longer relied upon to prevent wage pressure from raising wages beyond the long-term productivity of labour; nor do governments pin their hopes on continuous inflation to absolve them from their rôle as arbitrator or, at least, conciliator.

So defined, a policy of balanced growth resembles neither pre-1914 counter-cyclical policies nor the Hicksian alternative (at the end of his book) of 'monetary reform to re-establish monetary security' combined with 'a moderate use of public investment and fiscal controls'. It would be an interesting exercise to draw up two columns, one setting out counter-cyclical measures and the other the requirements of a policy of balanced growth. On one side there would figure open market policy; the manipulation of interest rates; and built-in stabilizers, fiscal and social. On the other side there would be long-term policy with respect to resources and population trends; policies designed to modify the propensities; and, finally,

---

[1] It would be wrong to say that the 'tensions' under discussion cannot be measured. Quantitative comparison of intended and achieved levels is quite possible. For a simple yet excellent numerical illustration, see Jean Baboulène (engineering consultant to the Compagnie Française d'Organisation), 'Résistances et disparités dans la croissance économique', *Semaine sociale de Marseille* (July 1956).

policies aimed at co-ordinating long-term and medium-term investment programmes and part of innovation. Such a table would not
be an anthology of contradictions in economic thought, but rather
an outline of attempts to surpass itself, resulting in a net gain.

It was, after all, only natural when the differences and connections between trends and cycles were not explicitly stated, nor the
relations between structure and growth explicitly analysed, that policy
should have been developed without explicitly seeking to support
and regulate short-term expansion and long-term growth. It is not
impossible to argue that the change that has taken place is one of the
distinguishing features of economic thought and practice in our day.

I accept this, at any rate for my present objective, in order to
discover what the policy whose objective and methods I have outlined
has to contribute towards solving our paradoxical difficulty : maximum growth with stability.

I now proceed to consider this question on a national scale.

II. The Content and Limits of a Policy of Balanced Growth on a National Scale

The fundamental question is the following : 'Is it possible, over
a long period containing several cycles, to speed up the rate of growth
of aggregate real output by innovation and public investment without
thereby increasing cyclical instability?' The question is not new
and must inevitably divide different schools of thought. I propose
to answer it in the affirmative, after having, for obvious reasons,
reformulated it by reference to the distinction between autonomous
and induced investment. I do this despite the inherent uncertainties,
the impossibility of accurate statistical measurement and despite my
own inclination to eliminate autonomous investment entirely when
trying to discover how the level of income and the structure of capital
respond to innovations, which we shall take as a first approximation,
to be exogenous. The essence of my argument does not depend upon
the Hicksian model, but it can be more conveniently expressed in
terms of that model and its well-known, controversial terminology : [1]

(1) In a large economy, which we assume to be closed, public
investment in research, in major innovations and their propagation,

---

[1] The most controversial point of all is, of course, Autonomous Investment.
This idol, born of a difference, is nothing more than a total (public investment + investment 'in direct response' to invention + firms' long-term programme
investment). It displays no great variety of effect : either in a straight line, or in
a switchback track of humps and hollows, it brings about the Increase in output
which sets off the Accelerator and its Lags. This is the Cycle which winds its

and in the improvement of human capital is an established fact.[1] This type of investment is more closely defined by reference to two other categories of investment. Upon it depends some of the investment based on the plans of large firms; upon it, too, depends part of the investment that would formerly have been undertaken 'in direct response to invention'. Thus to the investment induced by the growth of real output must be added investment generated by the public sector.

Public investment does not, of course, fall from Heaven; like any other form of investment it has to be financed by saving, that is to say, by levies of appropriate form and amount. No less clearly, excessive or misapplied public investment can over the short or long period reduce private investment as well as real output.

My point, however, is quite different: great innovations, the exploitation of new forms of energy, the creation of new large-scale industrial units, of new public or semi-public organizations or of new organizations of public importance, all these are today dependent upon propensities to public innovation and public investment. If such public innovations and investment, which set off other complementary innovations and investment in accordance with the law of modern technology and not in the disorderly fashion typical of Schumpeterian heroes, are not brought about no one will bring them about and the long-term rate of growth of real output will fall short

way between Floor and Ceiling, provided that the Saving and Investment Coefficients keep quiet. The *deus ex machina*, both the god and the machine, have been ferociously assailed more than once, but no one, it seems to me, has ever quite done away with some salutary truths which its — very free — worship can reveal.

No well-read economist would, of course, dream of crediting recent Anglo-Saxon contributions with the discovery of 'ceilings' and 'floors'. Anyone not familiar with the Italian literature, for instance, should read the special number of *Giornale degli Economisti*, Sept./Oct. 1952.

[1] In the twentieth century, in the major Western economies, the mechanism of the appearance and propagation of innovations has changed rather radically. If we under-estimate this change, we also neglect an opportunity. The past continues to live in the midst of the present forms, but these do, eventually, open our eyes. Therein lies the importance of public research in pure and applied science. (For the United States, see S. Colum Gilfillan, 'The Prediction of Technical Change', *The Review of Economics and Statistics* (1952).) Between 1940 and 1945, more than four-fifths of the sums spent on organized research were allotted by the Federal Government.) Thanks to self-financing, the large corporation has become a centre for economic and social experiment with an efficacy previously unknown. By a rather sweeping simplification, of which we are well aware, we may say that very large and vital parts of production depend upon public research and collective research centred on large oligopolistic firms. The private entrepreneur who first exploits a 'discovery' which he calls his 'own' and which brings him a purely temporary monopoly profit until such time as the new product has been diffused through the market, has by no means disappeared but has declined in importance. This is especially true of the major innovations typical of the twentieth century (atomic energy, automation). As a result, we get overlapping flows of inventions and innovations, which appear at deliberately chosen moments and are propagated in a prepared environment.

of its possible maximum. A third or a quarter of defence expenditure could in more settled times be devoted to increasing public invest- ment and innovation. In any case, the significant effect of increased public innovation cannot be measured purely in terms of the size of public investment, but rather in terms of the body of effective inno- vations generated by it. Owing to the technological changes that have occurred in recent times it has become difficult to decide *a priori*, dogmatically and systematically in favour of private innovation and investment. I would point out that I far from belittle their potency. I am merely suggesting that for a given increment of investment the maximum long-term increase of real product will depend on whether the innovations and investments set off by the generating action are greater in the case of public or private action. I would add that there are numerous cases where the advantage lies with public action.

Translated into Hicksian terminology this means that public innovation and its accompanying investment can raise the movable 'ceiling', that is, the bottleneck zone in which resources are fully used, because they make available natural resources which private action would not have released and because private innovations are elicited as a result of the impulse originating from the public sector. The same factor tends to raise the 'floor' above the level which it would have reached if account could have been taken only of the asymmetrical nature of the accelerator during the downswing in a purely private economy. Why? Because public research and inno- vation present private enterprise with innovation opportunities which are largely independent of cyclical movements. Such permanent pressure, relatively independent of counter-cyclical monetary and fiscal measures, stems from long-term development programmes. Fellner has shown how innovation has, over long periods, acted so as to compensate [1] for a falling output/capital ratio in the United States. My thesis is that nowadays part of this compensating action follows necessarily upon public innovation and its corresponding investment.

(2) Induced investment in the Hicksian sense of investment induced directly by an increase in real product or via profits, is inevitably reshaped in a schema which allows that the economy may be guided and co-ordinated by the forecasts inherent in flexible plans and programmes.

In the field within which induced investment depends on the profits being earned, such investment takes into account, to some

[1] 'L'Action compensatrice de l'innovation', *Économie appliquée* (Paris, 1956– 1957) ; for more detail see William Fellner, *Trends and Cycles in Economic Activity* (New York ; Henry Holt and Company, 1956).

extent, the subsequent demand for products, about which information is furnished by medium-term forecasts.

So far as the expansion programmes of large firms are concerned, they can more easily be made compatible by those responsible for carrying out, say, a five-year plan than through oligopolistic conflicts. (I do not, however, wish to cross swords with those economists who insist on reasoning in terms of a world entirely free from organization or forecasting.) The smaller degree of incompatibility between innovations and realized plans in the field of induced investment is the fact I am stressing when I say that induced investment has become 'capable of having its own purpose'; that such investment is neither purely that effected by a host of entrepreneurs rendered infallible by the market, nor that put in hand by some collective entrepreneur, automatically and unambiguously obeying a law of so-called 'induced' investment.

(3) An additional reduction in consumption is a necessary condition for a long-term growth of the national real product resulting from an increase in innovational public investment.

In this connection two dangers must be mentioned — one well known though inaptly named and the other less commonly considered.

The first is the set of permanent inflationary pressures in countries of long-standing growth, even apart from wars and preparations for war. Neither 'secular inflation' nor 'chronic inflation' seem to me appropriate descriptions. Some of the persistent inflationary pressures which depend upon structural characteristics, cannot be adequately controlled except through long-term — possibly very long-term — policies designed to alter the structure of institutions ; such policies have virtually nothing in common with counter-cyclical policies of a monetary and fiscal type. The ageing of the population, and the consequent burden of growing transfer payments, calls for a conscious adjustment between productive and total population, such as a higher retirement age. The slogan of full employment demands changes to eliminate or reduce rigidities. A falling propensity to create real wealth requires the reintroduction of the notion of profit as providing a reward for creation and responsibility ; a fall in the propensity to work in real terms needs to be faced with a long-term policy regarding types of wages and labour education. I confine myself to these points since I am absolved from dealing with monetary factors, these having been unequivocally taken in hand and mastered by Professor Haberler.

I should, however, like to dwell on the second danger, difficult though it is to define, since it presents both a risk and an opportunity. It relates to a fundamental and major change in the occupational structure of industrial communities. The General Staff of Industry — the technicians, foremen, skilled workers, office workers and staff employed in economic administration, all of whom go to make up what are called, not very happily, the new middle classes — grows rapidly not only in absolute terms but also relatively to both active and total population. Such persons earn high salaries, which certainly induces an element of savings; as a rising class they share in the dynamic features of industrial life. There is reason to believe that for this class new consumers' goods, especially durable goods, compete with past and even current savings. If that is so, a compensating reduction in consumption would need to be created by fiscal action.

(4) Suppose the global conditions outlined above are achieved by a long-term policy based on real factors and encompassing monetary counter-cyclical policy, automatic or discretionary, then our type of analysis makes it necessary to understand the relations between structures and balanced growth. In a long- or fairly long-term development plan, the state is not merely concerned with aggregate flows. It is concerned with industries and cannot ignore regions; whether it does so openly or not, it attempts to fashion a new structure for the economy.[1] The constituents of aggregate flows are seen easily enough; the state cannot be so deceived by the capital coefficient that it confuses an increase in investment in, say, housing with increased investment in light or heavy industry. My object, however, is to make a much more precise and practical point. The state and the nation can maintain a desired rate of growth only by resolving the contradiction between two kinds of balance: vertical and horizontal balance by industries, and balance by regions. Dynamic specialization and dynamic comparative costs are wholly determined by the deliberate backing of the key industries of the age: at the expense of keeping alive, be it from considerations of welfare or politics, all that is obsolete or merely traditional, wherever it might be found. Such a solution is not reached through the market and its free operation: it is achieved by the creation, with active governmental help, of 'poles of development' in an environment of propagation so arranged as to give every region the opportunity to draw new strength from them.

Such a policy of conscious and co-ordinated choice is altogether different from traditional business cycle policy, and is practised by many countries. It very clearly emphasizes the contradiction, which is new to our times, between the maximization and spontaneous

---

[1] Jean Weiller has developed very well the idea of preference for national structure. It stands to reason that authors used to thinking in terms of a market of small units cannot easily recognize the theoretical and practical implications of this idea.

stabilization of the real product on the one hand, and, on the other, the difficulties which these attempts at maximization encounter when they are combined with the simultaneous endeavour to eliminate interruptions in growth and the cyclical hazards of growth.

The choice between 'development poles' and areas, between function and location, brings us face to face with international politics.

III. The Content and Limits of the Policy of Balanced Growth on the International Scale

Different rates of growth of real output in different countries constitute one of the most important causes of instability ; they also, unlike wars, rearmament and other exogenous factors, lend themselves to economic analysis.[1]

These divergences must be related to a multiplicity of circumstances. Given the object in view we shall dwell only upon new industries possessing the threefold characteristic of indivisible plant, oligopoly and public intervention. It is such industries or new sections of industry (sets of firms) which M. Armand stresses [2] in his

[1] Links between different economies are no more 'classical' than links between the parts or sectors of the same economy. (In the countries of Western Europe, for example, price and income rigidities, social transfers, subsidies, etc., form networks of relationships which have nothing whatever to do with those implied by the models of free competition.) Let us leave aside intergovernmental trade ; but what about links through direct private investment ? Do they count for naught ? Drawing on the work of the National Bureau of Economic Research, H. B. Woolley (*Hearings of U.S. Congress Sub-Committee on Economic Stabilization*, Oct. 1955) notes that, between 1946 and 1950, one-quarter of the goods imported by the United States came from American-controlled firms abroad. For one-quarter of American imports, therefore, the volume and direction of trade would appear not to have been subject to the law of comparative costs nor to the law of capital transfers in a competitive system. (Woolley says textually : 'It must not be overlooked that United States (direct) investment . . . in great measure determines the direction of the flow of these foods and materials to the United States rather than, say, to Europe'.

By combining the structural inequalities of economies and non-classical links, we begin to understand the large groupings of 'affiliated countries' around their focus, which the National Bureau of Economic Research describes so well. This accurate (and statistically proved) picture is neither that of a world economy composed of small units subject to the limitations of the immobility of factors, nor that of an economy linking nations with no structural characteristic other than the relative abundance of one factor of production by comparison with another (cf., for example, P. A. Samuelson's model). It is the image — I repeat Woolley's own words — of 'affiliated' economies grouped around their focus ; one of these, the United States (I am still quoting Woolley), having 'a unique and asymmetrical position'.

[2] Besides the well-known official reports on energy, I should like to draw attention to an excellent study deliberately addressed to a wider educated public : Louis Armand, 'France et Afrique à l'ère des grandes entreprises', *Hommes et Mondes* (July 1956).

efforts to emphasize the weakness of small nations and to invite Europeans to pool their resources as a first step towards collective enterprise in Europe itself as well as in Africa. Despite differences that are so obvious as to require no elaboration, European industrial communities and the large industrial complexes operating in Africa bear some resemblance to the complex units, for instance, the *Kombinat* upon which the Russians lean so heavily.

In both cases we see 'blocks' of investment and innovation endowed with the capacity to initiate changes and to set off a whole train of complementary innovations.

The first thing to note is that not all nations possess the necessary resources for action on this scale in equal measure. In the atomic field this is painfully and embarrassingly obvious; a prime minister has, in this context, found it possible to speak of major and minor nations. But there is similar inequality in many other fields, though to a smaller degree. This major inequality rests on others: inequalities of liquid reserves and assets; inequalities in the proportion of the aggregate product which can be spared for public research and development work; inequalities in the ability to expand geographically over adjacent or neighbouring territories; and, finally, differences between the capacity of various governments to modify, either to their own advantage or to the advantage of their economic groups, the rules of the economic game.

This unequal ability to bring into being new industries, in the sense defined, can be examined from two standpoints.

Let us consider the case of a new industry set up within some major economy. Such an industry will, as it expands, generate external economies, *i.e.* successive reductions in costs for outside firms or industries. The effectiveness and the speed with which these economies can be achieved, depends on the surrounding circumstances, and it is only on the basis of a structural model that one can gauge the extent and the kind of reductions in money costs, or of reductions engendered by cumulative innovations. And whatever be the part played by external *diseconomies*, every major state nowadays pursues such a policy. That they should do so at the risk of harming their own interests is unthinkable. Diseconomies caused by increased factor prices are, in any event, smaller in large economies experiencing heavy unemployment and a high rate of growth of resources. Theory of the most orthodox kind would thus seem to justify the policies in question.

Two possibilities exist. Either prices fall proportionately with costs in the sector experiencing external economies, in which case, other things being equal, the rate of growth of the real product rises.

Alternatively, prices do not fall proportionately with costs, the result being that supernormal profits are earned in the above-mentioned sector.

The surplus profits may be used in three ways : (1) to finance new and cumulative research and technical developments; (2) in direct investment; (3) to subsidize prices and meet 'propaganda' expenditure abroad, that term being used without any pejorative intent.

In each case an asymmetrical and, for a time, irreversible effect is produced by the large national economy upon its environment. This mechanism helps to make intelligible the appearance of constellations of 'affiliated' countries grouped around *foci*, a pattern so clearly described in the most recent studies of the National Bureau of Economic Research.

Secondly, the big economy can export a new industry or part of it. I have in mind the 'exporting' of 'blocks' of investment and innovation, such as the Middle-Eastern oil-refineries upon which great stress is laid by Wassily Leontieff, an economist of realistic and practical bent, who, being averse to metaphorical language, must have meant something very explicit when he spoke of the emergence of 'a new economic order'.[1] The essential consequences are again brought out by an analysis of external economies. In underdeveloped, as also in developed, countries, the export of new industries brings in its wake the trade which follows investment, and new complementary types of enterprise supported by direct investment; and sometimes, though not always, the large economy secures preferential treatment for itself. When, for instance, three large nations vie with each other, through means that are rather unorthodox by market standards, for the privilege of setting up some great steel mill or automated industries in an underdeveloped economy, it is certainly

---

[1] Wassily Leontieff has described some of the effects of the export of automated units to 'underdeveloped' countries. It is the species of a genus. The big oil-refineries of the Middle East, he says, the integrated steel mill built after the last war in Brazil, the giant artificial fertilizer plants recently brought into operation in India, mark the beginning of a new economic order. Complex structures of real capital and services (management, skilled labour), which introduce innovations that are capable of opening up immense regions, are 'exported' (the term is used for the sake of brevity ; the use of local resources in the operation is implied) to underdeveloped countries by countries very unequally endowed for such initiatives. These initiatives reduce the extent of the transmission of economic progress by the terms of trade resulting from the activity of small units and invalidate the theory of the international allocation of resources according to costs, prices and profit potentials in a market of small units. These initiatives also show the importance of growth, and indeed of balanced growth, deliberately induced by one nation in another by contrast with counter-cyclical policies. (M. Byé has done pioneering work in studying the 'large multi-country firm' ('La Grande Firme pluri-territoriale', *Cahiers de l'I.S.É.A.* (Paris, 1956)) and its relation to the period of expectation.)

with the object of reaping a gain that is inadequately measured by the yardstick ordinarily applied to the market of small units. In advanced countries, the fact that strategic sectors grow at vastly unequal rates may expose the weakest of them to crippling losses, the only protection against which is speedy adaptation; it stands to reason that a threatened sector hopes to deal with its problems through programmes and plans.

The theory of international trade does, of course, still apply formally to the situation I have described, although in substance it tells us something totally different from what it has customarily been understood to tell us.

Without going into questions of description or hard fact, it must be admitted that, in an economic system in which profit maximization and state intervention — encouraged or imposed by technological development — are found side by side, it would be contradictory for major economies to renounce their own projects, however incompatible these may be from the point of view of maximizing gains all round. They will use every means, including their political power, to maximize their individual gains.

The policy of balanced growth on the international scale and with special reference to innovations and new industries has yet to be translated into practice. Allowance will thus have to be made every time I use the present indicative instead of the optative. Having no gift for prophecy, I propose never to venture to use the future tense.

There is a critical point at which organization of the economy on geographical lines and its organization on functional lines enter into direct conflict : this is also the point which marks the fundamental difference between a policy of balanced growth on the international scale and the juxtaposition of national policies consisting of long-term programmes accompanied by counter-cyclical monetary and fiscal policies.

Let us consider some actual group of countries, such as the arbitrary European economic group known, without any implied criticism, as 'The Six'. To raise the level of effective public investment of this unit and dovetail such a measure with a common counter-cyclical policy would, in the absence of a single government, require a joint authority controlling money and investment. One only has to state this proposition to realize that it is probably safer, and certainly makes for a quieter life, to refrain from delving too deeply into such 'institutional technicalities'.[1]

---

[1] Because of the preponderant influence of political factors weighing upon a current experiment (the European Coal and Steel Community), it is better to

When discussing general principles there is a lot to be said in favour of creating from scratch, sharing in common the costs and benefits, new 'leader' industries, that is, economic entities whose own growth in aggregate output and productivity in turn engenders greater increases in output and productivity within their environment.

This recipe is much commended by that distinguished French engineer and economist — M. Armand. Its effect would be to reduce the danger of duplication and of incompatible expansion plans ; it would secure capital and specialized services from countries where they happen to be relatively abundant ; and would possibly even foster the creation of international teams. As an example of this approach we may mention the 'International Public Services' which Henri Laugier, former French representative to the United Nations, upheld with all the penetration of a scientifically trained mind.

Whatever the model envisaged, the relative effect of a 'development pole' upon a given region depends upon the structure of that region. If one wishes to avoid aggravating disparities between the rates of growth of product and those of the variables of the 'external sector', one must unavoidably accept some minimum measure of programme co-ordination. Since both neo-classical liberalism and nationalism, old or new, oppose a policy of this kind, one is forced to conclude that there is a fundamental contradiction between modern forms of technology and forms of political organization.

In other words, an appropriate institutional response is not given to the turbulent development (there is no question of stagnation) of the forces which are the mainspring of production.

dwell on the economic aspects of a grouping, under one authority, of two or more industries producing energy or several complementary goods in a group of countries. One imagines that these allied industries will together achieve higher and more productive investment than if each had remained separate and independent. It is also to be expected that investment engendered in other branches of production in the countries belonging to the community will be greater and more productive. The increase in the combined real product should, on the one hand, raise real *per capita* consumption and, on the other hand, set off a series of 'induced' investments in the whole group of countries (this concept to be understood with the qualifications previously described). Given unequal rates of growth of real output in the participating nations, additional disequilibria in balances of payments are not excluded.

The logic of this reasoning is unassailable to the point of making one wonder why such an excellent formula should be applied only to the Europe of the Six ; but, like other arts, that of building a community is 'entirely a matter of technique'.

Apart from the innumerable difficulties of detail, the necessary conditions for such a policy to bear fruit are the following : (1) the authority must exist ; (2) additional national investment for the defence of national positions must not entail large-scale waste of resources for the group as a whole ; (3) conditions for 'workable competition' (harmonization) must be created in the so-called common market.

An objective discussion of these ineluctable conditions should make it possible to determine the balanced growth which a supra-national community achieves for a particular group of nations.

Stability and Progress in the World Economy

Perhaps it is a counsel of wisdom to stop here.[1]

It is time indeed to refresh and relax ourselves by gazing upon more cheerful and restful vistas. Behold that fine plain where the marginal productivity of homogeneous factors tends to equality amongst unequally endowed nations. Or the realm of Monomotapa, where all men are true friends, a land of Cockaigne wherein reign peace and plenty and the dividends of the one *single* Republic — and, what is more, a *trading* one!

[1] Do the real factors lead us, whether we want it or not, to reconsider the problem of stability in the capitalist system itself?

I would advise those who do not decide 'by convention' to stop at this point, to advance with extreme caution.

They could protect themselves with two shields : one hypothetical (though perhaps rather flimsy), the other documentary (but certainly solid).

The documentation is borrowed from the fine work of the *Sub-Committee on Economic Stabilization* of the United States (*Automation and Technological Change*, op. cit., especially the statement by Dr. Edwin G. Nourse, former Chairman of the Council of Economic Advisers, pp. 618 *et seq.*). The probable trend of future events in 'automated' industries is there presented as follows : the most skilled workers will demand, and will receive, a rise in their real wage rate and then, beyond a certain limit, a reduction of working hours. Should this reduction be granted? No, say the top-ranking experts, not so long as a large fraction of the workers have a comparatively low standard of living (this is the meaning of the 'ethical challenge' forcefully stressed in *Automation and Technological Change*, separate pamphlet (Washington, 1955), pp. 11 *et seq.*). This means that for the community, and in its name, these experts recommend refusing people the choice between more real wages and more leisure.

This position is intensely interesting at a time when Soviet Russia and the People's Democracies are exporting capital goods, skilled experts and money to underdeveloped countries, without limitations other than the effort which they, can obtain from their people. If the Western nations do not wish to be ousted they will have to give proof of an equal capacity for large-scale transfers to the so-called underdeveloped countries. In this context, the economy of comfort and leisure, the economy of accumulated wealth considered as the main source of power, might well lose something of its happy self-assurance.

From the documentation, we are thus led to the hypothesis.

Does it not seem as though the quasi-liberal and the collectivist economies were engaged in a battle beyond the logic which the text-books attribute to the systems?

Modern technology faces both sides with problems to which certain data are common (indivisibilities, technical dimensions, skilled personnel). Each side tries to solve these problems by taking all the necessary liberties with the logic of its system and taking into account the tacit coalition of the poor against the 'masters'.

These are some very embarrassing real factors.

Money (when R. F. Harrod says 'money is power' this is subject to more than one interpretation), the instrument of choice and the weapon of power, seems to have little hold on them. I say 'seems', because the ways of Money are inscrutable.

Must the economist go on dreaming of a Golden Age? Or must he definitely think of something entirely different?

THE DISCUSSION ON
PROFESSOR PERROUX'S PAPER

Chairman: PROFESSOR GUDIN (Brazil)

Professor J. R. Hicks (U.K.) was the first to comment. He said : I shall not be able to take up more than one of the ideas that Professor Perroux has been putting before us in his eloquent paper ; it is the idea that a policy of balanced growth is something different from an anti-cyclical policy. If one underlines the word policy, there is nothing in this with which one can disagree. For governments to take responsibility for the trend of economic progress is undoubtedly something different from the mere taking of responsibility for correcting deviations from the trend. But in the substance of his paper, if not in the thesis which he proclaimed, I felt that Professor Perroux went farther. He seemed to be saying that if we look to balanced growth, we shall automatically avoid fluctuation. If that is what he is saying, I think that at that point I part company.

It seems to me quite clear that the cycles experienced in the nineteenth and early twentieth centuries were in their nature phenomena of growth ; how else can we explain the way in which economies have begun to fluctuate just as they have begun to grow, or as they have come under the influence of growing economies. The fluctuating economy is a growing economy, but one which is growing by fits and starts. There was, in the old days, the danger (on which Sir Dennis Robertson has taught us so much) that a more regular growth would mean a slower growth ; there was a conflict between stability and progress. Professor Perroux would, as I understand him, wish us to believe that that conflict has now disappeared ; through the growth-mindedness of governments and of his 'massive oligopolies' we can avoid the risk of fluctuation. This is just the opposite of what we used to be taught. Though I would not deny that there has been a change — a very important change, which we must seek to comprehend as far as we are able — I doubt if it has been so complete a change as Professor Perroux thinks.

In support of his position — his rather extreme position, as I think it — Professor Perroux has made great play with the concept

127

of *autonomous investment*. As I have myself some responsibility for that concept, I may allow myself some remarks upon the use which he has made of it. We have been told that it is 'a sum which is born of a difference'. I would prefer to say that it was born of a qualification. I was attempting to qualify the extreme accelerationist view which would make all investment dependent upon increases in demand; autonomous investment, as I used the term, was meant to suggest that there was some investment which did not depend upon demand at all closely. But in fact the sorts of investment which are autonomous in this sense are rather a mixed bag; it might have been better (I am sure it is better, in general, though it was not absolutely necessary for my particular purpose) to have drawn distinctions among them. At the least, I would now draw a distinction between (1) autonomous investment proper, due to exogenous causes (such as investment stimulated by invention, and investment which is the direct result of public policy) and (2) *semi-autonomous investment*, which is independent of the actual level of demand at the moment, or in the current short period, but does depend on demand in the longer run. The main type of this latter would be the 'long-term' investment, of which Mr. Harrod had already spoken. When one is talking of balanced growth, the rôles which are played by these two kinds of investment seem to me to be distinctly different.

The bearing of this distinction upon Professor Perroux's argument seems to me to be the following. Let us grant him his view (which I agree to be in all probability correct) that the investment which springs from invention is becoming concentrated in certain sectors of the economy; and let us also grant (what seems to be common experience) that investment which springs from public policy has a bias towards particular sectors of the economy. Call these (both of these), for the purposes of the present argument, the Active Sectors; the remainder of the economy constituting the Passive Sectors. What I think that Professor Perroux is saying is that the Active Sectors have acquired, in the time through which we are now living, a greatly increased importance. Political and technological factors have combined to give them a pre-eminence that is, against the background of historical experience, altogether novel. With this I should in no way disagree. But I think he goes on to imply that this pre-eminence of the Active Sectors has pushed the problem of investment in the Passive Sectors right into the background. If that is what is meant, I think it is quite wrong.

For, after all, the Passive Sectors do use capital; they have a problem of keeping their equipment adequate and suitable. If development in the Active Sectors proceeds too fast (either through government preference, or, as may indeed happen, through the working of the price mechanism) the capital stock of the Passive Sectors will be under-maintained, or, if it is maintained, it will fail to keep pace with the growth of the economy. It will then in the end fall intolerably below what is felt to be needed for efficient production. This, it will no doubt be said, is not 'balanced growth'; but it is what growth-mindedness seems to come to, most often, in practice. It seems inevitable that every class of rulers will have a bias towards certain kinds of investment, and that other kinds will lag behind. This is the kind of instability to which a high-pressure economy is especially liable. Then the point is bound to be reached when the under-equipment of the Passive Sectors passes the limit of tolerance. The Active Sectors must then be chained back, and the Passive given their head. But investment in the Passive Sectors is, at the most, no more than semi-autonomous; much of it is simple induced investment of the old sort.

What I want to emphasize in this connection is not the *mechanical* relation between the level of demand for 'Passive' products and the desired level of capital stock in those sectors (the conventional 'accelerator'). I regard that as no more than a simplification which is useful in the construction of models — instructive models as one hopes they are — for the *ex post* analysis of what has happened in the past, of the common elements in many cycles of the past. But for policy purposes, it does not get to the root of the issue. More important here is the dependence of the desired stock on *expectations* of future demand — the expectational element in the accelerator which gives it a psychological character. If the dependence were purely mechanical, it is possible that we might find means of predicting its working; it is the psychological element which makes it, at least in the short run, so highly unpredictable.

In the light of this, I remain unconvinced that the economy Professor Perroux has been describing is likely to remain, in practice, as free from fluctuations as he supposes. These fluctuations may not be of the old type, but they must be expected to have a recognizable continuity with the old type. I believe that the phase of precedence for Active Investment must be succeeded by a phase in which Passive investment is given its head. It looks to me as if some countries have already got to the point where a change round of this sort has occurred, while others are still in the intermediate stage when there is intense competition between the two sorts of investment, so that, though it is not yet dominant, an appreciable proportion of the investment that is being carried out is of a passive character. I still believe that Passive Investment is inherently unstable,

K   129

so that a slump in Passive Investment is not merely possible; it is probable sooner or later. Such a slump would be the modern version of the downturn of the old cycle.

The vital question which will then arise is whether, from that point onwards, things will proceed differently. It may be that Active Investment will have been kept throughout straining at the leash, so that at the moment when Passive Investment falters, Active Investment will leap ahead. If that is so, and we must hope it will always be so, the Cycle will indeed have lost its terrors; it will have been tamed into nothing worse than a few temporarily 'depressed industries'. But if, as I have been suggesting, the downturn in the Passive Sectors proves rather unpredictable, it is not going to be easy for Active Investment to expand very fast at just the right moment. The difficulty of keeping plans in cold storage in such a form that they can leap into *full* activity at the very moment when they are wanted is an old crux of *anti-cyclical* policy. I am not convinced that we have put this difficulty behind us, for good and all.

Professor Erich Schneider (Western Germany) made the following comment. The central thesis of Professor Perroux's stimulating paper seems to me to be contained in the following sentence: [1] 'Policies of balanced growth cannot be reduced to counter-cyclical policies'. If I understand his meaning correctly, it is that a counter-cyclical policy is not sufficient to ensure balanced growth. But this conclusion follows directly from Professor Perroux's own definition of balanced growth. He means thereby: [2]

(*a*) Maximum real *per capita* product and minimum fluctuations in employment and aggregate output;
(*b*) Diminution of disproportions between sectors; and
(*c*) Diminution of tensions between social groups.

If the concept of balanced growth is defined in this way, minimization of fluctuations is clearly insufficient to ensure balanced growth.

I should prefer, therefore, to state the problem in somewhat different terms, without, however, departing in substance from Professor Perroux's line of argument. My remarks will be in the nature of an addition rather than of dissent. We are concerned here with the part played therein by real, as distinct from monetary, factors. If we take progress to mean growing *per capita* product, and stability to mean the absence of fluctuations in employment and aggregate output, then a progressing and at the same time stable economy

---

[1] This is a translation of a sentence from p. 7 of the original French draft, circulated at the Congress.   [2] See pp. 113-116.

would be marked by a combination of a continuously rising real *per capita* product and permanent full employment. The question we have to ask ourselves is whether such a course is at all possible within a free, or predominantly free, market economy.

In the past, the most distinguished business cycle theorists — such as Wicksell, Spiethoff, Schumpeter and others — have answered this question with a clear 'no'. We have been told that short-run fluctuations in aggregate employment and output are not only unavoidable, but are indeed the very path of progress, or of economic growth. Economic growth rests on real factors which necessarily create instability, because 'technical progress and commercial progress are by nature such that they cannot rise in an even series as demand has done in our time', and because 'they are now accelerated, now retarded'.[1] If this is so, counter-cyclical policies exclude all economic growth.

But since the last war, we have seen that many countries with a predominantly free market economy have experienced continuous growth without significant fluctuations in aggregate product and employment, but that such growth does not exclude fairly considerable, mutually compensatory, fluctuations in the separate sectors of the economy. It is not difficult to see why such partial fluctuations are bound to be endemic even in a steadily growing economy. Rising real income causes the volume of demand to rise. But it cannot be expected that demand for all the separate consumption goods will rise *evenly*. There will always be areas in which demand increases more quickly than does the social product as a whole, and others in which demand increases more slowly. It is even possible for some demand (for inferior goods) to decline within general expansion. Statistical observation often shows a remarkably constant general rate of expansion, but this is, in fact, a weighted average of rather divergent (positive or negative) rates of expansion in the different sectors. Moreover, the fact that the rates of expansion of the demand for separate consumption goods must necessarily always be unequal, exercises a decisive influence upon the capital goods industry. Hence the economy is subject to continuous structural shifts. Some sectors contract, others expand, both in the field of the consumer goods and of the producer goods industries.

Similar processes are set in motion by cost-saving investment, that is, investment not induced or called forth by demand. Given even constant demand, the introduction of cost-saving production methods will cause the size of some firms to grow, while others, using obsolescent methods, contract. In this sense, partial fluctuations are

[1] K. Wicksell, *Lectures*, Part II, p. 241 (German edition).

the form 'by which the market economy effects the transition from one set of tasks to another'.[1] Such sectoral fluctuations are necessary concomitants of all progress. Joan Robinson was right when she said : 'The stocks of specific equipment of various kinds and the supplies of particular types of labour in existence at any moment, have been moulded by the past history of demand and are usually out of gear with current demand'.[2] This is one of the very important real factors, and it shows up as unrealistic the assumptions of Harrod's model of a continuously growing economy, because it is one of the basic conditions of that model 'that productive capacity in the various sectors of industry is adjusted to the division of demand between their products'.[3]

It is, furthermore, most important to remember that transition from one set of tasks to another is by no means an automatic process. Here, too, the driving forces are the independent decisions of entrepreneurs, and these decisions cannot be expected to be compatible with each other so that the process of transition might be accomplished along the path of a moving equilibrium.

Nevertheless, post-war experience (though, of course, too short to allow of final judgment) does suggest that the unceasing stream of structural displacements (sectoral fluctuations, shifts due to technical progress) are in themselves sufficient to provide the impulse for rapid expansion without *general* fluctuations in economic activity.

If this conclusion is correct, then it is obviously not true to say that any policy designed to stabilize employment at high levels — or to minimize employment fluctuations around a high average level — must impede the growth of a market economy, let alone that such a policy makes growth impossible. No doubt certain stabilization policies do hinder economic growth, but there is no doubt either that some employment policies directly further it.

Full employment policy aims at full use of available labour resources ; a policy of expansion aims at the highest possible rate of increase in the real social product with given labour resources, which means nothing other than an increase in the productivity of labour. This in turn can generally be achieved only by means of an increase in capital equipment. The rate of increase in real product is hence immediately related to the size of investment. We can readily appreciate that an employment policy which, for instance, seeks to remedy falling employment by stimulating consumption is devoid of significance in terms of progress, while a policy designed to maintain

---

[1] H. Gestrich, *Kredit und Sparen* (Jena, 1944), p. 90.
[2] J. Robinson, 'The Model of an Expanding Economy', *Economic Journal*, 1952, p. 52.   [3] *Ibid.* p. 52.

employment by stimulating investment directly encourages the process of growth.

The question arises, however, whether full employment policy as such is at all apt to create a propitious climate for the deployment of entrepreneurial activity in the Schumpeterian sense. Very distinguished economists have held that entrepreneurial activity prospers best in an atmosphere of the 'the carrot of profit in the boom, the stick of necessity in the depression' (Spiethoff), and that any policy designed to stabilize employment at high levels therefore deprives the entrepreneur of the very conditions of his existence and of his activity. It is true that some forms of full employment may create a climate hostile to innovations. But it is equally true that periods of severe general unemployment are no less hostile to economic progress. In a world in which maintenance of high employment levels has become an ineluctable object of the economic policies of all countries, only one path remains open, and this is to pursue employment policies only by means which at the same time allow of the greatest possible progress without social tensions (such as might be created by undue reduction of consumption). In the sphere of real factors this involves the maintenance and furtherance of the 'capacity to create and to manage new industries and to improve existing industries' (Perroux), keeping 'the channels of innovation clear' [1] and an increase in the mobility and flexibility of labour.

I should like to raise one final question also touched by Professor Perroux in his paper. How far are the macro-economic growth models which have been constructed so far — and they are all models in real terms — able to indicate the conditions of stable growth. Inasmuch as these models work with large aggregates and are concerned only with the expansion of global income and investment necessary to avoid disturbances in the shape of disappointed entrepreneurial expectations with regard to capacity and sales, these models do not shed much light on the problems of stable growth. What we need is a model which disaggregates into sectors, that is, one which uses an input-output table and includes in the analysis the relation between sectoral rates of increase as well as the different capital coefficients. It must be said that the dynamic input-output systems elaborated during the last few years cannot show the conditions of sustained growth, since they are usually based on given consumption. The level and the structure of consumption demand must themselves be included in the analysis of equilibrium and may not be regarded as autonomous. Professor Perroux seems to hold

[1] G. C. Allen, 'Economic Progress, Retrospect and Prospect', *Economic Journal*, 1950, p. 474.

the same view, since he says: 'If we knew the laws governing the separate parts of overall growth, we would be in a position to proceed to the synthesis of analysis by aggregate flows and analysis by sectors'.[1] And we are bound to agree with him when he adds: 'We are nowhere near such knowledge. However, not even the most modest concrete policy can be formulated without trying to eliminate the most blatant disproportions between sectors by means of medium-term forecasts and flexible programmes.'[2] We are indeed only at the beginning of any theoretical analysis of economic growth without disproportionalities. At the same time, it is no less important to examine the problems created by divergences in the rates of expansion of two or more connected open economies. Shifts in the ratio of the rates of growth may well upset the balance-of-payments equilibrium and thereby cause internal fluctuations which in turn may have a bearing on the process of growth. But these are problems which can no more be separated from monetary problems than can the important questions which Professor Perroux has raised in his paper.

Professor Jöhr (Switzerland) was the first to speak from the floor. He said that Professor Perroux had defined real factors as non-monetary influences. Certainly, a great number of these influences had to be treated as autonomous. But was this equally true of factors which could be classified as psychological? These had not been dealt with so far, except in Professor Hicks's very interesting remarks on the psychological interpretation of the acceleration principle, and in Sir Dennis Robertson's paper. The latter gave them an important place, speaking of the 'contagious forces of over-confidence and gloom' and mentioning, as cause of the upswing, the fact that 'cheerfulness breaks in'.

Professor Jöhr doubted whether we did full justice to these factors in treating them as mere outside influences. They were rooted in the structure of the economic system, which, in the Western World, implied a great number of independent units, all making their own decisions. But these decisions were not fully subject to the law of large numbers. They influenced each other through unconscious imitation, unconscious propagation of optimism and pessimism, the fact that certain behaviour gave rise to similar thoughts and objectives, and through the endeavour to get ahead of others. From this, there resulted the inherent instability of the economic system. This failing of the economic system could be illustrated by a situation often observed during bicycle races, like the Tour de France. Often, said Professor Jöhr, though it was a

---

[1] Page 8 of the original French text.   [2] *Ibid.*

race, all the competitors crawled through the countryside. But this 'rate of progress' represented a very unstable equilibrium ; it needed only one of the participants to increase his speed and most of the others would follow, chasing each other at high speed.

From this followed certain conclusions for economic policy. For example, the level of activity could not be left to the automatic regulation of the market. The government had to watch over the flow of incomes, and eliminate inflation and deflation. This problem could now be regarded as solved, but some similar problems were not so easily overcome. First, there were the big economic organizations which tried to influence economic policy so as to maximize the share of the national product going to their members. This had the great disadvantage that economic policy, which had to guarantee a steady income flow, was itself a dependent variable, subject to the influences of competing pressure groups. The only way to overcome their influence was through political decisions, independent of the economic organization.

Finally, one had an inherently unstable system of international relations, as had been shown by the competitive depreciations of currency during the 'thirties, the increasing tariff protection during the same period, and the outburst of world-wide inflation after 1950. This source of instability was certainly the most serious one, and he saw no hope of attaining stability otherwise than by extending the tasks and the efficiency of the international organizations set up since 1945.

Professor Jöhr said he would conclude by questioning Professor Hicks's thesis that growth was the main cause of business fluctuations. He himself regarded the instability resulting from the psychological interdependence of decision-makers as the principal factor.

Professor Papi (Italy) said he would like to comment on two methodological points in Professor Perroux's paper. First, when he spoke of real factors underlying the cycle, ignoring monetary factors ; when he dealt more especially with innovations, which led to the production of new goods or enabled existing ones to be produced more cheaply, he referred to 'favourable events'. The presentation was certainly 'up to date' with reference to structures and systems, but the facts remained unchanged. Only 'favourable events' enabled output to rise from the level reached during a depression. We had already seen that a rise in *per capita* real income depended on a series of 'favourable events'. These influences, spread by foreign trade, provided the impelling force behind economic progress.

Many authors, including Sir Dennis Robertson, thought progress depended on savings, capital accumulation and the efficiency of production. This was agreed. But why did individuals save, and, more important, lend for productive purposes? For a sort of inner discipline; a sort of spirit of co-operation? This was not likely. Saving and capital formation were conditions of progress. But it was 'favourable events' that increased activity.

Professor Papi said he wanted to thank Professor Perroux for supporting theories which regarded exogenous factors — favourable events — as the factors impelling progress. Professor Perroux had said that innovation would raise real income, even if the investment coefficient were constant; and, with rising income, even though the rate of increase fell off, consumption would rise. But Professor Perroux was mainly concerned with *real* factors affecting stability, and had shown how *public* investment could occupy the rôle of innovator through the great importance of fundamental applied scientific research, and as the private innovator declined in importance.

Professor Perroux had stressed the need for co-ordinating real factors to achieve balanced growth. The need for a policy to stimulate innovation, to co-ordinate investment, and so on, was needed to sustain growth. This led to a second consequence of Professor Perroux's argument. He proposed a policy of regular growth, leaving aside a policy for stabilizing economic flows by using built-in stabilizers, which would give such control over innovation and investment as led to greater investment, bigger consumption and smaller fluctuations. Perhaps Professor Perroux had not wanted to say this explicitly, but to attain such an objective one had to plan. It was therefore necessary to develop the theory of economic planning so as to enable individual and communal plans to be reconciled. In order to develop planning on a sound basis, economists had to study the consequences of the activity of the state and public bodies. Only thus could the state avoid conflicting with too many individual actions, or what was even worse, trying to reduce or suppress individual choice.

Professor Suranyi-Unger (U.S.A.) said that Professor Perroux's illuminating comments on the structural link between economic stability and growth opened promising fields for research. In particular, his 'pari en faveur d'une structure nouvelle' had the earmark of a powerful tool to be used in quantitative and qualitative enquiries into relations between the 'spontaneous' and 'controlled' allocation of resources. However, Professor Perroux's hints on the relations between small and large firms, old and new industries, agriculture and manufacturing, and so on, did not cover all the structural problems raised by economic stability and progress. He himself would like to comment on general aspects of these problems. Both in theory and in practice, greater attention should be paid to the overall intensity and methods of short-, medium- and long-term planning for a stable and growing economy.

More or less erratic fluctuations in the depth and volume of this planning had recently damaged some richer countries and had substantially slowed progress in some poorer countries. Experience revealed a correlation between the size of such damage and the abruptness of structural changes. Unfortunately, but understandably, some poorer countries tended to change suddenly from private enterprise freedom to global collective planning, or vice versa. Most of the changes in question were between 'post-Keynesian interventionism' and 'private business initiative' in the West, and between alternate 'new economic policies' and renewed drives for collectivization and industrialization in the East. Such shifts inevitably interfered with propensities to save and to consume, with private capital formation, with private plans, and with the efficiency of labour and entrepreneurs. *Ex post*, such misuse of productive resources could be seen to have menaced both stability and growth.

His conclusion was that in research and in discussion on economic stability and growth, the complex and neglected structural problems of linking private enterprise and state planning should be further explored, with special stress on the crucial relation between capitalism and communism. One also had to stress, with Professor Robertson, Alice's profound statement that, 'one does not like changing so often'. Frequent and wide structural changes were more likely to hamper than foster economic growth.

Professor Howard Ellis (U.S.A.) said he did not want to criticize either the whole or a part of Professor Perroux's paper. He merely wanted to call attention to the fact that his theoretical system bore a close resemblance to new models of economic growth. An important line of analysis was now being opened up, and he wanted to mention the recent works of Professor Fellner and Mrs. Joan Robinson.

In Professor Fellner's study, the three crucial factors for growth were innovation (and its connection with monopoly and competition), the mobility and relative supplies of factors, and monetary management. In Mrs. Robinson's work, the four main protagonists were innovation (and whether it was capital- or labour-saving), the increase (and rate of increase) in real wages, accumulation and population growth. Professor Perroux had three autonomous variables : institutions (including monopoly and competition, structural adjustments, etc.), innovation and the growth of population. Professor Ellis felt, however, that Professor Perroux implied that the distribution of income, and monetary and fiscal policy, also played a major part in his system. This meant that there was a striking similarity in the views of these three economists. It was, perhaps, inevitable that the Keynesian idea of underemployment equilibrium should become dynamic, and that the rate of accumulation and investment needed to ensure full employment should now be studied, as, for example, in the Hicks-Harrod-Domar models. But these models raised several questions. Was it full employment of labour or capital which should be preserved ? Again, population growth was important both for the level of employment and the rate of growth of the economy.

Professor Ellis suggested that the usefulness of the model was growing as its application spread. It was not, now, a monolithic unemployment theory, based on the relation between savings and investment. One could have underemployment of specific types of capital goods, because processes of innovation were inappropriate to the relative amounts of the other factors which were currently available. A variety of types of stagnation and underemployment became factors affecting the speed of development, as the model was extended. Professor Perroux was following this trend, and we were, in a sense, moving back to the old-fashioned business cycle theory, which envisaged a plurality of sources of maladjustment in the process of growth.

Professor Ellis recalled hearing a speech by Jacob Hollander on the economists' spiral, and the way in which economists kept reverting to old themes. This was happening to the model builders, who were once again dealing eclectically with the various factors of the business cycle, though we were now moving at a much more sophisticated level.

Sir Robert Shone (U.K.) said he would speak as an industrialist and would take the parochial view of the problem of progress in Britain. He had been able to recognize many landmarks in Professor Perroux's paper, but he had found it difficult to follow the whole geography. He followed Professors Viner and Robertson, but questioned one of their fundamental assumptions. They rested their analyses on the underlying assumption that free consumer choice could be relied on to give a satisfactory rate of growth. Yet, the system in the Western economies was biased *against* rapid growth. Because of the electoral system, politicians were liable to take the same short-sighted view as consumers — and a high price, in the form of a high rate of interest, had to be paid to secure growth. If we competed with no one but ourselves, this might not matter. But when we were competing, as Professor Rubinstein had shown, with a sector of the world where progress was the fundamental objective, it mattered very much. His recent visit to Russia had shown him the great progress being made there in heavy industry, in contrast to the progress, so far, in consumer goods. The main problem of the West was how to produce by education and leadership results which the East achieved by more direct control.

Sir Robert agreed with Professor Perroux that our world was one of large units. He did not think that, in Britain, the public sector was more progressive than the private. But the problem of getting people to take a dynamic view of progress went much deeper. In the U.K., for example, the recent increase in the profits tax and in interest rates called for a 5 per cent higher steel price to justify development. This made it difficult to keep prices stable and also secure development. Higher taxes and interest rates might be needed in the short run; but in the long run, one needed more investment in new plant. There was a conflict between the policies adopted for stability and those needed for growth.

Professor d' Alessandro (Italy) said that Professor Perroux had rightly emphasized the importance, for the aim of maintaining economic stability, of enforcing political stability by reducing tensions between social groups. These tensions were aggravated by political ideologies, and often grew out of economic ideologies. Therefore, stability clearly required the formulation of a universally accepted economic theory, since the existence of different economic ideologies proved that economic analysis had not succeeded in reaching generally agreed principles. The theoretical propositions of physics, chemistry and biology had been major factors in man's continuous struggle to improve his standards of living. But the theoretical propositions of economics did not appear to have assumed a comparable rôle.

Professor d' Alessandro said difficulties had certainly been caused by the complexity and mutability of economic phenomena, and by the rarity of opportunities for social scientists to carry out experiments. Nevertheless, economics might obtain better results if more attention were paid to the natural elements of the economic system, the firm and the family. Whereas technical progress had shown the importance of the economic problems of the firm, economics had hitherto given only marginal consideration to them. It could not be denied that the problems of the firm were often basic, nor that a full analysis of them might throw new light on general economic problems. As firms showed a remarkable uniformity of behaviour, it was consequently possible to formulate generalizations which might open up new paths for research. Financial statements, and special surveys covering shorter periods, would provide checks on such deductions.

It did not seem that the unwillingness of firms to provide data was a sufficient justification for the present situation. Perhaps the problems of the firm had been insufficiently examined because many experts in social economics thought such studies were at too low a level. On the contrary, the study of the firm called for a complete mastery of refined and modern econometric techniques.

Professor d' Alessandro said that in his forthcoming work on plant capacities and inventories, he had tried to show how a study of the basic problems of the undertaking could help to assess modern economic theories, such as the theory of cycles, the principle of acceleration and theory of full employment. He appealed to economists to pay the greatest possible attention to the problems of the firm, for this might bring about substantial advances in economic thinking and lead to greater economic stability.

M. A. Hahn (France) said that a few remarks by an old-fashioned liberal economist might perhaps appear outdated. Nevertheless, although necessarily incomplete, they might serve to clarify somewhat the problems under discussion.

The idea that there was a connection between progress and cyclical movements was an old one, whether progress was considered dependent on cyclical movements, or cyclical movements on progress — especially progress resulting from new inventions. It should be recognized, however, that basically, and from the standpoint of pure theory as applied to a market economy, progress and cycles were not dependent on each other, although they might have been connected in the past and might be again in the future. From that point of view, most of our problems appeared as *Scheinprobleme*, as *seeming* problems that became real only under the assumption of certain institutional rigidities (of wages and interest rates, for example) or of political goals. Progress could be, and had been, achieved, without cycles; and cycles could originate, and had originated, without progress.

Progress, in so far as it was dependent on capital accumulation (*i.e.* increased investment), set in when the demand for capital increased because its productivity rose, and/or when the supply of capital increased because savings rose. As long as increased demand was met by increased savings, and increased savings by increased demand for capital, all changes were cyclically neutral.

So far as the cycle was concerned, its causes depended on the business cycle theory that one held. Personally, he tended to a monetary cycle theory which interpreted the cycle as alternating inflations and deflations, which were self-reinforcing because of mass psychology. According to this view, if, on the one hand, the demand for capital increased in the wake of technical progress and, on the other, interest rates were not raised accordingly, inflation and a boom must develop. If inflation was prevented, for instance, by higher interest rates, then progress must lead to a non-cyclical, more or less evenly proceeding, development, depending on the availability of genuine savings. This was an eventuality which Schumpeter had judged unfavourable to progress, but which must appear as highly desirable to those seeking stability. It was, in any case, clear that progress was not *a priori* incompatible with stability, and that the cycle was not dependent on progress. It could originate, for instance, in the simple fact that profit expectations had improved under the impact of inventory liquidation.

He knew, of course, that *real* problems could arise if, for instance, population increased without a corresponding increase of the capital supply — provided wages were inflexible downwards. Nevertheless, it seemed important at least to start every analysis from the basic fact that, within the framework of flexible data, most of the problems discussed in connection with growth were not of a fundamental character. And, consequently, there was no real connection between progress and cycles, except that when the demand for credit grew, inflation was often allowed to develop.

M. Hahn said he would close with the still more general remark that, for a conservative economist, progress was the result of, and flowed naturally from, the propensity of people to work, to save and to improve production methods. It flowed from these rather than from the establishment of goals, the drafting of plans and so on. Governments, as distinct from the individuals who had to make their own economic decisions, could influence progress only by influencing those decisions. But government measures would have only a limited success, and might even be self-defeating, in an economy where people were still essentially free to make their own decisions.

Professor Okyar (Turkey) said that the discussion had now moved to a new world which was at once more beautiful and yet more concrete. Coming as he did from one of Professor Viner's countries, he was interested to see where Professor Perroux's paper applied to these lands, and would like to comment on the concept of economic growth. Professor Perroux had distinguished between growth and an 'economically progressive economy'. Professor Okyar wanted to try to remove the confusion between these terms. Growth occurred when there was an automatic process of increase in size in a steady way without major interruptions — but leaving room for cycles. On the other hand, a net investment of a given size in a poor country would not give rise to the same automatic process as in a richer one ; for the institutional framework was different. Any increase in activity to which it gave rise might be temporary or might display marked irregularities with periods of stagnation.

Professor Okyar said that whilst he could not go into these institutional differences very fully, he would like to point to a major one which, whilst essentially psychological, was none the less real. This was the absence of a capitalistic attitude to wealth. By this he did not mean the absence of the ideas of any particular political system. He simply meant that the behaviour of firms and individuals was not based on any distinction between capital and income. So capital was often not maintained intact, but subjected to concealed or open consumption, and an increase in the capital stock was hard to ensure. It was consequently important to distinguish between economic growth which was automatic, and economic development, which was not.

Professor Jaffé (U.S.A.) claimed to have come to Rome resolved to behave like the Victorian child, who was seen and not heard. Had there been only the five lectures, he would not have departed from this resolve. But the discussion suggested that his incompetence in the special subject under review was not absolute but only relative. He would therefore add his own speculations, as others had done.

He felt that the gulf between Professors Robertson and Viner on the one hand, and Perroux on the other, was only apparent. The bridge between them was to be found in Professor Perroux's remark that the fundamental problem was not to iron out the cycle but to render its effects more tolerable. This neat system started from a given income distribution which was accepted as just. Its unreality was only partial and its conclusions could be useful for all economies. The danger was that, as distinct from the masters, pygmies drew conclusions which they presented as dogmas. It had to be remembered that, in practice, economies were dominated by monopolistic competition, and had some planned, but unco-ordinated, sectors. There was competition in world markets; but integration, planning and control all occurred; there was the difference between poor and rich; and so on. And all of this was subject to the overriding influence of cyclical and long-term fluctuations.

How could we make the situation tolerable and reduce strains? The analysis of a competitive market was not everything, but one should not reject what it could offer. Like Professor Hicks, in his distinction between active and passive sectors, we proceeded by trial and error; each method became more fashionable in its turn. And in a changing world, remedies had to be palatable to all nations.

Finally, when we talked of making progress 'tolerable', what did we mean by 'tolerable'? Professor Jaffé agreed with Professor

Baudin's view that socio-psychological aspects should not be under-rated. When welfare was being considered, ordinary aggregate indices were not enough. We needed other indices to show departures from tolerable limits. For example, one might study the extent to which a country had departed from Wicksell's criterion of an optimum population.

Professor Rugina (U.S.A.) said he wanted to raise an explosive topic, namely, the idea that an attempt to put into practice the policy called 'balanced growth' would mean opening the back door to socialism. Professor Perroux had said that the new economic policy was a combination of 'flexible medium-term programmes and plans (five-year periods, for example) and measures of monetary stabilization (regulating the volume of monetary flows, of interest rates or built-in stabilizers)' (Note 1, original text). This criticism was not directed at Professors Perroux, Hicks and Nurkse, but he doubted whether the policy of 'balanced growth' — as expressed in this quotation — would enable us 'to determine by trial and error, on a national basis, the maximum product in real terms, with the minimum of fluctuations' (*ibid.*). In other words, he doubted if it could achieve economic progress with normal stability.

Professor Rugina gave a number of reasons for this.

(1) The policy of 'balanced growth' did not use as its criterion the fundamental conditions for economic equilibrium, *i.e.* the only way of reaching normal economic stability.

(2) It worked with the same method of trial and error which had been unsuccessful under the previous anti-cyclical policy, which also attempted to bring the national economy towards stability.

(3) He specifically stressed that the method of trial and error would be satisfactory if we had some objective standards by which to measure the intensity of various evils in economic life (inflation, deflation, disproportions between investment in capital and consumer goods, etc.). Unfortunately, we had no such objective standards or instruments and, consequently, the method of trial and error was fruitless.

(4) So the new policy of 'balanced growth' might in the end be as unsuccessful as the previous 'anti-cyclical' policy. Yet the situation today was very different from that in the century before 1929. Indeed, at that time, the Central Banks were relatively independent and the issue of money was ordinarily beyond government manipulations.

If the policy of 'balanced growth' were tried today, the governments in question would be so widely and deeply involved in day-to-day economic affairs that the political leaders would not recognize eventual failure. Instead of declaring their failure openly, they might well resort to more regulations, on the ground that people did not react in a 'normal' way — which, in this case, would mean as expected by government experts. Thus, in a country of the Western world, with traditions of true choice in the spending of earned income, there would be a struggle between the private and public sectors of the economy.

The result of this antagonism could be either a revolution to restore freedom (a possibility which was doubtful in our time of uncertainty and insecurity) or the government, under the pretext of promoting social welfare, might take over the entire economy, so that a completely planned economy could be introduced.

This was why Professor Rugina feared that the policy of 'balanced growth', if put into practice, might well represent a further step on the road to a planned economy. This, however, would be nothing else but socialism introduced by way of the 'back door', whether the promoters of the new policy of balanced growth anticipated that or not.

Professor Delivanis (Greece) suggested that the government could intervene not only through innovation, as Professor Perroux had suggested, but also by influencing the growth of population and the form of institutions. For instance, the immigration policies of the Australian and New Zealand governments had been most effective; and in totalitarian countries governments could exert tremendous influence on economic activity by drastically modifying institutions.

On Professor Perroux's general contention, he doubted whether one could distinguish between an anti-cyclical policy and balanced growth. Professor Perroux had also contended that entrepreneurs could not expect great profits from the development of atomic energy. It was no doubt true that the initiative in planning such developments no longer rested with private industrialists; but it was nevertheless open to them, by planning their factories efficiently, to obtain larger profits than their less powerful rivals.

Professor Perroux had asked whether capitalism could solve the economic problems of the atomic age. His own view was that capitalism in the orthodox sense no longer existed. Finally, he agreed with Professor Perroux that analysis often lagged behind economic developments, but he thought that Professor Perroux's own writings were admirable examples of constructive analysis.

Professor Perroux closed the discussion by thanking those who had commented on his paper, either in writing or verbally. He would like, first, to clarify the main ideas and concepts in his own analysis, for there appeared to have been a few misunderstandings.

First of all, Professor Perroux could not accept the increase of real product as the criterion of economic progress. He wanted to pay tribute to the very precise analysis by Professor Marrama, and to sum up the essential points in his own work. Economic progress could be expressed by indicators of average quantities, indicators of structure and combinations of simple indicators. But a progressive economic society was one in which innovation spread with great rapidity and at least *social* cost.

Professor Perroux again criticized the vagueness of the notion of stability. He distinguished between periods of increase or decrease in the rate of growth, cyclical fluctuations and secular interruptions in growth. He emphasized that one should not be concerned with eliminating alternations in growth, nor with fluctuations, but primarily with making bearable the disequilibria of growing economies.

Second, Professor Perroux replied to Professors Hicks and Schneider. Professor Hicks was wrong in supposing that Professor Perroux's model failed to take account of investment in the 'passive' or 'private' sectors. On the contrary, he had been very careful in both oral and written communications to emphasize that private investment was of major importance. He was not an 'optimist', as had been suggested by Professor Hicks; he had confined himself rather to being objective. Professor Perroux noted the introduction of a new category in Professor Hicks's system — *semi-autonomous investment*. He said he would like to pay a special tribute to Professor Hicks's work on the trade cycle, which, in his opinion, was of capital importance in understanding the relations between trends and cycles. He would like to extend a similar tribute to the whole of Professor Hicks's work.

Professor Schneider seemed mistaken, perhaps unconsciously, in attributing to him a certain predilection for making deductions. In his own analysis, said Professor Perroux, balanced growth was an idea. The operational and econometric concepts used in the expression of this idea became apparent in experimental research.

On other matters, he was glad to find himself in agreement with Professor Schneider; in particular, he fully agreed with his contribution to the development of 'partial conjunctures' (*Teilkonjunkturen*). In his own models, said Professor Perroux, he had made a more extensive use than Professor Schneider of asymmetry and irreversibility. However, he fully agreed with Professor Schneider that Professor Harrod's path of balanced growth was entirely unrealistic. Professor Schneider had argued in terms of full employment, but he himself had been reasoning in terms of products.

Professor Perroux mentioned a correspondence with Professor Tinbergen which had given him great pleasure. Professor Tinbergen had stated his agreement with the idea of balanced development, but thought that all such problems could be treated as problems of anti-cyclical policy. Whilst finding this objection both important and stimulating, Professor Perroux preferred to continue to defend his own point of view.

Third, Professor Perroux passed on to the various interventions. He thanked, in particular, Sir Robert Shone, with whom he fully agreed. Sir Robert, with his realistic and open mind, had helped to shake off certain old and very dangerous illusions.

Professor Perroux was glad to learn from Professor Ellis that the research on balanced growth which he himself had directed in France for ten years was being pursued along similar lines in the United States. The classification of dynamic forces promoting growth, which he had decided upon many years previously, was now generally accepted in current French works, as, for instance, the excellent work of Professor Barre.

Professor Perroux said he had had the pleasure of corresponding with Professor Fellner, and he appreciated the tribute paid to him by Professor Fellner in recognizing his work as a new contribution. He wanted to mention that the recent admirable work of Professor Fellner, *Trends and Cycles*, was used extensively in the work of the Institut de Science Économique Appliquée in Paris. But he regretted that he had not yet had occasion to study the important new work by Mrs. Joan Robinson on the accumulation of capital.

Professor Perroux referred to Professor Papi's valuable contribution which had brought out a point of fundamental importance, namely, that innovation was of even greater importance than capital saving. He considered that Professor Papi was right in emphasizing the significance of a scientific theory of planning. He would like to pay tribute to Professor Papi's numerous works on cycles, on programmes and planning, and on the pure theory of the financial activity of the state. He extended this tribute to all Italian scholars who, so often the initiators in the theory of general equilibrium, had also frequently been the originators of ideas in theories of trends and cycles.

Monsieur Hahn was quite right in his dissociation of progress and the cycle as distinct elements; an idea which merited detailed discussion. The works of Professor Sayers on invention and cycles represented an escape from traditional views.

In Professor Perroux's opinion, Professor Okyar was right to distinguish between growth and development. An analytic study of this distinction would probably yield important results. Professor Suranyi-Unger had insisted on the importance of structural phenomena. The conception of 'plasticity of structure', discussed by

Professor Suranyi-Unger in an interesting article, was worthy of further consideration. Professor Delivanis had raised some very interesting technical points, like those of Professor Tinbergen, claiming that anti-cyclical policy was always a basic conception; a point, however, on which he himself was unable to agree.

Professor Jaffé, by insisting on the idea and concept of a bearable disequilibrium, had fully understood his own point; and he himself would agree that it was not a question of eliminating fluctuations, but, above all, of rendering them tolerable. He also appreciated the remarks of Professor Jöhr; he would certainly not deny that psychological factors were capable of acting as 'de-stabilizers', but the question whether such factors were autonomous was not essential to his own model. In the cases of balanced growth which he himself had described, the de-stabilizing effect, due to 'waves' of optimism or pessimism, could be reduced.

Professor Perroux thought that perhaps Professor Rugina had not quite understood his own position. Professor Rugina had depicted a supra-liberal world enjoying perfect stability — he would enjoin his best wishes for the success both of this universe and of its theoretician.

Professor d' Alessandro was critical of economists. How right he was! But, nevertheless, economists seemed to have their uses both to the econometricians and to the business analysts. Professor Perroux said he would take advantage of the opportunity handed to him by Professor d' Alessandro of recalling a really rather important counsel in the history of human civilization: 'Don't shoot the pianist! . . .'

In conclusion, Professor Perroux recalled that the divisions of the world as decided upon by the supreme authorities, even when pontifical, were sometimes challenged in the course of historical development. And amongst the 'real' factors with which we had to contend, there were those of the relations between East and West. The two worlds pursued their struggle without troubling unduly about the 'logic' of their 'systems'. As M. Merleau-Ponty (Professor at the Collège de France) had said in his recent work, *Les Aventures de la dialectique*, a 'generalized' economy would be an economy where Capitalism and Communism were nothing more than 'special instances'.

Professor Perroux said there were many economic examples to show how different institutions could fulfil similar economic functions. He hoped that economists might be sufficiently vigilant and clear-sighted to enable such a world economy to come about without catastrophe.

FOURTH DAY

THE QUEST FOR STABILITY:
THE MONETARY FACTORS

MONETARY FACTORS AFFECTING ECONOMIC STABILITY

BY

PROFESSOR GOTTFRIED HABERLER

Chairman : MONSIEUR RUEFF (France)

I. INTRODUCTION

WHEN I was informed how the world had been divided between Robertson and Viner, and then a part of it subdivided between Perroux, Lundberg and myself, I at first judged myself lucky, because, unlike Robertson and Viner, I could forget about Progress and concentrate on Stability; moreover, 'real' factors are taken care of by Perroux and international aspects by Lundberg.

But I soon discovered that this was an illusion. In order to expound what I have to say on the scope and importance of 'monetary' factors, I cannot avoid referring to 'real' factors, for the double reason that the dividing line between 'real' and 'monetary' factors is by no means unambiguous, and that, however we draw it, real and monetary factors interact in complex patterns. And while dealing primarily with the problem of stability, one cannot well ignore the claims of the related and possibly conflicting objectives of progress and growth. There, again, the reason is that stability and growth, and factors making for growth and factors affecting stability, overlap and interact in a complicated fashion.

There will thus be some repetition and trespassing on other territories. But in view of the great complexity, the interrelatedness and the manysidedness of the various topics of these meetings, this is not only unavoidable but perhaps not altogether undesirable.

II. CRITERIA OF GROWTH

It is now fashionable to define economic growth or progress as the sustained increase in *per capita* output or real national income. While I shall conform to this short formula, I should like to remind you that maximum progress in this sense cannot possibly be regarded as an absolute and exclusive objective of economic policy. First, real income per head must be interpreted broadly, making allowance for leisure, steady employment, utility and disutility of work and other intangibles. Second, allowing for all this and disregarding possible ascetic or puritan value systems, the composition of total output and changes in that composition must surely be accorded a prominent place among policy objectives, in addition to overall size and annual increase of *per capita* output. Composition refers to commodity composition, especially between consumption and investment goods, as well as to the distribution of income between social classes and individuals.

The rate of growth of overall *per capita* income will clearly be related to the composition of, and possibly to changes in the composition and distribution of, income. For example, the larger the proportion of output invested, the greater can be the sustained rate of growth. Similarly, relations certainly exist between the rate of growth of income and the mode of its distribution between social classes, although the concrete form of dependence is not very clear ; it may vary according to social conditions and is, within limits, amenable to change by policy.

I cannot pursue these matters any further. Suffice it to say that I accept an increase in *per capita* output (broadly defined) as the criterion of economic growth, and maximization of that rate as the objective, subject to the reservation that the composition and distribution of income do not change in a way that is deemed undesirable. The fulfilment of this condition is often tacitly taken for granted — which is perhaps not altogether unreasonable in view of the fact that historically the composition and distribution of national income often remains surprisingly constant for long periods of time.

III. THE MEANING OF INSTABILITY

Let me now turn to the problem of stability as distinguished from growth and progress. By economic instability we refer primarily to fluctuations in aggregate output and employment. Here again, as in the case of growth and progress, the aggregate criterion must be qualified. But, by adding employment to output, an element of income distribution is implicitly introduced, viz. as between employed and unemployed. However, even with stable aggregate output and employment, price instability is possible ; this would introduce instability into the income distribution which might well present very serious social and economic problems. Sharp changes in the terms of foreign trade, an especially serious matter for highly specialized primary producing countries, is an example on the international level. But there can be no doubt that, in most cases, violent changes in the terms of trade between large segments of the economy, on the national or international level, are the consequences or concomitants of fluctuations in aggregate output and employment in the industrial countries.

For this reason I shall deal in my paper almost entirely with phenomena originating in the highly developed regions of Professor Robertson's part of the world. I fully agree with what Professor Viner has to say on economic instability in underdeveloped countries. Economic instability there is very largely, although not entirely, either a reflection of the business cycle in the industrial countries or the consequence of autonomous inflationary policies. Much has been made of changes in demand, in technology and in import policies which may de-stabilize the external balance of highly specialized primary producing countries. Without wishing entirely to discount their importance, I venture to say that, from a global standpoint, these sources of instability are of minor importance compared with the business cycle and autonomous inflation.

Inflation, to which I shall return briefly later in my paper, is by no means an unimportant matter. On the contrary, I am convinced that long-run, continuous or recurring inflation not only introduces price instability, but is also a factor seriously retarding economic growth (although it is easy, applying the modern theory of the 'second best', to think of conditions which make it appear as the lesser evil). Intellectually, however, the problem of rapid secular inflation (continuous or intermittent) is much less challenging than the problem of the business or trade cycle, to which I shall turn my attention now. On the question of long-run instability, the so-called 'long waves', 'trend cycles' or 'Kondratieff cycle', I shall say a few words later.

Business cycles I take in the sense in which the term is used by the National Bureau of Economic Research — that is, ups and downs in aggregate activity, more precisely in aggregate output and employment, changes in output due to changes in employment.[1] (Output can, of course, change without changes in employment — harvest changes being the most important example. But the short-run changes in aggregate output that constitute the business cycle are

[1] In identifying fluctuations in activity with fluctuations in aggregate output and employment, I deviate somewhat from the masters of the National Bureau. The deviation is, however, slight because their cyclical chronology for 'activity' matches almost perfectly the cyclical chronology of aggregate output and employment.

clearly not of that nature; this does not, however, exclude the possibility that crop changes, as well as other exogenous disturbances, may have great causal significance for the cycle.)

I follow the National Bureau in defining the cycle as the shortest observable fluctuation in activity. In their words, 'business cycles vary from more than one year to ten or twelve years and are not divisible into shorter cycles of similar character with amplitudes approximating their own'.[1] Furthermore, I make no attempt at finding a regular sequence or pattern of 'minor' or 'major' cycles (as Hansen thinks there is). Cycles do, of course, differ greatly in duration and enormously in amplitude; some depressions are mild, others severe; some upswings are strong, others weak and abortive.[2] But the careful investigations in *Measuring Business Cycles* have convinced me that no regular and persistent pattern exists, or at any rate has not yet been discovered; that it is not possible to interpret the succession of cycles of different length and amplitude as resulting from the superimposition of independent or interdependent cycles of different length (Schumpeter's three-cycle scheme); that it is even less defensible to assign different quasi-independent cyclical mechanisms to the different superimposed cycles. Each cycle or depression is, in a sense, an historically unique case; that is to say, it is the joint product of endogenous and exogenous forces. The result of the interaction between the cyclical mechanism, the historical environment and external disturbances is a complicated chemical compound, and not a mechanical mixture whose constituent parts are separable by more or less mechanical statistical devices. The statistical decomposition of time series into cycle and trend is an insoluble problem.[3] But this by no means excludes the fact that it is often possible to explain particular cycles or phases (depressions or expansions) in

[1] See Burns and Mitchell, *Measuring Business Cycles* (New York), p. 3. Seasonal fluctuations are not of 'similar character'.

[2] This makes me doubt the usefulness of the averaging procedure adopted by N.B.E.R., even with all the cautions and reservations expressed by the illustrious authors of *Measuring Business Cycles*.

[3] It is perhaps more correct to say that the problem is meaningless, at least in the sense in which it is — or rather was, for it is no longer a very live issue — usually formulated. The question is usually framed as a causal one: how can one separate the effects of the causes responsible for the cycle from the effects of the causes responsible for the trend? The further assumption is made that the two sets of effects are additive. This assumption is surely unwarranted. The causes making for cyclical fluctuations, when impinging on a growing system, will produce very different results than they would produce in a stationary system. And, similarly, the growth factors would produce different results in an economic system that, unlike the one we live in, is not subject to cyclical fluctuations. As a consequence, if we would make the experiment of abstracting from the actual system, which is subject to the joint operation of both sets of causes, first those that make for cycles, and second those that make for trend, the sum of the two effects would not be equal to, but would probably greatly exceed, the total observed change.

terms of exogenous forces or endogenous processes, or to point to strongly intensifying or mitigating factors which explain the mildness or severity of a particular depression, or the weakness or strength of a particular upswing. Let me mention only one or two examples — more will follow later. The intensification of the boom following the outbreak of the war in Korea does not require any explanation beyond reference to the wave of governmental and private spending engendered by the war.[1] The great depression of the 1930s in the U.S.A., whatever its deeper causes, was undoubtedly tremendously intensified by the collapse of the banking system.

It is disturbing that economists do not see eye to eye on all these matters. But we can take consolation in the fact that, despite great divergences in interpretation and explanation, different writers agree about the dates of cyclical turning-points and about certain basic characteristics of the short cycle. For example, cyclical chronologies established independently by the most careful investigations of the N.B.E.R., by Edwin Frickey's painstaking researches,[2] and by Schumpeter's more impressionistic methods, agree almost entirely. (Divergences of a few months in the dates for turning-points are hardly surprising or serious, in view of the complexity of the underlying data.)

While the contours of the short-run business cycle are, thus, fairly clear and generally accepted — further characteristics which throw light on the rôle of money in its causation will be discussed presently — the long 'waves' which go under the name of Kondratieff cycles, secondary or trend cycles are a much more hazy thing. They find their expression mainly in wholesale prices and interest rates. But the chronology varies considerably from writer to writer and from country to country; and it is not quite clear whether the ups and downs in prices are always associated — as they invariably are in the short cycle — with ups and downs in output and employment.

It is better not to identify the problem of long-run stability with a hypothetical long cycle — a phrase which suggests an endogenous mechanism and a degree of regularity that simply do not exist. We should rather think of the occurrence or recurrence at irregular intervals of rising or falling price trends, stretching over several short cycles, which may or may not be associated with similar trends in real output.

[1] It should be observed, however, that in the U.S.A. the lower turning-point following the mild recession of 1948–9 had occurred already in the middle of 1949. The war in Korea was therefore not necessary to pull the American economy out of a depression, but was superimposed on an upswing that had started independently.

[2] Edwin Frickey, *Economic Fluctuations in the United States* (Cambridge, Mass., 1942).

IV. Connections between Stability and Growth

There are various possible connections between stability and growth. Some questions arise on the normative level, the level of what is desired and of policy objectives. Suppose there is a choice between : (*a*) a high rate of growth associated with a high degree of short-run instability ; and (*b*) a lower but more steady rate of growth. Some may prefer the latter to the former, although the preference will obviously depend upon the degrees of instability and the rates of growth in question. It is not suggested that people have firm convictions and governments well-articulated policy objectives with respect to these matters, though it is as well to be aware of the problem.

But are we actually confronted with such a choice ? Is it not possible to combine a maximum rate of growth with a high degree of stability ? More concretely, is cyclical instability really the price we have to pay for rapid growth ?

This is a question on which there is, always was and always will be a good deal of disagreement among economists. For the modern apostles of full employment, any deviation from full employment, however slight, is an unnecessary and unmitigated evil. According to them, instability can be eradicated by filling in all, even short and shallow, valleys of depression. Far from endangering the rate of growth, this policy will maximize long-run progress, almost by definition.

For many others — let me only mention Schumpeter and Spiethoff, Perroux and Robertson — the problem is not so simple. For them, cyclical fluctuations, although not necessarily the actual historical cycle, are an unavoidable concomitant of growth. At least under capitalism, the economy progresses in cycles. Cyclical depressions cannot be entirely prevented without seriously endangering the long-run rate of progress. However, both these extreme positions have perhaps been a little overdrawn. It may be possible to find some middle ground on which many economists would agree.

Most economists would probably agree that exceptionally severe slumps, like the great depressions of the 1930s and 1870s, are not conducive to long-run economic growth ; that it is possible to alleviate them — in fact, the more severe depressions are, the easier it is to combat them ; and that, with respect to severe slumps, anti-depression policy is calculated to raise the rate of long-run growth. It is over the milder fluctuations that disagreement is likely to persist as to their function and their relation to long-run growth.

Similar issues arise concerning the type of measures used to combat depressions, and the point up to which anti-depression policy should be pressed. For example, most experts would agree that mild methods in moderate doses, let me say monetary policy and built-in stabilizers of fiscal policy, are conducive to long-run growth, though they are probably insufficient to eradicate the cycle altogether. But stubborn disagreement can be expected about the advisability of the more powerful measures of stabilization that would be required to guarantee the permanent maintenance of full employment within narrow limits. Many would argue that such policies would reduce the incentive to work, save and venture, lead to creeping inflation, diminish the flexibility of the economy and so decrease the long-run rate of growth.

I do not propose to discuss these most difficult problems any further at this point. I rather turn now to a discussion of the monetary factors bearing upon stability.

V. A STRIKING CHARACTERISTIC OF THE SHORT CYCLE

One of the most striking and revealing characteristics of the short cycle is that the ups and downs in output are closely correlated with ups and downs in price levels. *A fortiori*, fluctuations in *real* magnitudes (output, employment, real income) are paralleled by fluctuations in *money* flows (money income, money value of output). It should be noted that this does not follow from our definition of the cycle, which runs in *real* terms. Conceivably, prices as well as money values could be uncorrelated or negatively correlated with fluctuations in real output.

It seems to me that this actual, almost perfect, parallelism cannot be a chance phenomenon.[1] In fact, an increasing number of business cycle analysts explicitly or implicitly agree that the *proximate* cause of fluctuations in output and employment is fluctuations in aggregate expenditure or effective demand. To be sure, there is plenty of disagreement on the deeper forces and processes that are responsible for the cyclical fluctuations in aggregate expenditure. It is nevertheless highly significant that very diverse theories agree

[1] I say '*almost* perfect' because there are sometimes short-lived deviations at the turning-points between the movement of prices on the one hand and of real activity on the other. But note that even if the timing between prices and real volume is not perfect, it is still possible (and probably the case) that money flows (prices *times* quantities) are perfectly correlated with volumes.

For the hypothetical long cycle, the parallelism is certainly much less close. This surely is a reflection of the fact that, in the long run, price and wage flexibility is much greater than in the short run.

on the rôle of expenditure fluctuations. To this group belong not only the various types of monetary theories of the cycle, but also all the modern 'capital stock adjustment theories' which rely on some sort of interaction of multiplier and acceleration principle to construct an endogenous oscillating mechanism. Even Schumpeter's theory, whose logical structure is entirely different, belongs to this group. All these theories explain in different ways why expenditure fluctuates in cycles; it is easy to produce cycles in output and employment — so easy indeed that the necessary assumption of some sort of price and wage rigidity is rarely made clear. Let me add that a very large part of currently employed methods of forecasting the future course of business consists of attempts to form a judgment on the probable course of various segments of the expenditure stream — business spending on investment (plant and equipment, inventories), consumer spending, government spending, foreign demand, etc.

The proposition that fluctuations in aggregate effective demand or expenditure are the proximate cause of the business cycle by no means implies that it is always monetary factors, in the sense of active measures of monetary policy on the part of the monetary authorities or of the banks, that bring about fluctuations in expenditure. The line of causation does not necessarily always run from the monetary to the real factors, although it can hardly be doubted, in my opinion, that monetary factors do often contribute greatly to cyclical instability and that, on the other hand, skilful monetary policy can help to counteract instability caused by autonomous monetary factors or 'real' factors.[1] Suppose our economic system were not subject to cyclical fluctuations; it would then be an easy task to produce, by monetary measures, a business cycle with all the familiar features of alternating periods of expansion and contraction in output and employment associated with ups and downs in prices and aggregate demand. All that would be required to bring about that result is to expand and contract credit or to produce sufficiently large surpluses and deficits in the government budget.

[1] Hardly anybody doubts any more that counter-cyclical monetary and fiscal policy can damp down the cycle. In that respect the situation is very different from what it was at the outbreak of the Great Depression. Let me point out, however, that this statement does not imply endorsement of a naïve theory of 'functional finance'. The objections turn on the formidable difficulties of proper dosage and timing of anti-cyclical measures, due to unavoidable lags and uncertainties in the diagnosis of the underlying situation and the execution of policies; modern objections (see, for example, Milton Friedman's strictures in his *Essays in Positive Economics*) do not call in question the basic proposition that the maintenance of a steady flow of aggregate expenditure will go a long way to stabilize real activity.

VI. Real and Monetary Factors behind the Fluctuations in Aggregate Expenditure

In order to gain perspective, and to illuminate the problem of drawing a line between 'monetary' and 'real' factors, let me briefly enumerate and survey various possibilities of explaining cyclical fluctuations in aggregate spending by 'monetary' and 'real' factors and their interaction — starting from cases of 'purely monetary' causation and proceeding to cases with an increasing preponderance of 'real' factors.

At the one extreme we have the purely monetary explanations of the cycle which assume that the real economic system is inherently unstable and that instability is introduced by the misbehaviour or mismanagement of money. (It should be remembered that what may be purely monetary is the causal mechanism ; the thing to be explained — the cycle — we have defined in real terms.)

Monetary explanations have always been popular, especially in earlier periods. This is not surprising, because monetary symptoms and concomitants of the cycle were especially conspicuous in the nineteenth century, before rules and institutions for more efficient monetary management had been evolved in the developed countries.[1] Of modern writers who have proposed purely monetary explanations, Irving Fisher and R. G. Hawtrey come at once to mind. Fisher flatly denied that there was such a thing as a cycle except to the extent that quasi-cyclical instability was introduced by monetary instability ; this he conceived in terms of changes in the purchasing power of money. Professor Hawtrey's endogenous theory is well known.[2] It consists of a dynamic mechanism of lagged interactions of monetary circulation, cash drains, and credit policy of the banks, changes in short-term interest rates inducing changes in inventory investment.

Another school that explains the cycle by monetary factors starts from Wicksell's distinction between the market or money rate of interest, on the one hand, and the natural or equilibrium rate on the other. Wicksell himself did not hold a purely monetary theory of the cycle, but Mises and Hayek, to mention only two, did. They

---

[1] It is true that our own age has not distinguished itself by monetary stability ! But the conspicuous ups and downs in the price level since 1914, as well as financial crises, have been caused by wars and their aftermath and are not the concomitants of a peace-time business cycle as they so often were in the nineteenth century. Extreme monetary instability in peace-time is a scourge afflicting countries in Professor Viner's world.

[2] It seems safe to say that his theory would have become more popular if it had been worked out in mathematical form.

believed that the initiating cause of the cycle could always be found on the monetary side, on the supply side of money. Excessive supply of credit (that is to say, credit creation in excess of 'voluntary savings' — the precise criterion of excessiveness not being always the same) depresses the market or money rate of interest below its equilibrium level; this starts a Wicksellian cumulative process which necessarily ends in crisis and depression. As distinct from Hawtrey's, these theories are not fully endogenous. Each cycle starts fresh from a new inflationary bout, that is, from a renewed attempt to depress the money rate below the equilibrium level.

In these monetary theories, which stress changes in the supply of money, it is assumed explicitly or tacitly that the demand for money and credit, or, to put it differently, the natural or equilibrium rate of interest, is determined by the (physical) marginal productivity of capital which is fairly stable over time, although perhaps subject to a gradual downward shift as the capital stock increases.

Non-monetary factors make their appearance as soon as it is realized that the demand for money and credit (the equilibrium rate) is neither stable nor determined solely by the physical productivity of capital.

The main factors making for instability of investment demand, or, in the terminology of the Wicksellian School, for changes in the equilibrium rate of interest (if we still permit ourselves under these circumstances to think of an equilibrium rate existing at any given moment) are as follows (I have arranged them in order of increasing 'physicalness'): 'Psychology' (*i.e.* waves of optimism and pessimism); investment changes induced by changes in income or consumption as postulated in the different variants of the acceleration principle (including that of Kaldor); inventions and innovations and the forces giving rise to the 'bunching' of innovational investment as described by Schumpeter; 'lumpiness' of investment due to the durability and indivisibility of capital instruments, together with the asymmetry in the operation of the accelerator, the replacement waves and 'echo effects' which follow from the fact that capital goods are durable. Speaking of the bunching and lumpiness of capital investment, we cannot forget, in the world in which we live, the most powerful external factor causing intense concentration (and hence instability) of investment, namely, wars and preparation for wars.

All these factors have been used, singly or in combination, to explain the business cycle. But in all these theories, although they are no longer purely monetary, monetary factors enter more or less importantly — and not only in the trivial sense that everything that happens in a monetary economy (as distinguished from barter) wears a monetary garb.

The theories which use the various 'building blocks' just mentioned vary greatly, not only in content (for example, in the importance they attribute to the monetary factor), but also in the degree of formal refinement.

Let me first say a word on the latter aspect. The earlier theories relied on verbal analysis and the rough estimation of magnitudes. Since the pioneering article of Frisch, 'Propagation Problems and Impulse Problems in Dynamic Economics',[1] Lundberg's celebrated *Studies in the Theory of Economic Expansion*,[2] and especially since the formal marriage of multiplier and acceleration principle (which earlier lived together under different names in ill-defined relationship), a great change has come over business cycle theorizing. The theory has been formalized in complete endogenous sequence models, using difference and differential equations. The earlier models were linear but soon non-linear models with 'floors', 'ceilings', 'asymmetries', 'stochastic variables', and 'exogenous shocks' were added. Not only mathematical blueprints, but full-blown econometric models relating to individual countries or even to the whole world, with constants and parameters statistically evaluated, are pouring from single scholars' studies and statistical laboratories like automobiles from the assembly line.

This surely is a very interesting development ; and the type of approach is worth trying and perfecting. But there can hardly be doubt any more that so far the results have been most disappointing. The multiplicity of more or less inconsistent models, many of them based on broadly plausible assumptions, and, if of the econometric type, fitting the data from which they are derived fairly well — but none of them standing up to the test of extrapolation beyond the period from which the data were taken — is a spectacle that is not calculated to inspire confidence.

. But let me return to the substantive question concerning the rôle of monetary forces in the cycle. It would seem to be a valid generalization that purely monetary explanations have become increasingly unpopular and, although most current theories are mixed in the sense that monetary and real factors interact, the monetary factor has been more and more de-emphasized and relegated to a merely passive or permissive rôle.

In the 1920s attempts were made to uphold the preponderance

---

[1] *Economic Essays in Honour of Gustav Cassel* (London, 1933).
[2] Stockholm, 1937.

of the monetary factor in the presence of the de-stabilizing real factors mentioned above, by saying that the trouble arises not from the 'real' side but from a failure of the money rate of interest to adjust promptly to changes in the equilibrium rate — a defect which is due to faulty monetary arrangements (fractional reserve banking, inflationary policies and the like). The 'neutral money' school (see especially Professor Hayek's writings) tried to formulate rules which would assure neutral behaviour of money. Unfortunately, these rules, after some reflection, became so involved that it was practically impossible to visualize an institutional set-up which would assure their automatic observance, or administrators sufficiently knowledge-able and skilled to apply these rules even if, and this is a large 'if', the theoretical problem of formulating the rules were soluble in all cases.

It is not surprising that the notion of 'neutral money' has been abandoned, and that the problem is no longer approached in terms of a deviation of the market rate or rates of interest from a hypo-thetical equilibrium rate or complex of such rates.

The modern approach has become much more direct and pragmatic. There is a theory of the various broad branches of ex-penditure — consumption, investment, government outlays, exports and imports, with suitable subdivisions.[1] These parts are then integrated into a closed dynamic system which is capable, depending on the magnitude of certain parameters, of producing all sorts of oscillations.

In most of these models, money, banking and credit institutions as well as the rate of interest and prices have definitely taken the back seat. Let us consider, as an example, Professor Hicks's cele-brated *Contribution to the Theory of the Trade Cycle* — the most elegant and most carefully elaborated specimen of a great variety of similar systems.

His principal model runs almost entirely in 'real' terms. Con-sumption expenditure is a function of *real* income; investment is a function of the rate of change in *real* income; there is a *physical* ceiling which may or may not be hit and, owing to the *physical* impossibility of using up durable capital faster than it wears out,

---

[1] It is interesting to compare the methods of the economic theorist with those of 'practical' economists who are currently watching the economic weather and are trying to make short-run forecasts; for instance, the Council of Economic Advisors in the U.S.A. and similar institutions elsewhere. The latter, too, put forward explanations ('theories') of various branches of expenditure — but the disaggregation goes much farther. Investment, for example, is divided into inventory investment, plant and equipment, residential construction, commercial construction, public construction, etc. Also, the number of explanatory variables is much greater and the analysts refrain from setting up an invariant and rigidly interconnected system.

the accelerator is weaker on the downgrade than on the upgrade. Wages are supposed to be perfectly rigid and so are prices (with minor qualifications). In the basic model, money plays a purely passive rôle; monetary circulation automatically expands during the upswing and automatically contracts during the downswing of the cycle.[1]

Money is a mere veil, or rather a tricot (as Mises used to put it),[2] which faithfully reflects without distortion the contours of the economic body and all its changes.

Although Hicks regards the 'real' model as the heart of his theory, and the latter as an adequate picture of reality, he is too much of a realist to rely entirely on the 'real' part of his theory for the explanation of actual cyclical experience. In the last two chapters of his book he introduces the 'monetary factor' as a very active element, and thus modifies his theory more drastically than appears on the surface or than he himself would seem to admit. But let me spend a few more minutes on the 'real' models.

Although money plays no active rôle in these models in the sense that no deliberate inflationary measures, or rising prices, falling interest rates or lowered credit standards, are required to explain a cyclical upswing (nor the opposite of all that to account for the depression phase), money is nevertheless essential because the upswing could not proceed unless the supply of money were elastic in the sense that either M or V can increase without sharp rises in the interest rate.[3] If there is not sufficient scope for V to expand, the monetary authorities must permit the necessary expansion in M; if V can expand, it is sufficient that they refrain from counteracting the increase in V by contracting M.

The downturn is brought about entirely by the 'real' mechanism, and during the downswing the rôle of money is even less important than in the upswing. For, while the monetary authorities can always stop or slow down an expansion, they can do nothing or very little to soften a contraction (although they could presumably intensify

---

[1] Monetary complications are, however, invoked to explain one feature of actual cyclical experience which in Hicks's opinion cannot be accounted for by his 'real' model. He thinks that, after the downturn, contraction of output usually proceeds faster than the multiplier-accelerator mechanism would lead one to expect. So he introduces as an intensifier what Pigou many years ago (in his *Industrial Fluctuations* (1926), which to this day has kept remarkably fresh), called the detonation of bankruptcies and business failures into which the upswing explodes. For this concession to realism, Hicks was promptly rebuked by Kaldor, who believes that this particular feature of the cycle can also be explained by the 'real' mechanism.

[2] Needless to say, Mises did not accept the view that money was a mere tricot.

[3] It is true there has been a strong tendency to discount the importance of the interest rate, but it has hardly gone so far as to deny that sharply rising interest rates would act as a brake on an expansion.

it). When the 'real' forces 'decree a contraction', MV shrinks inexorably, and if monetary policy prevents M from shrinking (or expands it) the result is simply an offsetting drop in V.

There can hardly be any doubt that this account greatly underestimates the importance of monetary factors in producing the major cyclical swings of actual experience. What is open to question is the degree of distortion of the true picture. While I realize that many of those who have put forward real models of the cycle would be ready to admit that their picture of the cycle is liable to be changed somewhat by the operation of monetary factors, I do believe that modern theory has tended grossly to under-estimate the importance of the monetary factors. Not only in the field of business cycles, but in other areas as well, alleged stubborn 'structural' and 'real' instabilities and impediments to necessary adjustment have been over-emphasized and over-estimated — at the expense of monetary factors and the closely related element of price- and wage-rigidity. This is a matter of great importance which has far-reaching policy implications.

VII. Monetary Factors in Depressions

The operation of monetary forces is especially conspicuous in depressions. But the seeds of depression are sown during the boom, and they are not entirely of 'real' origin !

Let me enumerate a few notorious instances in which monetary factors have greatly intensified depressions, although perhaps not brought them about.

The great depression of the 1930s in the U.S.A. was made much more severe than it otherwise would have been by the wholesale destruction, through bankruptcies, of banks and of bank money. It is surely not an essential feature of the real cycle that the banking system should collapse during the depression. The same thing happened in several other countries, and the breakdown of the international gold standard, the liquidization of the gold exchange standard and the international scramble for liquidity are essentially the same monetary process on the international level.

It is gratifying to see a prominent champion of the 'real' cycle theory, like Professor Hicks himself, emphatically stressing the basically monetary nature of the great depression, thereby flatly rejecting 'real' explanations of the events of the 1930s — his own multiplier-accelerator theory as well as the 'secular stagnation' thesis.

Let me quote the relevant passage :

I do not see that there is any adequate reason to suppose that the *real* boom of 1927–9 was at all an exceptional boom ; if the accelerator mechanism, and nothing else, had been at work, it should not have been followed by an exceptional slump. But the slump impinged upon a monetary situation which was quite exceptionally unstable. The main cause of this instability was not the purely superficial speculative expansion which had occurred in New York in 1928–9 ; its roots went much farther back. The monetary system of the world had never adjusted itself at all fully to the change in the level of money incomes which took place during and after the war of 1914–18 ; it was trying to manage with a gold supply, which was in terms of wage-units extremely inadequate. Difficulties in the post-war adjustment of exchange rates (combined with the vast changes which the war had produced in the creditor-debtor position of important countries) had caused the consequential weakness to be particularly concentrated in certain places : particular central banks, as for instance the Bank of England and the Reichsbank, were therefore particularly incapable of performing their usual function as 'lenders of last resort'.[1]

This explanation of the great slump has long been propounded by continental European economists, notably by the late Charles Rist, but has found few supporters among Anglo-American economists.

Two general observations are called for. First, it should be stressed that price rigidity, which is, in practice, primarily wage rigidity, is an essential prerequisite of any monetary explanation. This remark must not, however, be interpreted to mean that everything would be put right, and cyclical instability banished, by introducing wage flexibility. The problem is much more complicated, because of the existence of fixed contracts and the possible adverse dynamic and expectational repercussions of a perfectly flexible wage and price system.

Second, it is well known that throughout the nineteenth century the British monetary system operated on a very narrow gold reserve. This narrowness of the monetary base made for a jerky credit policy, because it forced the Bank of England to react sharply to slight cash drains. Thus it contributed to monetary instability throughout the nineteenth century.[2] The growing wage rigidity in the twentieth century made the system unworkable.

It is also well known, although often forgotten, that monetary

---

[1] *Loc. cit.* p. 163. This explanation does not quite fit the American case. It cannot well be said that the monetary (gold) base of the U.S. economy was too narrow, even though the dollar was later devalued in terms of gold. The speculative orgies of the late 1920s were not as superficial as Hicks thinks ; they surely contributed much to the collapse of the banking system.

[2] On all that, and for references to the contemporary literature, see especially Viner, *Studies in the Theory of International Trade*, Chapter V.

mismanagement, namely, the revaluation of sterling after the First World War, without the necessary wage adjustments, was responsible for the semi-stagnation of the British economy during the 1920s.[1] The great depression of the 1870s offers many parallels with that of the 1930s. It too was greatly intensified by monetary factors, both in the U.S.A. and in Europe. In the U.S.A., large budget surpluses followed the deficits during the Civil War, and the premium on gold was gradually reduced from 57 per cent in 1865 to zero in 1879,[2] the terminal year of the depression — a situation which in some respects resembles the British position in the 1920s. True, the general economic background — nineteenth-century America versus twentieth-century Britain — is entirely different, but the difference in the surrounding conditions makes the similarity of the outcome all the more remarkable, and serves to support the hypothesis that monetary factors were of decisive importance in both cases.

Turning from the U.S.A. to the world at large, there were several deflationary factors of a monetary nature at work during the last quarter of the nineteenth century. For example, the increased demand for gold, stemming from the introduction of the gold standard by several continental countries, and also speculative excesses, financial crises and their aftermaths in several countries.

These are conspicuous and notorious cases in which depressions have been intensified by monetary factors. Similar, though less conspicuous and serious, monetary disturbances, entailing credit contraction, pessimistic expectations and inducements to increase liquidity (reduction in V), can be found in practically every, except the mildest, depression.

VIII. Monetary Factors during Cyclical Upswings

While it is thus easy to point to instances in which depressions have been greatly intensified by monetary factors and policies during

[1] This outcome was correctly foretold by Keynes in his essay, *The Economic Consequences of Mr. Churchill* (1925).

As Professor Hayek has pointed out (*Monetary Nationalism and International Stability* (London, 1937), p. 44, Keynes's warning was based on orthodox teaching. A hundred years previously (1821) in a letter to Wheatley, Ricardo said: 'I never should advise a government to restore a currency which was depreciated 30 per cent to par; I should recommend . . . that the currency should be fixed at the depreciated value'. (Ricardo, Sraffa Edition, vol. IX, p. 73.) Under twentieth-century conditions of wage rigidity, most economists would say that a 10 per cent over-valuation is too much to be dealt with by deflation rather than by devaluation of the currency.

[2] See R. Fels, 'American Business Cycles 1865-79', in the *American Economic Review*, June 1951, pp. 325-49.

the depression, and while, following Pigou and Hicks, we may venture the generalization that in many less-conspicuous cases than those mentioned, the severity of depressions has been enhanced by the monetary repercussions of financial crises, the rôle of monetary factors in the upswing and boom phase of the cycle is much more controversial and difficult to assess.

I take it that hardly anyone would nowadays defend the pro-position, and I certainly would not do so myself, that the tapering-off of the upswing, and the subsequent depression, could be avoided by keeping M, or MV (in some sense), or some general price level constant. Hence the failure of money or monetary policy to con-form to any simple rule cannot be held responsible for the fact that booms do not last for ever and are always followed by depressions. But from the fact that it is difficult or impossible to discover a monetary rule which, if observed during the upswing, would guarantee perpetual prosperity, it does not follow that the behaviour of money or monetary policy during the upswing cannot greatly contribute to the severity of the ensuing contraction.

The length and severity of a depression depends partly on the magnitude of the 'real' maladjustment which developed during the preceding boom, and partly on the aggravating monetary and credit factors already mentioned — the scramble for liquidity by financial institutions as well as by others, the destruction of bank money by bank failures and similar events on the international level.

While monetary arrangements and policies during the upswing probably cannot entirely prevent the emergence of real maladjust-ments — except perhaps by preventing the upswing itself — im-prudent monetary policies can surely aggravate them. Moreover, the financial crises which frequently mark the downturn of the cycle, and the monetary and financial complications during the depression, are partly the consequence of monetary forces and policies operating during the preceding expansion.

The term 'real maladjustment' must not be interpreted in a narrow, exclusive sense.[1] There are alternative types of such maladjustments, and I do not want to suggest that there is a pre-sumption that every boom breeds the same kind of trouble. Let me mention only two or three types.

The Harrod-Hicks theory (envisaged also by other writers) that

[1] In the economic literature it is closely associated with F. A. Hayek's theory of the cycle. However, the 'real maladjustment' which Hayek describes, 'over-extension of the period of production' (the concept is not easy to define in operational terms), is only one kind of maladjustment out of a multitude of possibilities, and not the most likely or the most ascertainable one.

when an expansion runs head-on into a full-employment ceiling (which need not be a rigid barrier but may be a flexible bottleneck-zone), induced investments will collapse,[1] describes one kind of real maladjustment.

Another type of maladjustment is the one described by Schumpeter. It can be characterized as a temporary exhaustion of investment opportunities in the particular area in which the boom was concentrated. The chance that there should be a *general* and *chronic* dearth of investment outlets for current savings (as distinct from a temporary one in a particular area) is so remote and, *sub specie historiae*, so far-fetched, that we can ignore it.[2]

While these real maladjustments are closely tied up with growth and expansion itself, and are most difficult to diagnose and to avoid (except by preventing the expansion itself), most upswings are characterized in varying degrees by excesses which, at least *post-festum*, appear unnecessary, undesirable and avoidable. This is true even though the line which separates them from the maladjustments mentioned earlier cannot always be drawn neatly at the time when things are going well.

What I mean is that there are speculative excesses in the real as well as in the financial sphere; over-optimistic over-production in particular lines of industry and over-building; speculative land booms and speculative over-investment in inventories;[3] and, in the financial sphere, excessive speculation on the stock exchanges.

It is mainly in this area that money and monetary policy become important during the upswing. These 'unhealthy' developments are not possible, or at least not possible on a large and disturbing scale, without excessive credit expansion. It is, of course, often difficult to diagnose such developments when they occur, and it is a most difficult task of monetary policy to prevent inflationary excesses without endangering expansion itself; no easy rule, such

---

[1] In other words, 'capital widening' comes to an end and, since 'capital deepening' cannot quickly take up the slack, aggregate investment is bound to fall, and a depression ensues.

[2] This does not, however, alter the fact that in every severe depression we experience a revival in lay and expert circles alike of the theory that most, if not all, depressions are the consequence of a chronic lack of investment opportunities — only to be given up during the following upswing and replaced in the minds of many by the opposite point of view to the effect that we have at last conquered the business cycle and entered the 'new' era of perpetual prosperity. This illustrates the *Konjunkturgebundenheit* of economic thinking, and can be claimed as supporting evidence by those economists who stress the importance of the 'psychological' factor in the generation of the business cycle.

[3] I suspect that the 'non-speculative' inventory cycle based on a multiplier-accelerator mechanism (analysed in a masterly way in Metzler's celebrated articles) is only a small part of the real story and that inventory cycles without price speculation and monetary stimuli (elements which play no part in Metzler's theory) would be mild and uninteresting affairs.

as stabilizing some general price level, will be sufficient. It is nevertheless a fact, I believe, that these things do happen in every major upswing and that they breed financial upheavals and revulsions which then greatly contribute to the severity of the succeeding deflation and depression.

IX. The Comparative Importance of Monetary and Real Factors in the Cycle

My general conclusion is that monetary factors and policies play an important rôle in generating economic instability. A large part of modern cycle theory has unduly neglected monetary factors and has overplayed the 'real' factors, although most proponents of 'real' theories of the cycle find it necessary to bring in monetary factors as modifying elements at some stage before applying their theories to the cycle of the real world. This neglect of monetary factors and institutional rigidities is partly a general characteristic of modern theory, which finds expression in other areas besides the field of business cycle theory. It can partly be understood as reaction to the fact that some earlier monetary theories of the cycle have been discredited by over-statement and over-refinement.

Let me now raise the quantitative question. Suppose the various de-stabilizing monetary complications which I have enumerated could be avoided by institutional reforms and skilful monetary policy; would that damp down the cycle drastically, or would it not make much difference? In other words, is the 'real' cycle, without the so-called 'complications', really a very serious problem? This is, of course, an extremely complicated question. I cannot hope, in the course of one lecture, to formulate it with all the care and precision which it requires, let alone give a well-documented answer. But let me make bold and suggest tentative answers to some subdivisions of the main query.

If the wholesale destruction of bank money during depressions, through bank failures, runs on banks, and lack of confidence in the financial institutions (as well as analogous phenomena in the international sphere), could be avoided — a modest minimum programme of monetary reform — catastrophic slumps like the one in the 1930s would be eliminated. Avoidance of mistakes like the revaluation of the pound after the First World War and a modest policy of monetary expansion (I am speaking now of monetary policy, not of fiscal policy, *i.e.* the creation of counter-cyclical budget deficits in depression), would make prolonged periods of semi-stagnation, like that of the British economy in the 1920s, extremely unlikely.

If, in addition to that, inflationary and speculative excesses during cyclical expansions were prevented, and a mild counter-cyclical budget policy adopted, cyclical instability would be damped down to moderate proportions. In other words, the 'real' cycle without the monetary 'complications' (comprehensively defined) is, in my judgment, a rather mild affair.

What are the chances that the 'monetary complications' will, in fact, be avoided henceforth? I think that a majority of economists would agree that the chances are good so far as anti-depression policy is concerned. Runaway deflation, like that in the 1930s, is, I believe, out of the question everywhere, even in the most capitalistic countries. More than that, so far as anti-depression policy is concerned, there is certainly more danger in most countries of 'too soon and too much' rather than of 'too little and too late'. Does that mean we have now reached the millennium of economic stability? Now, as far as employment is concerned, there is probably little chance anywhere of prolonged mass unemployment caused by deficiency of effective demand. True, this does not exclude unemployment due to a lack of co-operating factors; but dislocations, where that happens on a large scale, are exceedingly rare.[1]

X. SECULAR INFLATION

But for dimensions of economic stability other than employment, for example, for price stability, the outlook is definitely not so good. The small willingness to tolerate unemployment, the disposition to

[1] Such conditions existed after the war in war-ravaged countries because of a lack of raw materials, machinery and transport. The spectre of that kind of unemployment arose in some countries, for example, in Britain, during severe balance-of-payments crises ; but it never came to pass. Some theorists have played with the idea that this kind of unemployment exists *chronically* in disguised form in underdeveloped countries. It is based on the assumption of constant coefficients of production ; that is to say, that capital and labour can be combined only in one or two fixed proportions (rectangular, or at least angular, production functions). Capital is scarce, hence much labour must remain unemployed. The assumption that such conditions could exist in the long run, not for particular narrowly defined industrial processes, but for industry as a whole or for broad subdivisions, seems to me unrealistic to the point of being preposterous. It must be pointed out, however, that this same assumption underlies the famous Harrod-Domar model of long-run economic growth.

These theories constitute other extreme examples of the modern propensity to over-emphasize real factors and to look for real, in this case literally physical, rigidities, instead of for monetary factors, price and wage rigidities and the like. (For an able criticism of the Harrod-Domar model, see L. H. Yeager, 'Some Questions about Growth Economics', in *American Economic Review*, March 1954.)

suspect an incipient major depression in every slight actual or imagined dip in economic activity, the strong propensity to apply anti-depression measures — all that, coupled with the powerful urge to invest and develop, the constant pressure of organized labour for higher wages, and, in some countries, of organized agriculture for higher prices, makes for secular, intermittent or continuous, creeping or galloping inflation.

Continuous galloping inflation is found in some underdeveloped countries; Chile is perhaps the most extreme example. There can be no doubt that it retards growth (through lowering the allocative efficiency of the economy and discouraging saving) even if acute depressive reactions can be avoided.

In the advanced industrial countries secular inflation threatens, in the form of a creeping and intermittent rise in prices. That is to say, prices rise over the long pull at an *average* rate of a few per cent per annum, not steadily, but in waves; periods of rapidly rising prices are interrupted by shorter periods of stable, or even slightly falling, prices. This is an insidious process which is not easy to diagnose and on the consequences of which there is little agreement between economists, at least so long as the average price rise is not more than, say, 2 per cent to 3 per cent a year.

Let me deal with a few aspects of this problem. It is misleading to say, as it is sometimes done,[1] that the world has lived for the last 150 years or longer under a régime of secular inflation. I would not speak of secular inflation if the rise of the price curve over 150 years is due to towering peaks caused by major wars with no upward trend during the intervening periods of peace.[2] Price rises caused by political catastrophes are very different from similar intermittent price rises during periods of peace. The reason is that, in the first case, inflation is likely to be accepted as an act of God, while, in the second case, unless the intervening periods of stable or falling prices are long enough, inflation psychology is bound to develop, which will bring with it the danger of a galloping inflation and must have adverse and undesirable effects on saving habits, the distribution of income, and eventually on the allocative efficiency of the economy.

I am not going to speculate on the average annual speed and time shape at which secular inflation will begin to have serious

[1] See, *e.g.*, M. Bronfenbrenner, 'Some Neglected Implications of Secular Inflation', in *Post-Keynesian Economics* (ed. K. Kurihara, New Brunswick, 1954). This is a very suggestive paper with which I find myself largely in agreement apart from the point mentioned in the text.

[2] This is roughly the picture of the American price development from 1900 to 1950.

consequences. I shall discuss instead one aspect of the causal mechanism which brings about this condition, and one of its consequences on the international level.

As Bronfenbrenner (*loc. cit.*) points out, there are two different explanations of the tendency towards secular creeping inflation in the industrial countries of the West. One school blames the pressure groups of organized labour and organized agriculture; the other blames a monetary policy which has become lax under the influence of the Keynesian thinking. According to the first, the price level is gradually pushed up by rising wages; according to the other view, it is pulled up by monetary policy.

Money, of course, plays its rôle in both schemes. Labour unions could not push the price level up unless monetary policy gave way. It should also be observed that it is not necessary that labour should be organized in one huge bloc (as it actually is in some countries) and should force up the whole wage level in one big push. For this mechanism to work, it is a sufficient condition that big chunks of wages be forced up here and there by some of the large unions. The competitive mechanism, and the actions of other unions, can then be relied upon rapidly to generalize these increases. Pull and push always interact once the upward movement has started. Thus the difference between the two schools seems to degenerate into one of the chicken-and-egg variety.

But there remains an important operational difference. Both schools agree that, despite union pressure on wages, the price level could be held if monetary policy stood firm (as it had to, under the gold standard). The pressure-group school, however, asserts (or implies) that if monetary policy does stand firm, wages (or some wages) will be pushed up anyway. As a consequence, unemployment will appear and the monetary authorities will be confronted with the dilemma that they must either 'create' a certain amount of unemployment, or else tolerate, at least from time to time, a rise in the price level.

The other school takes a more optimistic position. According to it there is no such dilemma. If the monetary authorities stand firm, wages will not rise, or will rise only a little. A small amount of unemployment or the mere threat of unemployment will sufficiently restrain the unions to persuade them to desist from wage demands in excess of the gradual increase in overall labour productivity.

Given the fact that the willingness to tolerate unemployment in our time is low, this difference of opinion between the two schools thus reduces to a difference in estimates of the power and policy of labour unions and employer reactions. Obviously much depends also on public opinion and government policy.

I am inclined to side on this issue with the pessimists.[1] But this is certainly a question on which it would be unwise to take a dogmatic position. The power and policies of labour unions, as well as the behaviour of employers, reactions of public opinion and government policy differ from country to country. And although the trend has been everywhere in the free world in the direction of increased union power, towards a 'labouristic society' (Slichter), this trend obviously depends on political and social forces whose future course cannot be foreseen. The economist certainly has no special expert qualifications for such prophecies.

XI. Instability of the International Balance of Payments

I now come to my last topic, which dramatically illustrates the modern tendency to look for deep-seated structural defects, and to see stubborn real stumbling-blocks to the maintenance of stable equilibrium where in reality faulty monetary policies, and the rigidity of certain key prices, provide a perfectly satisfactory explanation of the existing disequilibrium or instability.

While in a closed economy, with a unified monetary and banking system, free mobility of funds and a fair degree of mobility of labour, a secular inflation of 2 per cent to 3 per cent per year may not have deleterious effects for quite some time, at least not clearly visible ones, in the actual world, consisting as it does of different countries with different monetary systems and policies, little or no mobility of capital funds and labour between them, even a small deviation in the rate of inflation between different countries must almost immediately lead to balance-of-payments disequilibria.

What holds of differences in the degree of secular inflation is, of course, also true of deviations in the timing and magnitude of cyclical and other short-run expansions and contractions. Analytically, moreover, it is only the other side of exactly the same problem if the disequilibrium in the balance of payments has been caused initially by a shift in international demand (however brought about). In that case the persistence of the disequilibrium can be said to be

---

[1] Bronfenbrenner too (*op. cit.*) is on the pessimistic side and so is the Dean of American 'labour economists', S. H. Slichter. The optimistic view is represented by members of the 'Chicago School', *e.g.* Milton Friedman, 'Some Comments on the Significance of Labour Unions for Economic Policy', in *The Impact of the Union* (New York, 1951), and W. K. Morton, 'Trade Unionism, Full Employment and Inflation'. *American Economic Review*, March 1950.

due to the failure of the monetary mechanism to bring about an *equilibrating* divergence between the rate of expansion in the surplus country and that in the deficit country,[1] while, in the cases mentioned before, the disequilibrium in the balance of payments was caused by the appearance of a *disequilibrating* divergence of the same sort.

But let me concentrate on the chronic case, because it illustrates most clearly the point I wish to make, namely, the contemporary propensity to over-emphasize 'real' factors and to neglect monetary factors and institutional rigidities.

There is today much more agreement than there was a few years ago on the proposition that the basic reason for the chronic (continuous or intermittent) balance-of-payments deficits, alias 'Dollar shortage', from which many countries are suffering is to be found in the fact that the deficit countries have, for a variety of reasons, a higher 'propensity to inflate' than the surplus countries. It must be stressed, however, at the outset, that it is grossly misleading to speak of a shortage of the U.S. dollar only. The same shortage applies just as much to the Canadian dollar, the Mexican peso, the Venezuelan bolivar, the Swiss franc, and, more recently, also to the German mark, the Dutch guilder and other currencies which are more or less freely convertible into U.S. dollars.

The reasons for a high propensity to inflate are, of course, many. Some are of an 'ideological', 'political' and 'social' nature; others are deeply rooted in the recent, or more distant, historical development of a country; still others are very 'real'. It is, for example, easy to understand why some time after the war it was almost impossible for war-torn and ravaged countries to restrain inflation (of the 'open' or 'repressed' variety); moreover, it stands to reason that countries with a small willingness to tolerate unemployment, an elaborate social welfare system, exorbitant rates of direct taxation and aggressive trade unions, will constantly strain against the leash. Similarly, it is not surprising at all that poor and backward countries, when they wake up and set their minds to develop in a hurry and to catch up with the more developed countries, are continuously tempted to overspend their meagre resources and to live beyond their means.

With such a wealth of explanatory material available which

---

[1] The equilibrating mechanism can be of the gold standard type (stable exchanges, expansion in the surplus countries and contraction in the deficit countries) or it can use the technique of flexible exchanges under which no expansion and contraction in the local currency circulation is necessary. Complications caused by price and wage rigidities and consequential changes in employment or by speculative movements of capital cannot be discussed here.

offers unlimited opportunities for bringing into play 'propensities', 'asymmetries',[1] 'demonstration effects' and many other gadgets dear to the heart of the economic theorist, it is difficult to understand why anyone should find it necessary to fall back on such implausible and far-fetched hypotheses as the sudden appearance in the fourth decade of the twentieth century of stubborn real inelasticities of international demand (of whole continents and a great variety of countries!) or on the equally bizarre theory that, again beginning with the third or fourth decade of our century, balances of payments (and terms of trade) must turn inexorably in favour of the most rapidly progressing countries.

XII. Summary and Concluding Remarks

My main conclusion is this. Monetary factors, comprehensively defined, bear a heavy share of responsibility for short-run economic instability — for the ordinary business cycle (again comprehensively defined) as well as for the short-run instability and chronic disequilibria in the international balances by which the world has been plagued for the last thirty years. It hardly needs mentioning explicitly that the same is true of long-run instability of price levels.

By 'monetary factors' I do not merely mean active policies of inflation or deflation — the latter having become almost inconceivable since the great depression and the rise of Keynesian thinking — but also monetary repercussions of the financial crises which frequently mark the upper turning-point of the cycle or occur during the downswing — irrespective of whether the downturn itself can or cannot be attributed to monetary factors. For example, the collapse of the American banking system in the 1930s, the downfall of the gold standard, the ensuing sudden liquidation of the gold exchange standard, the withdrawal of international credits, the flows of 'hot money' and the general scramble for liquidity — all these and similar events on the national and international level are monetary factors. If these things could be avoided, catastrophes like the great depression would be impossible and other cycles would be mitigated.

If we define the concept 'monetary factors' somewhat more comprehensively, so as to include in its effects that part of existing instability which would disappear in the event of monetary policy succeeding (in addition to preventing the monetary disturbances

---

[1] See, *e.g.*, C. Kindleberger, 'L'Asymétrie de la balance des paiements', *Revue économique* (1954), pp. 166-89.

mentioned above) in imparting a mildly anti-cyclical pattern to the supply of money and credit — monetary factors would be responsible for a still larger share in economic instability. In other words, the amplitude of the cycle would be sharply reduced if monetary factors in this comprehensive sense became inoperative (which would require, of course, acts of commission as well as of omission on the part of the monetary authorities).

This, however, by no means implies that non-monetary factors are of no importance.

First of all, monetary factors operate in an environment or impinge on a system which possesses certain non-monetary features that make the system respond to the monetary forces as it does. One could easily imagine an economic system in which the monetary factors would not produce large swings in output and employment but only fluctuations in prices, which would be a much less serious matter. If, for example, deflation did not breed pessimism and inflation did not produce exaggerated optimism,[1] and if, in addition, wages and prices were flexible and there were no large fixed monetary contracts, the effects of monetary instability on aggregate output and employment would be much smaller than they are in the real world.

The 'monetary' factor, the 'psychological' factor and the 'rigidity' factor are complementary in the strict sense of the word, and re-inforce each other. The resulting instability is their joint product and it is therefore quite legitimate to attribute to each of these factors a substantial share of the existing economic instability in such a way that the sum of their (alternative) shares greatly exceeds the total.[2]

Second, I do not wish to discount completely — for short-run purposes — the approximate fixity of capital coefficients as postulated by the acceleration principle — although even in the short run the capital-output ratio (and labour-output ratio) is not as rigid as many modern business cycle models assume.[3] Nor would I ignore the multiplier. But the accelerator plus the multiplier, unless combined with and reinforced by monetary factors, psychology and rigidities, would hardly produce more than mild and inconsequential

[1] Prolonged and too rapid inflation may, of course, produce pessimistic reactions.

[2] This was pointed out many years ago by A. C. Pigou, in his *Industrial Fluctuations* (2nd edition, London, 1929), Part I, Chapter 22. He says: 'It is possible that more than one factor may be a dominant cause of fluctuations in the sense that, if it were removed, the amplitude of these fluctuations would be reduced to insignificant proportions'. (See *op. cit.* Table of Contents, p. xiii.)

[3] To assume that it is rigid in the long run, or subject only to autonomous changes (due to technological innovations) and not to equilibrating adjustments, seems to me hopelessly unrealistic.

fluctuations. All these factors together bring it about that our economic system is subject to cumulative, self-reinforcing processes of expansion and contraction.

Third, there are autonomous changes in aggregate expenditure, especially the concentrations, followed later by slumps of investment demand (including demand for consumer durables), caused by technological innovations and, above all, by war and preparation for war. These 'real factors' obviously do contribute their share to economic instability. But in my judgment it is mainly in their rôle as starters, intensifiers and interrupters of cumulative processes that they do their de-stabilizing work. That is to say, the 'propagation problem' is more important than the 'impulse problem'. And in the propagation mechanism, the way in which the economy responds to outside impulses, the monetary factor plays a decisive rôle.

The reason for this hypothetical evaluation is the historical experience that modern economies frequently take terrific impulses and shocks in their stride, while on other occasions they seem to react strongly to modest shocks. Recent history offers numerous examples. Let me mention the transition from peace to war and from war to peace, the latter entailing a tremendous sudden drop in government expenditure; another example is the reconstruction of some war-torn countries, such as Germany, Italy, Japan, Austria, and the subsequent levelling-out of these economies to a more normal course of development. These shocks, which were absorbed with surprising ease, were certainly incomparably more severe than those that are supposed to have started the Great Depression.

I conclude that the response mechanism is more important than the severity of the external shocks; and in the response mechanism monetary factors play a most important rôle.

If it is true that monetary factors greatly contribute to economic instability, does it follow that they adversely influence economic growth? Not necessarily. If there is anything in the Schumpeterian theory of creative cyclical inflation followed by 'creative destruction' — and I find it difficult to believe that there is not a great measure of truth in it — monetary forces may produce instability and speed up progress at the same time. We must, however, remember that cyclical inflation is only a part, though an indispensable part, of the Schumpeterian mechanism. Prolonged rapid inflation is undoubtedly inimical to economic growth. And a good case can be made for the proposition that the stimulant of inflation has been so much abused in our times in war and peace — during peace especially in poor, underdeveloped countries — that the Schumpeterian mechanism can no longer be relied upon to work, even if the basic non-monetary condition for its functioning, namely, a sufficiently free enterprise economy, still exists.

Furthermore, to the extent that monetary factors are responsible for the occurrence of exceptionally severe slumps, such as the great depression of the 1930s, they certainly hamper long-run economic growth.

We thus reach the conclusion that monetary factors, and the instability they breed, may help as well as hinder economic progress ; but it is easier to think of authentic and dramatic cases of the latter than of the former.[1] While, for the problem of stability, a great deal of importance has to be attributed to monetary factors as compared with real factors, I have no doubt in my mind that for the problem of long-run growth this judgment has to be completely reversed. The economic future of nations over long periods and the persistent differences in the level of well-being as well as in the rate of growth of different countries are primarily determined by non-monetary factors, real as well as social in the broad sense. Favourable labour-land ratios, or more generally labour-natural resources ratios (resources defined broadly to include climate and geography) ; the quality of the people, innate and acquired ; political and social stability ; the propensity to save and to work — these things, and the factors and forces standing behind them, determine long-run growth. Monetary arrangements and policies can do much to retard, but little to speed up, the rate of growth, except by avoiding monetary disturbances and impediments to economic progress. The exception is not unimportant ; but let us not forget that, from a broader long-run standpoint, monetary arrangements and policies are themselves shaped and determined by deeper social and political forces.

Few would question these somewhat platitudinous statements. But economic policy, especially monetary policy, often seems to proceed on the assumption that monetary policy can do little to promote short-run stability, because stubborn real factors and structural defects decree persistent disequilibrium, while long-run growth depends on, or at least can be greatly speeded up by, monetary measures. This seems to me the exact opposite of the truth.

[1] Applying the modern theory of the 'second best' it is, however, not hard to think of cases in which inflation promotes economic progress in the sense of being the lesser evil ; in other words, with all its deleterious effects it may tend to offset some of the even more deleterious effects of other conditions. Suppose, for example, that wages are pushed up relentlessly by powerful labour organizations ; then it may be argued that it is the lesser evil to let prices rise continuously, because the alternative would be a large volume of chronic unemployment.

THE DISCUSSION ON
PROFESSOR HABERLER'S PAPER

Chairman : PROFESSOR HOFFMANN (West Germany)

Professor Erik Lindahl (Sweden) was the first to speak. He said : Professor Haberler has given us the instructive lesson in the theory of business cycles that we have come to expect from the learned and perspicacious author of the famous book, *Prosperity and Depression.* A characteristic feature of Professor Haberler as a scholar is that he will not jump to hasty conclusions, but is anxious to take all the relevant points into consideration. Thus in his paper today we have been given a masterly presentation of the subject in all its aspects, which provides an excellent starting-point for our discussion.

For my own contribution, which will only deal with a few of the questions considered by Professor Haberler, I should like to put the problem of the influence of monetary factors on economic processes as follows. Since economic processes are the result of monetary and real factors — we can hardly abstract completely from the former — we have to find out how the process would develop under different monetary systems, other things being equal. By comparing these different developments, we can draw certain conclusions as to the importance of the various monetary factors.

I should like to distinguish four different kinds of monetary system.

(1) Let us first imagine a monetary system which guarantees a fixed price level but is otherwise completely passive. Opinions are divided as to whether any business cycle would arise under this assumption. The advocates of purely monetary theories of business cycles, such as Hawtrey and Irving Fisher, would give a negative answer to the question, whereas the adherents of more real explanations would answer in the affirmative. Like most contemporary economists, Professor Haberler belongs to the latter group. But, within this group, opinions differ about how great these cycles would be compared with actual cycles.

(2) For comparison, therefore, we should choose a mechanical monetary system such as we had up to the 1930s. As Professor Haberler points out, the characteristic feature of the cycles during this period was that ups and downs in output and employment were closely related to ups and downs in price levels. In his opinion,

the cyclical movement was made *considerably* larger by these 'monetary complications' than it would have been with an unchanged price level. Without monetary complications in the form of inflationary and speculative excesses during cyclical expansions, with subsequent financial crises, the real cycle would have been a 'rather mild affair'. On this point, Professor Hicks, for instance, has quite another view; for he has been able to construct beautiful models of cycles where the price level is constant. By stressing the importance of monetary factors, Professor Haberler to some extent stands in opposition to the purely real explanations of the cycle. Here, I am inclined to side with him; but I will leave the matter open for discussion by the experts assembled here today.

(3) Meanwhile, I shall proceed by introducing a third monetary system as a further basis for comparison, namely, the present one. This system has been with us since the 1930s, and, unlike its predecessor, it is not of the mechanical type, but in most countries is directed towards a new goal of economic policy, namely, full employment. This policy can be characterized broadly as an effort to avoid, by monetary and other means, the periods of depression with heavy unemployment which were so typical of the earlier system. Looking at the unemployment figures, which in many countries have been lower in the past ten years or so than was formerly thought possible, and have displayed comparatively small fluctuations, we have to admit that the policy has so far had the desired effect. But the price that has been paid for this has been rather high — a continuous depreciation of the value of money. Even during the new era, certain cyclical movements have appeared, although in many respects they have been of a different kind from earlier ones. I will not explore these byways farther, however, especially as I here lack the sure guidance of Professor Haberler, but I will leave these too for the experts to follow up.

(4) My own contribution to the discussion will chiefly be a comparison between the policy that has been pursued hitherto and the policy that I hope will be pursued in the future, namely, one which aims at attaining a high and stable level of employment on the basis of a stable price level. A feature common to both is the attempt to maintain as high and stable a level of employment as possible. Indeed, one of the lasting results of the thinking of the Keynesian period has been that in some way or other this goal has come to be included in all political programmes. The difference between the two monetary systems is that in the past inflation has been used as a means of increasing employment, whereas in the future (I hope) the same result will be attained without inflation.

In consequence, I must here tackle the question of the importance of inflation as a method of promoting economic stability
and growth in real terms, a question which, in my opinion, is
relevant and controversial enough to be discussed during this
Congress.

Here I can again refer to Professor Haberler's paper. He reminds
us that there are two schools of thought, each explaining inflation
in a different way. According to one school, inflation is due to a
lax monetary policy, while according to the other it is due to exaggerated income claims from organized labour and organized agriculture. He seems to suggest that it is not easy to make a distinction
between these two factors in an inflationary movement, and this is
perhaps true. But I would like to emphasize that, in making a
theoretical analysis of the effects of inflation, it is appropriate to
make a distinction between two different *kinds* of inflation, whose
fundamentally different character could be conceived of in isolation,
even if, in reality, they are usually found together, reinforcing one
another. This distinction was, in fact, made long ago, by Keynes
in his *Treatise on Money*, where the one kind is called 'profit inflation' and the other 'income inflation'.

'Profit inflation' arises when a general excess demand drives
up prices, while 'income inflation' arises when wages, salaries and
other costs bring about a rise in prices, thereby causing, at the
same time, the increase in demand that makes the price rise possible.
In the former case, the increase in demand is the active force in the
price movement, whereas in the latter case the increase in demand
is a result of the higher prices.

First, I should like to say a few words about the causes and the
effects of pure profit inflation. This can most easily be regarded
as the result of a process of expansion which is caused by an excess
of investment over saving *ex ante*. As long as there are productive
resources which are not fully used, this process of expansion will
result in an increase in employment and in real output, without
raising the price level to any considerable extent. This process has
become well known to us through the Keynesian system. When
the expansion can no longer proceed in real terms, because the
available productive resources are already fully used, it will continue
in the monetary sphere, and will result in a rise in prices. On the
labour market there will be an excess demand instead of an excess
supply, and the result will be what is sometimes called over-full
employment. Even if total real output cannot be increased beyond
a certain limit, the existing excess of monetary investment will cause
an increase in investment in real terms, because the rise in prices

will give firms such large profits that these will constitute the basis of the required increase in savings. The losers will be all those income receivers who are not able to increase their incomes to the same extent as prices have risen. From their point of view, the rise in prices will have the character of a tax, which hits lenders particularly hard; for, as far as they are concerned, it will be equivalent to a confiscation of their property.

So long as such an inflation is on a moderate scale, it is looked upon rather favourably by many economists. It even seems to have found favour in the stern eye of Professor Haberler. If the spectre of unemployment has disappeared, if the whole economy is working at full capacity, and if, in addition, economic growth is being promoted by a level of investment higher than would have been achieved by a constant price level, then the advantages seem to be so great as to outweigh the disadvantage of a fall in the value of money by 2 or 3 per cent per annum.

For my own part, however, I should first like to say that it is illogical to set up such a moderate inflationary process as a long-term aim of economic policy. The result would be that the public would try to adjust itself to the inflation, both by taking advantage of it on the one hand, and by avoiding its disadvantages on the other. When borrowers become aware that they can repay their loans in depreciated money — an annual price rise of 3 per cent means a doubling of the price level in twenty-four years — they will increase their demands for loans for investment purposes. On the other hand, those who save part of their incomes will try to protect themselves against the inflation by making direct investments, to the disadvantage of banking and insurance. Consequently, the inflation will tend to accelerate, the more so as the workers gradually increase their wage demands to compensate for the lowering of real wages brought about by the inflation. To keep the inflation within bounds, the authorities have to intervene by means of strict regulation of the capital market, as well as in other fields. The result will be that the allocation of investment will be distorted, and also that its volume will increase by less than before. In the end, as Professor Viner explained the other day, the inflation will bring only disadvantages (except for some minor groups in society). This can readily be seen in countries, in South America for instance, where inflation has become a lasting phenomenon. I think we can all agree that such an inflation is not to be desired, and, in view of the difficulty of getting back to normality, it is particularly important to avoid getting into an inflationary rut. Thus we see that a policy declaration in favour of a mild and advantageous inflation will have consequences which conflict with the programme itself. In this lies its illogicality.

A condition for the success of such a policy would be that it was kept *secret*, and that the public was given the idea that the rise in prices each year was due to chance and would not be repeated. The thesis that morals should be sacrificed to the good of the state has, as is well known, been propounded in the past by a famous statesman in this country, namely, Machiavelli. But I very much doubt whether his theory can be carried out successfully for very long in an enlightened democracy, especially if it has at its disposal economists who consider it their duty to reveal that the public is being hoodwinked. The benefits to be derived from such a two-faced policy would therefore be rather limited. Having regard both to its immorality and to the risk that after a short time the economy would slide into an inflationary rut that few would consider desirable, I would dissociate myself in principle from schemes implying a 'mild' and 'pleasant' profit inflation.

The other kind of inflation, 'income inflation', to which I now turn, is usually caused by the efforts of organized groups in society to increase their shares of the national product. When aggregate disposable income exceeds the estimated value of the national product at constant prices, the conflict will be resolved by an increase in the money value of output through a rise in prices. In this way, the real shares will be so adjusted that their sums will correspond to the total product.

A pure income inflation has not such pleasant qualities as those ascribed to a profit inflation. It will neither promote capital formation nor increase the volume of employment. Indeed, it is quite conceivable that such an inflation may be associated with unemployment and trade depression. It can, however, be used as a last line of defence against excessive income claims when these cannot be reduced by other means.

Income inflation is thus to be regarded as an evil: but it is sometimes defended as being the lesser evil among the alternatives to hand. This line of thought, too, is to be found in Professor Haberler's paper. 'Suppose, for example,' he says, 'that wages are pushed up relentlessly by powerful labour organizations; then it may be argued that it is the lesser evil to let prices rise continuously, because the alternative would be a large volume of chronic unemployment.' (p. 178 footnote.)

Looking at each case separately, this line of thought seems very plausible. While a profit inflation can be counteracted by monetary measures which will restore the balance between saving and investment, the monetary counter-measures to an income inflation would upset that balance by creating deflationary pressure. This in itself would be very bad, especially as it could affect branches of industry other than those where the rise in income had occurred.

In the long run, however, the choice between these alternatives has to be made on other grounds. The real antagonism between social groups, with which we are faced here, can only be temporarily concealed by a depreciation in the value of money. If we were to accept the principle that excessive income claims should be corrected by price increases, it would result in the continuously rising price level to which the term 'wage-price-spiral' has been applied. Then the principle of a stable value of money would definitely have been abandoned, and the price movement would slide back into the disheartening inflationary rut of which I spoke earlier.

It may also be claimed, in favour of the stabilization alternative, that wage negotiations on the labour market would take on a more realistic character if they could be based on the assurance of a stable value of money. The parties would then know what they were discussing, and would not have to make exaggerated claims in order to hedge against the risk of further price increases.

Furthermore, it should be remembered that there are other means of solving such problems besides monetary measures; processes of arbitration, different kinds of government intervention, etc. I should be very pleased if the discussion today were to make any contribution towards resolving this difficult dilemma with which we are now faced.

My comparison of these two monetary policies, both aiming at a high and stable level of employment, the one with inflation and the other without, has led me to favour the latter. Time does not permit me to go into detail concerning the problems connected with the structure of this stabilization policy. I shall therefore restrict myself to a few general remarks.

(1) By a stable price level I do not necessarily mean a fixed price level. In Sweden we have, in theory at any rate, although unfortunately not in practice, some sympathy with the idea that the price level should vary in inverse proportion to productivity. Prices would then be allowed to rise when there was a shortage of goods, caused for instance by poor harvests or political complications, but fall when there was an increased supply of goods, due to technical progress. In view of the rapid technical progress of our time, such a policy would lead to a falling price level in the long run, and would probably stabilize the economic process — the crisis of 1929, for example, might have been avoided by such a policy. It would

also have the advantage that pensioners and others receiving fixed incomes would be able to share in the increased welfare, instead of seeing their real position progressively worsened, as has hitherto been the case. This policy would also permit a gradual increase in nominal wages, if the accumulation of capital proceeded satisfactorily, provided, of course, that the workers could accustom themselves to accepting an increase in real wages in the form of lower living costs.

(2) The fact that the policy aims at a high and stable level of employment means, first, that employment can be kept as high as possible without inflation, and, second, that those trade cycles that can be described as an alternation between periods of general excess demand and general excess supply will probably be mitigated. On the other hand, it should be regarded as a normal condition of an expanding economy that boom conditions in certain branches should be balanced by declines in other branches, so that some kind of equilibrium is attained between total demand and total supply. This means that temporary unemployment in some places cannot be avoided because labour is immobile. Total unemployment can, however, as a rule be kept at a low level if special measures are taken to facilitate the transfer of labour to new employment.

(3) In order that the aims just mentioned shall be attained, it is necessary to use not only monetary policy, but also fiscal policy and other forms of government activity. The various aspects of economic policy must be co-ordinated in a suitable way. In this context, I should like to express the view that monetary policy should be used in the first place to protect the value of money, and not for the redistribution of income, which could be achieved more effectively and more openly by fiscal policy. In some countries, experiments have been made in which the functions of these two policies have been interchanged, so that responsibility for the value of money has fallen on fiscal policy, while monetary policy has been used to reduce rents and to influence the distribution of income in other ways. These experiments have not, however, had a very good effect on the value of money.

(4) For an individual country, complications will also arise over foreign trade and the balance of payments. It is difficult, of course, though not technically impossible, for an individual country to stabilize its price level if world prices are rising. Experience shows that small countries easily yield to the temptation to exploit the inflationary margin that accrues to them through foreign price movements. The big countries therefore have a great responsibility, and I should like to express the hope that the stabilization policy in the United States, which has kept the retail price level

stable during recent years, will be maintained. This policy has already stimulated, and will go on stimulating, other countries to devote greater attention to breaking inflationary tendencies at home.

I have already suggested that we now face a new era in the history of monetary systems, where the value of money is no longer determined by mechanical factors, but is the result of economic policy. The old monetary system was certainly imperfect, a fact to which the crises and depressions of that time bear witness, and at the beginning of this century many economists were dreaming of a happy future when a more stable value of money would be guaranteed by active policy. It would have been a great disappointment to them if they had realized that our newly won power over the value of money would not be better used during the last two decades than to cause an exceedingly powerful and persistent worldwide inflation. Personally, I do not think that this process can go on. Considering the progress made in other fields, it would be an anomaly if, in the future, the need for a rationally organized monetary system should be neglected. What is needed now is, above all, the drawing-up of new rules of behaviour to replace those that were used during the gold standard era. Professional economists have an important contribution to make here, and it would be heartening for the participants in this Congress if our discussions were to provide a stimulus to this activity.

Professor Ugo Papi (Italy) said : Professor Haberler's paper abounds in wisdom and learning and offers rich food for thought. I shall concentrate my remarks on some points of clarification rather than dissent.

My first point concerns the significance of certain indicators. Professor Haberler accepts the 'increase in *per capita* income as a criterion of economic growth'; which is, after all, not very far from the truth so long as the composition and the distribution of income remain constant. He also accepts maximization of that income as an *aim* of economic development.

In going on to discuss the characteristics of business cycles, Professor Haberler — in common with many other writers — adds the consideration of employment to that of *per capita* income. And he makes the point that, both in short and in longer cycles, income fluctuations and employment fluctuations occur in the same direction and are often, though not always, accompanied by fluctuations in expenditure — that is to say, by fluctuations in money flows and hence in prices. However, there may be a certain degree of price instability even with stable aggregate output and employment.

I agree entirely with Professor Haberler, and with many other writers, that, in examining the cycle, it may be useful to consider *both* income and employment. But we must remember that income and employment are only indicators of economic fluctuations; the maximization of income and employment are *not* objectives to be simultaneously pursued by any given country. This needs to be stated clearly, lest there should be confusion of thought. Such confusion may arise when we try to establish relations between the two aggregates — aggregate income and aggregate employment. The statement, for instance, that fuller employment gives rise to a higher income is far from being proven, except in the very short period. Another occasion for confusion of thought — and this has happened in my country with respect to the so-called Vanoni Plan — is when a national development plan aims at increasing both employment and *per capita* income at the same time and by the same measures. This is an altogether untenable position. It is true that, given the conditions prevailing in the country, maximization of *per capita* income, together with a suitable income distribution, does help also to achieve the fullest possible employment. But the reverse is not true: the fullest possible employment does not guarantee the highest possible *per capita* income. We need only recall our experience in this country with the so-called 'compulsory allocation of manpower' in agriculture and industry. We see at once that this scheme has greatly raised the costs of exports, and placed serious obstacles in their way. For a country that wishes to achieve economic development, the fundamental objective always remains an increase in the volume of output which can be sold at remunerative prices, and consequently an increase in *per capita* income.

Lasting employment of the factors of production, more especially of labour, can only be conceived of as a result of productive activities which succeed in finding an outlet at remunerative prices on the home or the world market. Only as indicators of the phases of the cycle may *per capita* income and employment be considered jointly. And even as an indicator, income is of the greater importance.

The second point is more complicated. It concerns the importance of monetary factors in determining long-term development — the trend — on the one hand, and short or longer cycles on the other. Professor Haberler reminds us that, according to a commonly held opinion, long-term growth depends on monetary measures — or at least is susceptible of being speeded up by them — while short-run stability is but little affected by monetary policy. In his paper, Professor Haberler reverses this view. Monetary factors, he says, exercise but little influence in shaping long-term economic development; but they exercise a determining influence in shaping the cycle. I should be inclined to go a step further than Professor Haberler on this question of long-term development.

What are the causes underlying long-term development? A trend can hardly be defined *a priori*. It is only after the event that we are able to observe how the fluctuations of economic activity have oscillated around a line which, in the long run, is seen to be ascending, in spite of some regressions, later made good. This upward trend can be traced back to factors whose influence outlives the depression phases of both short and long cycles. Paramount among these factors are the growth of world population — a *net* increase of 100,000 each day — and the sustained effort made by man, not merely to increase the supply of essential goods so as to keep step with the population growth, but to improve the living conditions of a large part of the world's population. Unfortunately, the results of this effort still lag far behind its aims. Nevertheless, it is to this effort that the rising trend is due.

What part does money play in this sustained human effort? The characteristic feature of money is that it acts as an instrument to help translate into practical benefits the results of 'favourable events' affecting productive activity. In monetary systems far removed from the gold standard, money begins to exercise an influence on human effort and on long-term development as soon as it transcends its instrumental function and gives rise to inflationary pressure.

Many authors have described the motives which work towards inflation, and some of them have also shown why inflation hinders the accumulation of savings. Forced savings are rapidly offset by the shrinkage of voluntary savings; domestic savings are transferred abroad whenever possible; the influx of foreign savings is discouraged; the incentives to production and the principles guiding the choice of investment are modified; speculation is favoured; controls multiply; the country's real income falls and, as a result, economic development is hindered. So economic development is neither promoted nor accelerated by monetary factors. But it certainly does feel their influence whenever they neutralize the beneficial effects of the 'favourable events', that is, as soon as they compromise the results of that human effort which is directed to increasing living standards.

The position can be likened to that of any productive enterprise. Real factors favourable to productive activity — such as inventions, the better organization of production, the discovery of mineral resources or the opening up of new markets — mean 'economies' in the productive process and act as incentives to greater and more

economical production. Monetary factors — once they become anything more than instruments for translating production incentives
into practice — mean rising costs and inflationary pressure that is
harmful to long-term economic development.

The influence of monetary factors on cycles is more obvious.
Experience has shown that those human efforts designed to adjust
the supply of goods to the increasing population, and so to improve
living conditions, have never succeeded in calling forth a linear
increase in production. Professor Haberler has, in a masterly way,
surveyed groups of business cycle theories. In my view, cyclical
movements represent the outcome of a series of errors in deciding
on the supply of goods. First, there are the errors of under-supply
in relation to the prospects opened up by 'favourable events'. Later,
there are errors of over-supply in relation to the concrete opportunities deriving from those events. Both groups of errors are due
to the difficulty of foreseeing the dynamics of supply and demand,
or divergences between the rate and the direction of changes in
production costs and sales prices for goods and services on the
domestic market. But, whatever theory we adopt for the explanation of the cycle, we must be clear on one point. When do monetary
factors come into play in influencing the cycle ?

An inflationary spiral, and with it the influence of monetary
factors on the cycle, starts when incomes, which have to purchase
on the market at higher prices all that is produced, rise less than
prices themselves. So, in many productive processes costs rise
faster than prices, and the margin between them quickly narrows.
It is true that monetary forces can prolong the period of rising prices,
if credit is granted to firms with sharply rising costs. But monetary
forces thereby merely aggravate the ultimate consequences of the
depression.

Some authors speak of 'creative' inflation. The fact is that
there is only one case in which credit creation can justifiably be said
to anticipate the production of a larger future income, and thereby
promote output. That is when temporary inflation is followed by
an actual expansion of real wealth. If future incomes do not increase,
all that credit expansion has done will have been to cause inflationary
pressure. It follows that it is of the greatest importance for any
study of the rôle of money in the cycle to know precisely at what
moment inflationary pressure begins.

Monetary factors do exercise a very considerable influence, even
if only a negative one, on economic expansion. Together with
psychological factors, and rigidity, they exert a decisive influence
on both short and long cycles, intensifying the volume and

amplitude of swings. In the context of the quest for stability, these conclusions imply that monetary policy must be cautious. It must look ahead so as not to create obstacles to long-term development nor to aggravate the cycle. A prudent attitude on the part of the monetary authorities represents a real contribution to a country's stability.

This brings me to the third point I should like to make. We have seen that monetary factors play an important part in hindering long-term economic development and in determining the size and amplitude of cycles. Can these monetary factors somehow be transformed into instruments of a cautious counter-cyclical policy?

Professor Haberler is rather sceptical. He says that when business is good it is far from easy to diagnose inflation. It is not enough to keep the general price level stable — which in itself is a policy which the monetary authorities may not always find advisable, or be able to pursue. Only *ex post* can it be said whether credit has been excessive. In our present monetary systems, which are all but deprived of important brakes, monetary factors ultimately assume greater importance even than real factors, which are called upon only to act as mechanisms of impulse and intensification. However, I wonder whether monetary authorities, intent on pursuing the above-mentioned prudent policy, might not watch an index other than a stable price level ; for instance, equilibrium in the balance of payments.

Equilibrium in the balance of payments gives the maximum advantage which a country can derive from the sale of its own goods and services, on the home and foreign market. It represents an optimum position in terms of the appeal which a country makes to the incomes of other countries, to induce them to purchase its goods. And equilibrium in the balance of payments does not imply a rigid situation, so long as it allows for increasing exports over time. When exports rise, and the balance of payments remains roughly in balance, the country in question experiences a rise in national income. Provided the financial authorities are able to follow this growth of income closely, balance-of-payments equilibrium will sooner or later be followed by budgetary equilibrium. And the result of this double equilibrium will be a stable value of money.

Provided that they watch the equilibrium of the balance of payments, and given an upward tendency of exports, the monetary authorities may undertake a cautious credit expansion even in times of boom. The general level of domestic prices need not necessarily remain stable. The important thing is that the country should combine a movement towards balance-of-payments equilibrium with a growing flow of exports. Certainly, in any attempt to re-establish a country's balance-of-payments equilibrium, monetary measures, such as rises in Bank Rate, the manipulation of reserves or fluctuating exchange rates, must be accompanied by fiscal measures, heavier taxation and reduced expenditure — and possibly also by direct controls.

But all these measures, even if taken simultaneously, can have but a limited influence in keeping down upward fluctuations, unless they form part of an overall plan embodying real as well as monetary factors and designed to promote long-term development and expansion. The fact remains that it is possible for the monetary authorities to control an upswing, especially if they can precisely determine the moment at which an inflationary spiral begins in any given country. That moment is when the rise in incomes begins to lag behind the rise in prices.

Unfortunately, the use of monetary measures is definitely limited during the depression phase. To stimulate recovery and eventually lead to a boom, 'real factors' in the shape of 'favourable events' are indispensable. Monetary factors can help real factors, but they cannot by themselves cause incomes and prices to rise. Monetary factors alone cannot push the economy past the lower turning-point. This fact provides further proof that neither the short nor the long cycle, nor long-term development, can be traced back exclusively, or mainly, to monetary factors.

We are extremely grateful to Professor Haberler for the strong case he has made out for the rehabilitation of monetary factors as determinants of economic activity. But the real merit of his contribution lies in defining the limits of such rehabilitation. The limits he mentions may provide some guidance for practical decisions on the part of governments.

Professor Haberler opened the general discussion by saying that he was grateful to Professor Papi for putting a sharper edge on his definitions. The latter seemed to be in agreement on aggregate criteria, and his points were well taken. Professor Haberler agreed that the fullest possible level of employment need not mean the highest level of *per capita* income. He wished to stress that if these two aims conflicted, a high *per capita* income was more important than full employment.

Professor Haberler said he had used the term 'Creative inflation' himself to mean a 'Schumpeterian' inflation, followed by an 'auto-deflation'. Such an inflation would not be permanent or rapid. Professor Papi had said that the downswing was caused by an over-supply of resources compared with the available opportunities. This was an instance of the formal distinction between *conjuncture général* and *conjuncture généralisée*. The depression began in particular areas and then spread to the whole system. But he could not understand Professor Papi's claim that in inflation incomes lagged behind prices; for the national income equalled the total of all prices paid. However, if Professor Papi merely meant earned incomes (excluding profits) then he understood and agreed.

Professor Lindahl's remarks were in basic agreement with his own, but fortunately there were some points of disagreement on which he could comment. The distinction between profit and income inflation led back to Keynes's *Treatise on Money*, where profits were not regarded as part of income. Income was equal not to output but to disposable income, leaving out undistributed corporate profits and perhaps even distributed profits. This did not accord with modern usage, and it still remained difficult to make the corresponding distinction between types of inflation.

In any inflation which lasted for any time, the two forces merged; the initiating force might be a push from wages or a pull from demand, but after a short time the push and pull would be simultaneous, giving rise to a 'chicken and egg' problem. One could also make other distinctions. For example, one could have inflation leading to a rise in real output, when one had a cyclical expansion from the bottom of a depression. That might well be a profit inflation; but it could also be a wage inflation. On the other hand, near full employment a rise in demand would mainly raise prices, though the idea of a sharp break in continuity at the level of full employment was not tenable, as Keynes himself had shown in the *General Theory* with his discussion of bottlenecks and so on. The extent to which prices could rise also depended on the attitude of trade unions, and so the distinction between profit and income inflation was hard to make, though it might be important.

Professor Lindahl had discussed 'planned' inflation, and Professor Haberler said he agreed that an 'announced' inflation would not be pleasant. A regular rise of 3 per cent a year would soon be anticipated, and the inflation would soon degenerate into a galloping one; he himself had objected to Slichter on these grounds. But what was an 'announced' inflation? Who announced it? The Governor of the Central Bank, being in an official position, would surely keep silent; and academic economists might not be taken very seriously. It was true that inflation might sustain investment for a time, as Professor Viner had shown. But in many countries inflation to stimulate investment had turned into galloping, self-reinforcing inflation. What we needed was full employment *without* inflation.

On trade union policy, Professor Haberler said he had stuck to a pessimistic view, but he was open to persuasion. Perhaps he had been too pessimistic. But what would trade unions do if governments were firm in resisting wage rises? Views differed, and his own position was based only on experience in the U.K. and the U.S.A., where the advice of Swedish economists had not been accepted.

Finally, Professor Haberler said he had in the past commended the idea that prices should fall with rising productivity. He had thought it healthy for money wages to remain constant with prices falling. But he had now become more modest, and would be quite happy if prices merely remained fairly stable. There could be little danger if prices remained constant and the supply of money rose as output increased, whether this increase was the result of higher productivity or a bigger population. If productivity rose and prices were constant, all would be well. There had been over-refinement in older versions of monetary theory, and he did not wish to ask the impossible of monetary policy.

Sir Dennis Robertson (U.K.) explained that he was neither a Marxist nor a Hegelian; yet he could not help reflecting, in listening to Professor Haberler's paper, how truth seemed to proceed by way of thesis, antithesis and (we hoped) final synthesis. In his extreme old age, he felt impelled to remind his hearers of how, in the dim, distant past, before 1914, when he had first studied economic fluctuations, almost all the literature was of a crude, monetary kind, with all economic troubles blamed on monetary disorders. He still thought that, under those conditions, it had been right to lay emphasis on real income (output) and on the *real* causes of fluctuations — especially inventions, innovation and the lumpiness of investment.

But circumstances changed cases, and, after the First World War, there had been monetary chaos and also the teaching of Keynes, originally the prophet of the importance of money, in contrast to the classical 'veil'. He himself had then been ready to attach more importance to money. Now, one had the refurbishing of the accelerator and the introduction of the fixed coefficient linking capital to income that was embodied in the Harrod-Domar equation. Paradoxically, Keynesian theory was now so unmonetary as to require Professor Haberler's renewed emphasis on the forgotten elements of prices, costs and monetary happenings.

All this was general, but he wished to make two specific comments. First, what happened if monetary policy and trade union wage policy were in head-on conflict? In the past, he had been a 'moderate optimist'. While it was sometimes useful to distinguish demand-induced and cost-induced inflation, the two often blended together, and wage inflation in the past ten years had been a kind of secondary result of chronic demand inflation. Till recently, inflation had been tolerated by those in charge of monetary policy — governments and central banks. It had been unfair of them to put the standard of value in the hands of trade unions and expect them to behave moderately.

However, if governments and central banks *did* take charge, this altered the situation. If, in the face of a definite restraining monetary policy on the part of governments, trade unions made unreasonable wage demands, some kind of clash was inevitable. He hoped that this would not occur, because he felt that trade union intransigence had been largely the result of government policy. A restraining monetary system might 'take the steam' out of wage advances; if the average employer was less ready to grant wage increases, workers had less confidence in their ability to press their claims. But perhaps this was too hopeful, because news from home suggested that the T.U.C. had rejected the 'ear stroking' of the government and had given *carte blanche* to wage claims. Perhaps, however, in fact, the unions' bark was worse than their bite, and world conditions and central bank policy would make them more amenable.

Sir Dennis said that, on the international side, he and Professor Haberler had got a bit out of step. It was hard for the most academic of us to be non-national, and academics responsible for helping to frame government policy had sometimes found it hard to see eye to eye with colleagues across the Atlantic. He himself had always emphasized the link between inflation at home and balance-of-payments problems, but this was another side to the story. It had been said that the problems still besetting relations between the old and new worlds were purely monetary. But real factors came in too, and he felt that Professor Haberler had been a little slow to recognize them.

Sir Dennis said he felt that a policy of allowing prices to fall as productivity increased was desirable internally; but internationally difficulties would arise, and this was the chief reason against it. If prices were allowed to fall in full proportion to any rise in productivity within one country, this might cause very serious problems in other countries, which, to remain competitive, might need deliberately to contract the flow of money income. On these grounds alone, he might be willing to sacrifice the objective of falling prices. He still thought this would prove the ideal objective, but he would be fairly satisfied, when he looked round in a hundred years' time, if prices were no higher than today.

Professor Veit (Western Germany) considered the relation between secular inflation and technical progress. He did not regard the idea of stable prices, with the money supply increasing just enough to offset the depressing effects of rising output and falling costs, as the real solution. Indeed, we had to face the fact that a secular inflation was occurring. If one looked at the endeavours of monetary authorities and central banks in all countries, one found that the tendency was (and had been for five years) to fight inflation anywhere and everywhere it appeared. Yet it seemed to become harder and harder to succeed — even in countries in which a rise of prices was hardly felt. Something seemed to be going on behind the scenes.

What was needed, then, was a policy which would allow prices to fall as productivity rose and costs fell in the course of technical progress. In the 1920s, people in the U.S.A. had felt that, since prices were not rising, nothing serious could befall. Then came the collapse of 1929 and the following depression. Looking back to 1923–1929, we now saw that there had, in reality, been a great inflation, with prices fairly constant despite falling costs.

To explain what had happened completely, it was valuable to use the concept of inflation suggested by Professor J. Pedersen of Denmark. This appeared to be the only reasonable explanation of the concept in *real* terms. Thus, rising wages backed by bank credit would represent inflation, whether it looked like inflation or not. Even if prices were constant, there would be similar consequences for the distribution of income as there would be if prices were rising. If technical progress occurred, and costs fell without prices going down, this was only to the benefit of those whose wages rose. No one would have found any value in the development of modern technique if the advantage was not shared by all classes and income groups.

With the undercurrent of a veiled inflation, monetary authorities nowadays faced a real dilemma. They should, on the one hand, aim at falling prices, and therefore contract the volume of money per unit of real output. On the other hand, they knew that such a policy would be disadvantageous, and even dangerous to the banking system. The banks needed, at worst, a situation of constant prices, since debtors would not like having to redeem their liabilities to the banks in appreciated money. To be realistic, one might agree with a central bank policy of price stability, but one would nevertheless have to keep in mind that it would comprise a concealed inflationary element.

M. Rueff (France) thought it essential to go deeper into some problems raised by previous speakers, and in particular to give a closer definition of 'monetary authorities' and their powers. He had the impression that these authorities were often subconsciously compared to Jove, and that they were armed with an equally effective thunderbolt. Perhaps one should try to reduce this belief to its proper proportions.

He was glad that Professor Lindahl agreed that there were many types of monetary system, and that any discussion on monetary policy would lead nowhere unless the nature of the system under-lying the debate was first clearly defined. He himself thought it might be useful to define the two extreme types of monetary system — the active and the passive. The active system was the simpler. It issued a number of little pieces of paper, not backed by any metallic or other commodities. The number of these pieces of paper could be strictly limited, and so the value of the currency was geared to fluctuations in the economy. In other words, prices varied with economic circumstances. In the passive system, on the contrary, the amount of money varied with the total of desired cash-balances. This was 'neutral' money. Any actual system was somewhere between these two extremes. At present, all systems were much nearer the second type than the first.

The methods of controlling monetary policy open to the com-petent authorities were three in number. The first was variation in the discount rate. The second was open market operations, and it was usual to contrast active operations of this type with a passive, fixed discount rate. In his view, the difference between these two techniques was trifling. In open market operations the bank chose a certain rate at which it bought and sold securities. When the chosen rate rose, this rise was not fundamentally different from a modification of the discount rate. The third weapon available to banks was that of quantitative controls, *i.e.* ceilings and floors to the amounts of various resources they might hold. In addition, there were fiscal techniques for influencing the monetary situation, but these were in the hands of governments and not banks.

Active inflation of the type at present prevailing, consisted in letting the discount rate fall to a level below the equilibrium rate, which the market would have reached had the bank not intervened. When such a situation existed, the assets eligible for discount flowed into the bank and were converted into money.

He hoped that the subjects dealt with by Professors Haberler, Papi and Lindahl would be supplemented by study of the mechanics of the monetary system. The drama of monetary policy was enacted on a far wider scene than was generally realized, and the real actors in the drama were outside the offices of the monetary authorities.

Professor Lerner (U.S.A.) said that the problem under discussion was one of semantics and appropriate parables. The distinction between real and monetary phenomena was not a 'chicken and egg' problem. Nor was it a 'sun or moon' problem (the moon being the more important because it alone shone when it was dark !). It was not a question of what were real factors and what were not. It was a question of the causal relations between them. The appropriate parable for the present debate was the question whether people grew upwards or downwards. One man said that people grew downwards because they grew down below the bottom of their trousers. Another said they grew upwards, because he had seen a whole regiment marching along, and, on the ground, everyone was at the same level. The real-monetary distinction was not what we were really after. And yet economists were in the habit of thinking of an economy run without money, and then bringing in monetary influences. The point was that there were many different influences, some not 'real' but none the less genuine, all of which could increase or decrease the level of activity or cause it to fluctuate. The question was, how could the authorities prevent any harmful effects ?

At first it was thought that these harmful effects could be avoided by eliminating changes in the money supply. Then it was seen that monetary policy alone was inadequate, and other methods, often fiscal, were necessary. These two forces, monetary and fiscal, had, until recently, been considered the most important. Could they prevent cycles, it was asked ?

Professor Lerner declared that there were here two fallacies. First, there was the error of thinking that fluctuations were necessary for development. This error seemed to arise because economists had transferred to the economy as a whole conditions of progress which applied to the firm but were inappropriate to the economy. The firm needed difficulties to make it more efficient; but the economy did not, in the same way, need the business cycle.

The second error was to think that development necessarily resulted in fluctuations. This seemed to assume that the kind of rigidity in production techniques frequently found in the firm was found in the whole economy, so that one could apply a simple acceleration principle. And there was no point in adding riders about psychological factors, because that merely weakened the original argument.

Now, recent experience had shown that monetary and fiscal forces were not enough. In Israel, cost inflation (he preferred this term to 'income inflation' because it seemed more explanatory) had occurred with wages rising even in conditions of considerable unemployment. He agreed with Professors Haberler and Lindahl that the ideal thing would be to have stable prices and full employment ; but to attempt to achieve this by monetary and fiscal measures alone might necessitate the creation of massive unemployment to prevent wage increases. If prices could be kept constant by a small volume of unemployment, all was well. But there were many cases when unemployment would have to be very high to prevent wages and prices rising. It was not that the monetary and fiscal authorities had given up their authority ; their authority had been taken away by the trade unions. There was no point in the government trying to punish the trade unions by creating mass unemployment. If they did, they would not long remain the government. In this way, the power of the trade unions constituted a third element. One had not only a monetary authority and a fiscal authority, but also a wage authority. It was necessary to recognize this in order to understand the distinction between cost and demand inflation. It did not help to fudge this distinction ; one had to emphasize the differences in the forces which were at work and to separate the push from the pull. If one watched a horse and cart, followed by a motor car, going up a hill, it was hard to tell, from a distance, whether the horse was pulling the car or the car pushing the horse. But it was important to discover distinctions like this in order to discover whether one had to deal with the pull of demand inflation or the push of cost inflation.

Dr. Hershlag (Israel) said that Professor Haberler had introduced his subject by remarks on the criteria of growth. He himself wished to challenge the so-called 'fashionable' definition of the economic growth as 'the sustained increase in *per capita* output or real national income'. In 1952, Professor Viner had qualified this notion of growth by saying, 'It would be a superior kind of growth, to my taste at least, if it involved, in addition to an increase in the average income, an improvement in the standard of living of the majority of the people'.[1] Professor Haberler had also pointed out that a more accurate definition of growth implied something about the composition of total output, especially the ratio of consumer to investment goods. If this qualification to economic progress were included in the definition, it might not be enough to say with Professor Haberler (p. 152) that maximization of the rate of economic growth was an objective, 'subject to the reservation that the composition and distribution of income do not change in a way that is

[1] See *The Progress of Underdeveloped Areas*, ed. B. Hoselitz, p. 187.

deemed undesirable'. He himself would suggest adding the proviso that the 'composition and distribution of income should change in a way that *was* deemed desirable'.

As this question largely concerned the less developed countries, it might be important to draw more attention to the price that had to be paid for this kind of growth. This price might be expressed in terms of the rate of growth, or of alternatives and priorities in investment, or of the extent and nature of the financial resources drawn on during the process of growth. It might mean abandoning the *credo* of complete freedom of savings and investment. Dr. Hershlag felt it was difficult to assume that economic growth and economic stability would occur simultaneously. For example, a more equal distribution of income could have adverse effects on entrepreneurial incentives and investment, though it could also be a stimulating and stabilizing factor in the economy. Again, national economic policies intended to combat imported instability or home-produced inflation often increased distortions and instability. This could be seen in the patterns of international trade, in too early or too late devaluation, or in credit policies. The question arose whether monetary policies which were used to fight depression or curb inflation, could ever be understood as adequately as the distorting, but more predictable, real factors.

The answer depended largely on the influence of economists and governments on monetary developments. Sometimes it might be possible to maintain fairly rapid growth by a policy which almost extorted internal capital resources and thus avoided inflation. This undoubtedly raised the problem of the relation between average *per capita* income and the disposable income of the majority of people. Any decision on this hardly belonged to the economist, but he had to have his say. The choice was, perhaps, less acute in rich countries; but it was urgent in poorer countries.

Even accepting the existence of different economic levels within the richer countries, it seemed that while economic stability might be the main issue in richer countries, economic growth was mainly a problem of the less developed countries. Monetary factors and policies had recently become a burning problem in these countries, and this had a bearing on the extent and rate of economic growth. Even if the poor countries' problem was caused partly by imported economic instability and by the demonstration effect, it nevertheless merited more and clearer elaboration. He therefore suggested (*a*) a redefinition of economic progress; (*b*) an explanation of the cost and rate of economic growth; (*c*) a more satisfactory explanation of the impact of real and monetary factors on the poorer countries.

Stability and Progress in the World Economy

Professor Gudin (Brazil) suggested that the discussion hinged on the same old problem as that considered in Professor Pigou's *Industrial Fluctuations*. Capitalism, and also Socialism, if there were any freedom of choice for consumers, was subject to horizontal or vertical disequilibria. But this was the price of freedom and was worth paying.

Speaking of the influence of monetary factors on economic stability, Professor Gudin quoted an early writing of Professor Baudin in which he had stressed the fact that money, once it had replaced a barter economy, could do a great deal of harm, purchasing power becoming indeterminate in 'time, space, object and person'. But there had been, he thought, a tremendous improvement in monetary management after 1945 as compared with what had happened after 1918.

Professor Brus (Poland) wanted to comment on two problems. The first was the relation between real and monetary factors in stability. His approach to the problem, as a Marxian economist, obviously differed in many respects from that of Professor Haberler, and he would define the real factors, at least partly, in a different way. He would underline the fact that money played an active, although secondary, rôle because in the last resort the rôle of money was determined by a real process — the accumulation of capital. But most important was the fact that Professor Haberler had shown very clearly that the relation between real and monetary factors was of central importance to all those working on the problems of stability and progress in the world economy.

It seemed to him that it would not be right for any economist to pass over the views expressed on this topic by Marx, in the three chapters of the third volume of *Das Kapital* entitled 'Monetary Capital and Real Capital'. Admittedly one would not find there a final solution to the problem; that would be impossible. But if one considered Professor Haberler's approach as important and interesting, Marx would supply the instruments most necessary for solving the problem.

He believed that Marxists were often wrong in rejecting the achievements of Western economic science, and Eastern economists wanted to make up for this mistake in the interests of truth. But equally, and for the same reasons, economists in the West should stop committing the same error by ignoring Marx and the whole of Marxian economics.

The second problem was to decide on the significance of problems discussed by Professor Haberler for the socialist planned economy. Both in Marxist theory and, unfortunately, in the practice

200

of the planned economy, the rôle of the monetary factors had been greatly under-estimated. However, were we entitled to discuss it in connection with the problem of stability ?

He agreed with Professor Lipinski that in Poland the problem of stability did not exist in the same sense as in the capitalist economy; the planned economy had eliminated cyclical movements for ever. This did not mean, however, that in the process of development temporary disproportions could not arise in the socialist economy. It seemed to him that in the analysis of the causes of disproportions and of the means designed to eliminate them, monetary factors should be given greater emphasis than hitherto.

Professor Brus felt that his two points proved that there was a common field for discussion between Eastern and Western economists, and they should no longer regard each other as so exotic.

Mr. A. Heertje (Netherlands) said that for a long time economic theory had dealt with the business cycle, but more recently theorists had concentrated on economic growth. Though the older theories dealt especially with vertical and horizontal maladjustments, modern models like those of Samuelson and Hicks showed the possibility of inherent instability, based on Keynes's fundamental equations.

Since 1945, probably stimulated by the problems of the underdeveloped countries, economic theory had tried to explain income differences between countries. But it was remarkable that only a few writers had paid any attention to the relationship between economic structure and the cycle, for instance Mrs. Joan Robinson in *The Rate of Interest and other Essays*. It was therefore noteworthy that the Congress had devoted its attention simultaneously to the problems of stability and economic growth.

Mr. Heertje regretted that economists were still unable to produce a theory which fully integrated both stability and growth. Most speakers in the Congress had concentrated on policy, neglecting the underlying theory. Yet it was of great importance to formulate a synthetic theory, because only then could one see under what conditions a system was stable, and whether a stable system was capable of growth. In principle, this model was the same as Professor Hicks's (see the Mathematical Appendix to *A Contribution to the Theory of the Trade Cycle* (Oxford, 1950)).

Mr. Heertje said that all current cycle and growth theories constituted particular cases of a general theory, by holding particular variables constant. Which variables were needed for this solution ? Without attempting completeness, he would like to suggest some. These were : the growth of population, with workers classified according to their tasks in the production process; the accumulation of capital, classified according to branches of industry; other factors concerned with the institutions and sociology of the economy; and finally, the variables covered by cycle theory in the traditional sense, such as consumption, investment, etc., but more carefully differentiated than was usually the case. One must keep in mind that these variables were not independent of each other, but were interrelated. Thus, population increase might be related to the growth of national real income, and vice versa. Economic reasoning had to explain these hitherto badly neglected functional relationships. Of course, this could only be done in a mathematical model, while the coefficients had to be estimated by econometric methods. Otherwise one got only a list of factors. An important feature of the economic structure was the state of competition, so far rather neglected in macro-economics. We needed a systematic analysis of prices and macro-economic relations. He thought the best way to do this was by formulating a dynamic price theory. One could then determine the time-paths of the prices of the products with which one was concerned, and, by aggregation, trace the development of the general price level. This was the way to produce a synthesis of macro- and micro-economics, and lay the foundations for proceeding more fruitfully.

Professor Vickrey (U.S.A.) said that Professor Haberler's paper mainly considered how monetary factors might add to economic instability. He would like to add something on the rôle of monetary policies in combating instability arising elsewhere in the economy. The conclusion in Professor Haberler's paper, that monetary policy could be a powerful short-run weapon, seemed partly vitiated by the possibility that monetary policy might do little or nothing to soften a contraction. Indeed, the effectiveness of monetary policy in offsetting an incipient contraction was limited by the lower limit below which, in existing conditions, the money rate of interest could not be pushed. This also had repercussions on the extent to which monetary policy would be used to curb excessive booms, for it might be feared that if the brakes were applied too heavily their subsequent release might not cause sufficient increase in activity. This was particularly likely where, as was often the case, the relations between monetary and fiscal authorities were remote, or characterized by a lack of confidence. Yet to preserve the effectiveness of monetary policy was a highly desirable objective.

To have a fully effective monetary policy in the downswing there had to be, below the usual level of money rates of interest, a sufficient margin above the lowest rates which could conceivably be attained. Then monetary policy could act adequately in a stimulative, and also a sedative, direction. Yet, in a free economy, the desired rate of capital accumulation, and particularly of private net investment, might require a low real rate of interest. With a stable price level this might imply that the general prevailing money rates of interest were too low to allow enough margin for successful monetary policy.

A possible way out of this dilemma was by a deliberate, planned and steady rate of inflation, with a correspondingly higher money rate of interest. Professor Vickrey's suggestion was that in the long run such an inflationary economy might prove more stable and easier to control than one with a stable price level.

For example, if everyone confidently anticipated a price increase of 10 per cent each year, a normal 5 per cent yield on capital invested could be translated into a money rate of interest of 15 per cent. There was nothing inconsistent about such a situation continuing indefinitely, despite Professor Lindahl's statements, though the state he himself contemplated might be somewhat different from the one Professor Lindahl had discussed. An inflation that was fully anticipated and discounted need not be inequitable, nor need it alter fundamentally the distribution of income, or unduly depress or stimulate savings or investment. Moreover, in distinction to Professor Lindahl's type of inflation, it did not require additional controls — only an appropriately high money rate of interest. Indeed, it made detailed control less rather than more necessary.

Thus, if permitted to design an economic system on a *tabula rasa*, he would be inclined to suggest that a consistent inflationary trend would be easier to maintain than a constant price level ; while a system implying a deflationary price trend that required zero or negative money rates of interest in order to maintain equilibrium, would be violently unstable under most known types of monetary institution. Admittedly, it would be difficult to establish the sacredness of the desired rate of inflation of, say, 10 per cent, on the same plane as the sacredness of a constant price level. For people would regard a change in the rate of increase of prices from 10 per cent to 15 per cent with more equanimity than a change from 0 per cent to 5 per cent. But this psychological failing also might be overcome.

The 'normal' rate of money interest should not be too high, lest an undue amount of real resources should be used by individuals to economize in their use of cash, an asset which had a negligible social cost of production in these days of credit and paper money. Nor should the cost of repeated changes in price lists and of the currency and coinage itself be ignored. But the costs of this kind associated with a price rise of at least 5 per cent, and perhaps of as much as 20 per cent per annum, might be a reasonable price to pay for the added economic stability thereby secured. Such would be the prescription if one could start from scratch.

In practice, one had to start from institutions as they were. He was uncertain whether one could justify a long-run programme calling for an annual price rise of 5 per cent beginning tomorrow, or even next year. Nevertheless, it was time to increase the number of goals we were prepared to consider. After all, a constant price level was not an end in and of itself, but only one possible way of achieving the essential aim of a predictable and stable evolution of the price level over time.

Even if this point of view were accepted, there was the problem of transition. Some economies, where inflation was already generally expected, could perhaps make the transition with merely a more formal acceptance of the *status quo*. Others would require time for a wholesale revision of contracts as they expired. He did not want to be in the position of the town council which resolved to build a new school; then to use the old bricks to build the new school with; and finally to continue to use the old school while the new one was being built. But we should begin to think now about the longer-run aims to be sought for in thrashing out a major economic policy.

Mr. Swinfen (U.K.) said it had been suggested to him that, as he was not a professional economist, his point of view might be of interest. He felt that the object of the Congress, and, in fact, the object of everyone, was to improve our living standards by increasing productivity. This presented many difficulties, but one way had perhaps not received the attention it deserved. In the richer countries, techniques like method study and motion study, which observed and rearranged workers' movements and arranged training to teach workers the correct operations, were continually extending. These techniques were universal, in that the operator trained in them could use them in any process, small or large, simple or complicated. And the savings were often phenomenal. The possibilities for improving domestic industry were great, and he was convinced that if a poorer country could obtain the full co-operation of its influential elements, the use of these techniques would give an increase in productivity and a desire for greater productive efficiency sufficient to lift that country out of its 'economic rut'. These techniques could not be a long-term substitute for more power, more technical education, etc., but such things would follow naturally as peoples gained in efficiency.

Another advantage of these techniques was that skilled operators could be trained in a relatively short period, say, three to six months, for a work-study operator. A Training Within Industry *instructor* was trained by the British government in one week. Organizations similar to the British Productivity Committees could be introduced.

Mr. Swinfen felt that many people would be happier carrying out activities they had known from childhood, rather than being herded into factories to operate, or even to watch, machines. Probably the greatest effect could be produced in the small business of up to fifty employees, and this group formed the largest productive class in many countries.

He therefore suggested that stability could be effected by the methods used to obtain increased production ; and those he had mentioned would tend to produce stability while requiring relatively little capital. Their cost would also be very low compared with other methods of raising productivity. Finally efficient small-scale industries were less affected by trade cycles than highly mechanized ones.

Mr. Doyle (Ireland) suggested that while Professor Haberler had referred to the evils of unemployment, he had not considered the incidental benefits flowing from a moderate degree of unemployment. Would men really work hard if there was no risk of unemployment ? Where the level of employment was always high, and employers had constantly to offer new benefits to attract labour, then there must be some concealed unemployment ; fewer workers could do the same work if the level of employment were lower. The surplus workers were being 'carried', the quality of output suffered, and there was fertile ground for inter-union disputes.

Mr. Doyle was disturbed to find speakers endorsing the policy of a 'slight' inflation. Those who supported inflation were wilfully debasing the coinage. Once such a crime was punished by the loss of a limb ; nowadays, people who advocated inflation, which would rob the poor and thrifty, went scot-free.

Mr. Doyle concluded by declaring that, in a hundred years' time, economists would not be seeking stability and progress, because they would live in a world where these prevailed, as the result of a return to a genuine gold standard.

Professor Haberler replied to the discussion. He was glad to have the support of Sir Dennis Robertson, for there was no one from whom he had learned more ; but he did disagree on one point. This was on the international problem. He felt that *argumentum ad nationem* did not apply. Many American economists would agree with Sir Dennis ; many British and European economists would not. On trade unions Sir Dennis had changed his mind, and he himself oscillated in his views. The policy of trade unions themselves, of governments and the pressure of public opinion, all played a part — and all differed from country to country and time to time.

When one turned to the question whether technical progress should be accompanied by constant or falling prices, it was 'easy to argue both ways'. Professors Robertson and Veit had both restated the argument for falling prices. He himself would be satisfied if they remained stable. There was the case in terms of social justice — that some groups did not share the benefits of economic progress; there was also the more economic argument that, in our cycle-ridden world, prices rose in the upswing, and that in order to prevent a downswing we must let, or make, prices rise continuously. But the idea of stable prices surely implied that if prices rose at some times, they should be allowed to fall at others.

Professor Veit had rightly pointed to the experience of the 1920s, and the argument that since all prices had been constant, all was well. But all prices were not constant. The Stock Exchange and the real property market had experienced boom conditions. He himself was still not convinced that, if prices had been allowed to fall, and if the Federal Reserve had not taken vigorous action to combat a mild depression in 1927, the disasters of 1929 and 1930 would have been lessened. The only argument in favour of this was Professor Hayek's very complicated one. There was no answer, only a question mark.

Professor Haberler then replied to Professor Lerner's claim that 'real and monetary factors were inseparable'. He said that this distinction was surely useful, even if the dividing line between real and monetary forces was a little arbitrary. There were certain purely real factors. If one took any one separately, it might give rise to instability, and this in turn could be offset by monetary policy. Professor Lerner also argued against the notion that the cycle was the price of progress; this was a fallacy of composition. The problem was not so simple as this. Many factors entered in, rigidity, restriction, uncertainties and so on. He still felt that some instability was a necessary price of progress — as apparently did Professors Papi and Gudin.

Professor Gudin had also suggested that monetary management was more successful after 1945 than after 1918. This might appear to contradict his own footnote on p. 159. However, he thought Professor Gudin was right in the sense in which he meant his remark.

The next question was the alleged ineffectiveness of monetary policy in depression. He himself was not so pessimistic as Professors Papi and Vickrey. Even if the rate of interest could not fall below 1 per cent or 2 per cent, open-market operations could be more widely used than in the past. One could help the situation by continuing to pump money into the economy, even if the rate of interest had hit the 'floor'.

This led back to Professor Gudin's point. He felt that there had been much progress in U.S. monetary policy. It had been little used in the Great Depression, when the Federal Reserve had pursued a very timid policy. There had been no such big test since the war, but the 1953 'recession' had been met with a vigorous monetary policy. The chances were good that, if faced with a really severe test, American monetary policy would be much more effective than had been suggested.

Mr. Heertje had asked for a synthetic model including a cycle and a trend. He was sceptical about the possibility of this, and thought Mr. Heertje was asking too much. Some very recent econometric and mathematical models were much less deterministic than earlier ones.

Professor Vickrey had attacked Professor Lindahl's view that long-run inflation would lead to controls, saying he could construct models where this was not true. Professor Haberler did not doubt that such models could be constructed on the basis of plausible *a priori* assumptions. That was the trouble. Perfectly innocuous assumptions could lead to completely absurd conclusions, and that was true here.

Finally there was Mr. Doyle, who had doubts about the benefits of full employment. Economists were only too well aware of the problem of over-full employment and the waste it implied. But Professor Papi had dealt adequately with this.

FIFTH DAY
INTERNATIONAL STABILITY
AND THE NATIONAL ECONOMY

INTERNATIONAL STABILITY
AND THE NATIONAL ECONOMY

BY

PROFESSOR ERIK LUNDBERG

Chairman : PROFESSOR ELLIS (U.S.A.)

THE CONCEPTS

THERE are certain concepts which we are accustomed to apply
when considering whether a national economy does or does not
possess internal stability. A stable price level is often taken as an
indicator of stability, but most of us believe that it is not a reliable
criterion, and in any case not a sufficient condition, of stability.
General price stability may imply relatively little about the balance
between total demand and total supply of goods and services, and
even less about the situation on the labour market. In attempting
to find more general propositions of equilibrium (as determining
stability), we may try to establish criteria of excess or deficit demand
for the total supply of goods as well as of labour. An inflationary
gap would then indicate a deviation from stability in the internal
economy. But even though the definitions might be clear, and have
been given exact formulation in theoretical models, it remains an
illusion to think that these can be statistically applied and measured
with any degree of precision.

Criteria of stability of the type referred to above may be regarded
as necessary but not as sufficient conditions for a balanced economy.
There may be disequilibrium between sectors of the economy, such
as bottleneck situations and unused capacity with pockets of unemployment, within the framework of general balance. Wage-price
spirals may occur in spite of a certain amount of unemployment,
when the wage dispersion and income distribution are not accepted
by pressure groups of income earners. Furthermore, equilibrium
in the balance of payments does not follow automatically from a
situation of general internal balance.

We should include a number of aspects of this kind in our
concept of stability. And to all this we need to add some reference
to the time perspective. We ought to distinguish between short-
term and long-term stability, bearing in mind the problem of the

business cycle and of balanced economic growth. Short-term stability reached, for instance, by means of a high rate of interest or by import restrictions may generate tendencies towards unbalanced economic growth.

It follows from these introductory remarks about the difficulty of defining the concept of stability in a national economy that we cannot expect any simple notion of the meaning of the term *international* economic stability. Should international stability presume balance in the national economies forming the international community? Or only in most of them? Or in those that are most important to international trade, for instance, excluding the Eastern Bloc countries? Internal disequilibrium in one or more of the important economies is bound to imply actual or potential disturbance to the economic balance of other countries.

We might try to confine the notion of international stability to some kind of common-sense concept of equilibrium in the demand and supply of all currencies. By analogy with the concept of internal balance, we might define such equilibrium in terms of stable foreign exchange rates, with given tariff rates and (should we be so realistic?) with given 'degrees' of exchange and import regulations. Or should we try to give the concept of international stability more normative content by postulating stable exchange rates and the absence of direct import regulations, thus coming closer to the goal of general convertibility? Or should we perhaps only speak in terms of more or less stability, with reference to some index measure of such changes in exchange rates, tariffs or import regulations as may be needed to keep the current supply and demand for foreign exchange in 'equilibrium'? Or we might prefer to avoid being too fussy about details and — by analogy with the definition of internal balance — aggregate courageously, and then only consider the relations between the main exchange centres or between blocks of currencies such as the dollar, sterling, the currencies of continental Europe and those of the rest of the world. Even so, we again have the problem of the time perspective. The growth of the different economies, implying structural changes in the international division of labour, may have disequilibrating effects on international trade and flows of payments as between individual countries or blocs of currencies.

In the present context we need hardly be interested in fruitless attempts to find exact definitions of the concept of international stability. For this paper it is enough to have some vague criteria relating to the simpler problem whether a certain change or a certain development means more or less international stability — or rather an approach towards it or a retreat from it. The main problems to discuss are whether, to what extent, and how changes in the international economy of any one country may disturb the international payments system, and how such disturbances in their turn react on the individual economies, giving rise to economic policy changes on the part of the respective governments.

It is quite clear that my subject matter is unlimited; a vast amount of actual experience from a number of countries has been studied and analysed in a flood of books, papers and, not least, contributions from various international organizations. My modest ambition is only to raise some points for discussion which seem to be of interest in trying to ascertain the implications of stability for balance-of-payments relationships. It should be noted that my presentation of the issues will be on a very general level. I shall not try to analyse the experiences of individual countries nor refer to the specific studies I have been reading on this vast subject matter. If I were to refer in a more systematic manner to actual experiences and current literature, I could not confine myself to a short paper. I am fully aware of the dangers of the very general and therefore vague character of this way of presenting the problems. I am sure, however, that the discussion will give more concrete substance to the issues raised.

Internal Disequilibrium of a National Economy

The stability of international payments relations may be affected by the following types of disturbance within any single country.

(1) General fluctuations of income and employment arising from internal disequilibrium. There may be more or less permanent inflationary (or deflationary) tendencies compared with developments in other countries.

(2) Wage and price changes that are out of line with movements in other countries, more or less independently of the extent of internal unbalance. The general level of wage-costs and prices may get out of step with levels in other countries at given exchange rates.

(3) Shifts in the demand and supply schedules of import and export goods.

(4) Fluctuations in the scale and direction of capital imports and exports.

(5) Changes in the terms of trade.

(6) Structural changes in the economy, influencing the comparative cost situation.

(7) Growth trends in the economy that tend to create disproportions in the development of exports and imports.

It is evident that this 'catalogue' is only one of many possible ways of classifying types of disturbance. It is also clear that any one type of disturbance will not usually appear in isolation; they all tend to occur together, mutually influencing each other. In particular, it is not easy to differentiate between short-term and long-term disturbances. None the less, the catalogue will provide a basis for discussion.

I think that, since the war, the most usual cause of a balance-of-payments deficit has been excess demand at home. My argument is therefore concentrated on this issue. The causal relationships can be formulated in several ways. The essence of the matter is simply that excess demand — that is to say, a tendency for total expenditure to exceed the total short-term supply of goods and services — exerts strong pressure on the balance of payments. When there is practically full employment, and existing capacity does not allow much additional output, at any rate not in the short run, then any increase in the demand for consumption or investment tends to have big marginal effects on imports. If the average ratio of value of imports to national income is 20 per cent, the marginal propensity to import may easily be between 50 and 100 per cent. At the same time, an inflationary gap tends to restrict export supplies directly and indirectly, depending on the size and nature of the home market for the exportable goods and the mobility of the specific factors of production.

This phenomenon of a rapid increase in the volume of imports compared with the growth of national income and the volume of exports, can be observed in a number of Western European countries during the years of strong inflationary tendencies, namely, 1946–7, 1950–2 and 1954–5. There is not much point in trying to find any stable relations in these experiences, such as constant marginal import propensities, since the nature of the boom periods differed in important respects. Any effect on imports may be very different according to the extent to which the additional demand is for increased exports, investment in inventories, purchase of machinery, building activity or increased expenditure on private consumption. Generally, the marginal import propensities vary widely for these groups of expenditure. If the excess demand causes considerable price and cost inflation, then this development, and the consequent changes in price relations, will also influence import demand and export propensities. Expectations about the future course of the market, including expectations about government economic policy (which covers fiscal and monetary measures as well as changes in exchange rates and import regulations), differ from period to period, causing shifts in the marginal propensities to import.

The effects of an inflationary boom in any one country on its balance of payments depend, of course, very much upon developments in other countries. If there are inflationary developments of 'equal degree' in most other relevant countries, then no disturbance of the external balance need occur. Here, following the example of great economists, I use a good circular definition of the expression 'equal degree'. The essence of the problem, however, is that during international boom periods inflationary pressures become very 'unequal'. The deficits of the relatively much inflated countries then correspond to surpluses in the rest of the world — to which the United States tends to belong.

For the inflated economies loss of exchange reserves usually means an especially marked scarcity of dollars. The reserves of capacity of the American economy, its flexibility, the low ratio of foreign trade to national income, and many other factors seem to mean that a dollar crisis of varying severity follows upon the inflationary excesses of other countries.

How losses and gains of exchange reserves are distributed depends, of course, not only on 'the relative degree of inflationary pressure' in the various countries, but also on many other factors. There may be considerable shifts in the terms of trade during an international boom. During an extreme international boom (of the Korean type) excess demand for raw materials with relatively low short-run elasticities of supply tends to create very favourable terms of trade, and relatively large gains of foreign exchange, for the corresponding primary-producing countries. These gains in international liquidity may — as was the case in 1951 — start inflationary expansions in the countries concerned. After a time lag, new exchange difficulties are bound to arise for these countries, and that may happen when the inflationary pressures have been worked off in most of the industrial countries. The sequence of events by which changes of expenditure due to inflation are transmitted within the international system, with consequent changes in the terms of trade — both as between countries and as between sectors within each economy — produces a most complex pattern of development. Instability of the international system in this case implies that the reactions within and between the countries gaining reserves and those losing reserves do not work easily or quickly towards equilibrium. A chain reaction is started which may mean the propagation of new disturbances, giving rise both to more or less 'automatic' reactions by the various economies, and to responses in the form of changes in government economic policy.

The start of wage-price spirals in the countries of inflation would aggravate the disturbances. As the post-war experiences of many of the full-employment economies show, there is quite a lot of inflation-dynamite in the mechanism of wage and price determination. This may be the result of escalator clauses in the wage-contracts, but there may be an even stronger bias towards cumulative processes in a system with free collective bargaining (as was the case in Sweden in 1950–2). The internal disturbances arising from considerable excess demand thus led to a combination of high profits and over-full employment with a consequent upward 'drift' of wages and prices. There is no 'automatic' tendency towards equilibrium so long as unacceptable wage and income relations give rise to new claims for price and wage increases.

The effects on the current balance-of-payments situation of an additional internal disturbance arising out of a price-wage spiral cannot easily be assessed. On the one hand, a general rise in prices might bring about a reduction or elimination of excess demand and thereby diminish the marginal demand for imports. On the other hand, rising costs — if they rise *relatively* rapidly by comparison with those in other countries — tend to check exports and make imports more competitive. No generalizations can be made, and there is no clear approach to external balance on this route.

ECONOMIC POLICY REACTIONS

In countries with relatively strong inflationary pressure, governments may take measures aimed directly at solving balance-of-payments problems — for instance, by means of import regulations, higher tariffs and export premiums or depreciation of the currency. The first question is: Do measures of this kind tend to eliminate external disequilibrium? The second question, which is, of course, not independent of the first, is: What kind of repercussions will occur in the international payments system when countries try to solve their problems of external disequilibrium by such measures?

(a) *Import Regulations*

In Western Europe the introduction of import regulations to solve foreign exchange troubles is not supposed to be 'good form'. But in the rest of the world — outside North America — all kinds of direct import controls and exchange regulations are common, and used more or less continuously, a wider range of commodities being covered and more restricted quotas being enforced during times of severe exchange difficulties. This technique may be unavoidable for countries which have low exchange reserves and are in a process of rapid industrialization, where there is no possibility of finding a quick solution to an external disequilibrium. I shall return to this question. The danger is, however, that import restrictions do not entail a movement towards external balance for the country in question and — partly for this reason, partly for others — also cause disturbances to the international payments system. Such disturbances tend to be greater than those due to attempts to 'solve' foreign exchange troubles by other means.

The following types of internal disturbance tend to follow from restrictive import controls:

(1) Monopoly positions and profiteering in protected industries will readily occur. The unavoidable inflexibilities of a quota system tend to create bottlenecks that keep down productivity and must be solved by administrative action. When the supply of administrative ability does not correspond to demand, graft and corruption will sometimes be the result.

(2) A 'distorted' investment boom may occur in sectors of production where the country does not have comparative advantages. Import regulations generally aim at a quick saving of foreign exchange by cutting down imports of finished goods, especially consumption goods of the 'luxury' type. Stimulus to such lines of production through protective import controls easily leads to distortion in the use of productive resources — possibly at the cost of export development.

(3) To this is added the likelihood that the cutting down of supplies, together with the above-mentioned behaviour of profits and investment, tends to aggravate inflationary pressure.

(4) The method of solving recurring balance-of-payments difficulties by means of import controls easily creates speculative behaviour patterns which might perpetuate the controls. The lifting of import restrictions in all or some sectors of the economy at times when foreign exchange is in good supply will be followed by a rapid increase of imports in anticipation of a return to controls.

These remarks seem to show that there is no obvious road towards external equilibrium through the introduction of import (or direct exchange) controls. Increased inflationary pressure, an investment boom in protected home industries, and speculation over the perpetuation of controls, all imply the persistence of too high a level of potential import demand. Exports are certainly not stimulated — rather the contrary. In many countries the import content of investment is relatively high. Import replacement investment is a long-term affair, and in the short run may well occasion an extra addition to import demand (for machinery and other investment goods). In a situation of this type there will probably be a long sequence of short periods of 'transitional' import controls, while a cumulative import replacement boom goes on without having any appreciable ameliorating effects on the balance-of-payments situation. Australia seems to be a case in point.

As regards international stability, the solving of foreign exchange problems by means of import regulations tends to result in heavy disturbances. Export markets suddenly disappear or are seriously reduced with no clear possibility of adaptation. New disturbances may be created when exporters who are in trouble because of closed markets try to enter other markets — and new import regulations may follow. Uncertainties and risks regarding the timing and distribution of import controls make equilibrating adjustments difficult to conceive. One 'positive' type of short-term adjustment may be the stimulation of capital exports in the form of direct investment by export firms afraid of losing their markets in the import-regulating economies. This kind of capital export, which in some cases seems to occur on a considerable scale, helps in the short run, but may cause trouble in the longer run. The corresponding capital imports into the countries in question tend to be very expensive, since restrictive import controls and inflated demand usually mean high profits; the ploughing back of profits by foreign-owned companies, as well as new direct investment, create rapidly increasing potential claims for dividends — and also the danger of unstable capital movements when import and exchange controls are abolished.

(b) *Devaluation*

Little need be said about the dangers of devaluing the currency of an inflated economy. The immediate result may be an acceleration of the price-wage spiral; the equilibrating tendencies of the relative change in export and import prices will then be cancelled by rising internal costs. An unstable situation may involve flight of capital and speculation on further devaluation. Other things being equal, the result may well lead to more open inflation than in the case of direct import restrictions. The elasticity of demand for imported goods and the elasticity of supply for export goods both tend to be relatively low in the devaluing country, and it is possible that no long-term equilibrium process, with the help of the potentially high long-run elasticities, will ever appear. In such circumstances, devaluation will not work towards international stability.

(c) *Internal Stabilization Policy*

The conclusion of the argument so far is that less inflation and more internal stability are necessary, but not sufficient, conditions for a successful exchange policy. It is easy to make very sound and vague recommendations on the need for an anti-inflationary economic policy. Much eloquence has been devoted to this theme in the last decade, and also at this Conference. It is of interest to observe that during the years after the Korean inflation restrictive monetary and fiscal policies actually had a certain amount of success in a number of countries. The renaissance of monetary policy in one country after another has usually not meant the abolition of anti-inflationary fiscal policy. It is generally agreed that both kinds of policy are needed, and are complementary when the target is full employment without inflation and with external balance. However, from a short-term point of view, a number of factors limit the effectiveness of a general anti-inflationary policy in varying degrees for the different countries.

First of all, it takes time for decisions to be made regarding restrictive fiscal policies. Political pressure groups — representing interests pressing for low taxes or high expenditure in various sectors of the economy — make it difficult for governments in the West to introduce a restrictive budget policy in time, before inflationary pressure has become strong and an exchange crisis is imminent. Once that has happened, increased taxes may not be very effective in checking rising wages. From this point of view it seems, in most countries, more feasible to apply a restrictive monetary policy at an early stage of inflationary tendencies. The difficulty with the time lag here refers more to the lag in the reaction of long-term investment. Quite rapid results can be expected from the effects of credit restrictions on investment in inventories. This type of effect, as well as the influence of higher interest rates and the restricted availability of bank credit on short-term capital movements, may imply a rapid improvement in the country's balance-of-payments position. If, however, a profit inflation with a boom in fixed investment is already under way, then a moderately restrictive credit policy will tend to yield slow results. This is the experience of many Western countries during the last few years. A drastic monetary policy may certainly still be able to stop any boom, but the ultimate effects of such a policy cannot be judged and are feared. Restrictive policy applied step by step again means a long time lag before it yields results, and a consequent prolongation of the balance-of-payments difficulties.

In some countries, such as the United Kingdom and Sweden, production for export and for investment are rather close alternatives with high elasticities of substitution. Restrictive credit policy may, therefore, result in a rapid and smooth shift from investment to export. The same kind of effect might be achieved with the help of higher indirect taxes when it is easy to shift from consumption to export. High price (or income) elasticity of demand for durable consumption goods (especially motor cars) might make such a policy effective. In other countries — exemplified by Australia, New Zealand and Denmark — exports are mainly concentrated on certain special raw materials and food items with a generally rather limited home market. Restrictive monetary or fiscal policy cannot in such cases make much additional room for exports. The general anti-inflationary effect will have to be sought more exclusively on the import side. The delicate problems of how much dampening of total demand can be tolerated with regard to the targets of full employment and of rapid economic development then tend to become more acute than in the previous case. The marginal effect of a reduction in total demand on the volume of imports depends on constellations of factors so numerous and, at different times, so varying that they cannot very well be summarized in an expression of stable propensity coefficients. Hypothetical statements that the effectiveness of a generally restrictive economic policy in restoring external balance depends on a number of propensities and elasticities do not help very much. The main issue is that some countries find it much more difficult than others to bring about external equilibrium by means of a generally restrictive economic policy. In Denmark, a relatively high rate of unemployment has been brought about in recent years in order to stop the rise of imports. In a country like Australia such a firm policy would hardly be feasible because of the ambitious development targets (with a rapidly growing population).

Recognition of the fact that different countries have greatly unequal possibilities of bringing about external balance by means of a generally restrictive economic policy leads to some very broad conclusions. In order to obtain a high degree of international stability, it is most important that countries with relatively high 'income elasticities' of imports and exports should avoid erring on the deflationary side, thereby causing exchange difficulties for the 'low elasticity' countries. We have in mind the United States (and perhaps also to some extent Germany) as constituting a potential menace of deflationary disturbances to the international payments system. Recessions of the 1949 and 1954 type in the U.S.A. are likely to reappear, and next time the international payments system may perhaps not dispose of such good stabilizers against deflationary disturbances as in those years. Even if there is no great risk of the reappearance of a very strong deflationary competition for hard currency liquidity among the other countries (as in the 1930s), relatively large deviations from full-employment targets in some of the important countries would, without doubt, seriously disrupt the stability of the international payments system, and call forth many kinds of protective measures and exchange restrictions on the part of full-employment countries. The difficulty of harmonizing the levels of demand and employment in various countries — with respect to short-term targets and general economic policy measures — raises the question whether there are any efficient complementary methods which could help to give greater international stability.

Countries with foreign exchange troubles usually combine a generally restrictive policy with *more differentiated measures* such as high taxes (or tariffs) on imported goods and goods with high import contents, as well as export premiums. There are reasons for thinking that such measures are less disturbing to the international system than direct import controls. However, if many countries take numerous differentiated measures of this type, there will be a growing trend towards protection, and a danger of disturbance to international trade. From the point of view of international stability, more general lines of economic policy are preferable.

Good arguments can always be adduced for more flexibility, by means of larger exchange reserves or drawing rights on international funds, in order to give individual countries more time to reach external equilibrium. There is the dilemma, however, that larger reserves also tend to reduce the pressure on governments to check an inflationary process in their country and to carry out a policy designed to bring about an adjustment process. Large reserves, generous drawing rights or other forms of short-term capital movements in an international payments system do not in themselves necessarily work towards international stability ; the period of grace might mean postponing the introduction of necessary measures, and would thus mean wider deviations from equilibrium than would otherwise be the case. An elastic international payments system is therefore certainly not a sufficient condition of stability.

As mentioned above, a system with flexible exchange rates probably does not contribute much towards reaching balance and stability in a world of much inflation (or deflation). The price system functions badly — both internally within countries and externally on the world markets — when there is much excess or deficiency of demand. On the other hand, when a country is more or less in internal balance

— with high employment and a stable price level — and yet has a persistent deficit in its current balance of payments that is not expected to be covered by stable capital imports, then there may be something 'wrong' with the price and cost relations that can perhaps be corrected by means of devaluation. Prices and wages generally might be too high, or there might have been a downward shift in the demand curve for important export articles, or an upward shift of import demand. There is no easy way of finding out *ex ante*, by means of some dubious knowledge about the relevant price elasticities of demand and supply, whether and to what extent devaluation can be effective in restoring external balance in such a case. The process of adjustment — in the demand for import and export goods, in the use of raw materials, in the direction of production, etc. — is so intricate and variable according to circumstances that the fiction of stable elasticity coefficients might be quite out of place, and might even conceal the really significant problems.

There should be no doubt that in stable market conditions, including absence of cumulative price and wage developments, a sufficient depreciation must ultimately bring about an adaptation towards equilibrium. Such hypothetical knowledge is not very useful, however. In an economy with more or less full employment, with strong trade unions and, though in internal balance, not very far from inflation, the process of adjustment after a sizable devaluation can easily create inflationary disturbances that may not be quickly counteracted by a generally restrictive economic policy. There is also the danger that a system of rather flexible exchange rates will cause governments to be weak in their resistance to inflationary developments, if and when devaluation is taken as a comfortable and accepted way out of foreign exchange troubles.

This kind of dilemma has been very widely discussed. In the post-war international economic system much of the old flexibility is gone. The level of costs (wages) and prices is rigid downwards in most countries, and wage developments in the national economies tend to follow their own laws. Internal demand and total employment are more or less given, and in most countries very little downward flexibility is tolerated. Capital movements are of less relative importance than they used to be. In the face of these rigid national economic systems, in a world of dynamic changes, there are strong arguments for the need to introduce a new flexibility, namely, in exchange rates, in order to avoid exchange crises and a proliferation of exchange and import restrictions. The tragic element of this sound view on one of the most important aspects of international stability is that no general rules of the game seem to be possible.

In some cases a radical change in exchange rates may be a necessary condition for external equilibrium and for a balanced development of foreign trade. In other cases, devaluation would help in stable conditions — but conditions cannot confidently be expected to be stable. No definite conclusions can then be drawn in this case. In yet other cases, or types of countries, devaluation would quickly start a process of cumulative inflation, so that other measures, including physical import controls, are preferable even from the point of view of international stability. It need not be so, however. The conditions of economic policy might be changed. At this stage there is plenty of room for wishful thinking and fine sermons about a better world — but I leave this activity to the discussion.

INTERNATIONAL STABILITY AND ECONOMIC GROWTH

The method of reasoning has so far in the main referred to what economists call comparative statics. Positions of equilibrium (or disequilibrium) have been compared, picturing alternatives for a country with regard to changed levels of demand, employment, prices, exchange rates, etc. The conclusions have taken the form of a discussion of tendencies towards or away from a position of national or international balance. This method of reasoning is necessarily loose, but the conclusions may possibly be vaguely right. However, important problems of stability tend to be excluded, or are at any rate not brought clearly into focus, when the argument is founded on a number of static assumptions.

Behind the problems of internal and external disequilibrium, and the corresponding issues of international instability, there are problems of dynamic development that have to be studied. I am thinking more particularly of the problem of how national economic development is related to stability in the international payments system. This is a large subject, on which much has been said and written during the last five years. Here I shall only attempt, by way of some concluding remarks to what I have already said, to take up some aspects of the development issue for discussion.

In a number of countries very ambitious long-term development programmes are afoot. This is the case in 'underdeveloped' countries aiming at rapid industrialization, as well as in several highly industrialized countries with great schemes for housing, public utilities and other government works. Many of these countries suffer from very much the same type of unbalance in economic growth: too much investment in relation to the supply of savings that would be forthcoming with a stable general price level. The result is internal inflation and foreign exchange troubles. Restrictive monetary and fiscal policy designed to check the growth of investment would conflict with the development targets. If, as is the case in Australia, for instance, the development programme is bound up with rapid population growth due to an active immigration policy, then there will tend to be a long-term deficiency of savings. An annual population growth of 2 to 3 per cent means that perhaps as much as two-thirds of domestic net savings are absorbed in covering new capital needs of all kinds for the yearly increase in employment and population. In the poorer countries a slower rate of population growth may cause these capital needs to absorb all available savings, so that nothing is left for bringing about an increase in productivity and an improvement in the standard of living.

The development trends in countries with a rapidly growing population may thus imply a more or less permanent deficiency of savings. To the extent that this deficiency is not covered by capital imports, excess demand gives rise to internal inflation and to a current deficit in the balance of payments. Exchange regulations and import controls — as the better alternatives to repeated devaluation — will be more difficult to avoid than in countries with less population pressure. More or less permanent systems of exchange and import control will, at the same time, afford effective protection to the development of new and old home-market industries which give employment to the growing population.

From the point of view of international stability such a protectionist policy does not seem to be the best long-term solution. I have already discussed the consequences of import regulations. There is no *given* degree of inflation that is necessary in order to bring about the kind of economic development which is required to take care of the growing population (although, admittedly, it is, in general, more difficult to carry out an effective disinflationary policy in 'development countries' of this type than in a country like Sweden). I am convinced that in many of these countries the same kind of economic growth, with less risk of distortion in the structure of production, could be achieved at a lower degree of inflation and therefore with less pressure on the balance of payments.

It is inevitable that countries with ambitious development targets should tend to have a relatively severe shortage of savings. This disequilibrium could be 'solved' by less internal inflation and by less exchange regulation than prevail at present, if the gap were filled by capital imports to a greater extent than is now generally the case. It may be concluded that, in view of the development problems of a number of countries, international stability requires a stable flow, on a much larger scale than so far since the war, of long-term capital exports (including grants-in-aid) by countries with a relative surplus of savings. Statements of this general (and generous) type are very easy to put down on paper as important conditions of international stability, but it is not so easy to give them precise content as a practical form of international policy. One of the difficulties is that most of the highly industrialized Western economies themselves have such ambitious full-employment and investment programmes that there are no 'surplus' savings left for capital exports — on the contrary, there is often a demand for capital imports.

Much has been written during the last few years on the relation between international balance and differential rates of economic growth in the national economies. Any number of theoretical possibilities can be treated with more or less involved mathematics to show how divergent rates of growth in production, productivity and income, with given income and price elasticities of imports for the countries (or blocs of currencies) in question, will create disequilibria in the balance of payments. Looking at the problem this way, it is in a sense difficult to understand how even approximate international stability can be attained at all during any period of time, as, with generous tolerance, may be said about the period 1952–5. The danger with such exercises is that influential people come to believe in the stability of the given parameters, and therefore tend to under-estimate the long-run flexibilities of the international system of trade and payments.

From a very general but certainly most important point of view, the divergent long-run growth trends of productivity in different countries may give rise to increasing international instability. The high savings ratio in the highly industrialized countries is an important part of the explanation of the relatively rapid growth of productivity which has been going on in these countries for a long time. With the prevailing low rate of long-term capital export from the high-savings economies, the gap in productivity and living standards between poor and rich countries tends to widen in a cumulative manner. At the same time the rapidly increasing contacts between countries, thanks to modern means of communication, the spread of technical and commercial know-how, etc., provoke rising claims for improved living standards in the poorer countries and thereby limit the latter's possibilities of increasing the supply of domestic savings. These tendencies constitute more or less permanent causes of exchange difficulties for a large group of countries; their exchange troubles may diminish or even disappear in international boom periods with favourable terms of trade, but are bound to return and become serious in times of economic balance in the highly industrialized countries. As was said above, not much hope can be pinned on an efficient internal economic policy to solve this type of unbalance in poor countries with ambitious development programmes. Without a rapidly increasing supply of long-term capital for investment in countries with a large deficiency of savings, this type of instability may show a rising trend.

It is evident, however, that economics as a special method of analysis can deal only with a very limited aspect of the type of international instability discussed in this section. Many political, sociological and other issues are involved when we try to understand how or why our highly disintegrated world also shows economic instability. The economist must be very modest in his aspirations to explain these problems : and still more in his ambitions of making recommendations.

THE DISCUSSION ON
PROFESSOR LUNDBERG'S PAPER

Chairman: PROFESSOR JEAN MARCHAL (France)

Professor Maurice Byé (France) made the opening comments. He said: These comments are directed to the latter part of Professor Lundberg's lecture. They are concerned with the relationship between international stability and internal growth. Must growth be checked for the sake of external stability? Many countries have to face this problem, but it does not concern them alone; it is a serious question in a world of unsatisfied needs.

This is what we propose to discuss, and in order to proceed quickly we shall do so in terms of a formula — H. G. Johnson's application to the open economy of the ratio by which Harrod defines the equilibrium rate of growth.[1]

Johnson's ratio has as its numerator the sum of the 'savings' coefficient (Savings per period ÷ income per period) and the 'import surplus' coefficient (Imports per period – exports per period ÷ income per period), and as its denominator the capital coefficient (Stock of capital ÷ output or income per period).

Denoting these three coefficients by s (savings coefficient), b ('balance' of imports – exports) and k (capital coefficient), one can write the equilibrium rate of growth (g) for a given period as:

$$g = \frac{s+b}{k}.$$

This equality, which is widely used in the current literature, cannot claim to be a novelty, certainly not here. It is in itself not

[1] The main works to which reference has been made are: Fellner, 'The Capital-Output Ratio in Dynamic Economics', *Money Trade and Economic Growth*, in honour of J. H. Williams (New York, Macmillan, 1951). H. G. Johnson, 'Equilibrium Growth in an International Economy', *The Canadian Journal of Economics and Political Science*, Nov. 1953. H. J. Bruton, 'Growth Models and Underdeveloped Countries', and R. Nurkse, 'The Relation between Home Investment External Balance in the Light of British Experience, 1945–55', *The Review of Economics and Statistics*, May 1956. The second part of this intervention owes much to Bruton's paper; the whole has been greatly influenced by Nurkse's very important article. Finally, by reason of work carried out for the past ten years at the Institut de Science Économique Appliquée in collaboration with François Perroux, it is not surprising that certain basic notions, 'macro-decision', 'gift economy', 'dominant economy', 'poles of development', etc., have been borrowed, not always with acknowledgment, from my colleague and friend. In particular, I should like to indicate my agreement with the lecture he has delivered to this Congress.

even open to discussion — at least if the right conditions are satisfied. *Ex post*, and provided the coefficients remain constant through the time under consideration, it is none other than the equality, holding by definition, between domestic investment on the one hand, and the sum of domestic savings and borrowing from abroad on the other.[1] When used *ex ante*, the limits of its applicability are those of any formula in terms of global quantities. Recognizing these limits, we shall use it to examine, by giving different values to the coefficients, what consequences such manipulation of the coefficients has for growth equilibrium.

Let us consider this formula. Of the three coefficients which it contains, two may be 'controlled from within'; the savings and the capital coefficients depend on structural, technical, social and psychological factors over which the centre of macro-decision, called the 'state', has a controlling capacity. The third, on the other hand, the import surplus coefficient, is only partly tied to the structure and the behaviour of society. For the remaining part, it depends

---

[1] The reconciliation of the two *ex post* identities, which can be interpreted as *ex ante* conditions of equilibrium, is simple.

Let Y be the national income, or output, in a given period, S savings, M imports and X exports in that period. K is the capital stock existing at the beginning of the period. Let us denote the various increments in a given period by Δ. We substitute, for the rates and coefficients of the equality given in the text, the ratios which they represent. We then have:

$$\frac{\Delta Y}{Y} = \frac{\dfrac{S}{Y} + \dfrac{M-X}{Y}}{\dfrac{K}{Y}}.$$

To introduce domestic net investment, I, it must be noted: that $\frac{K}{Y}$, or the average capital coefficient, is equal to the marginal coefficient $\frac{\Delta K}{\Delta Y}$, provided that there is no change in the capital-output ratio during the period; that the increment of capital during the period corresponds to domestic net investment during the period ($\Delta K = I$).

The above equality can then be written:

$$\frac{\Delta Y}{Y} = \frac{\dfrac{S+M-X}{Y}}{\dfrac{I}{\Delta Y}}.$$

In order that the equality may be an identity, it is clearly both necessary and sufficient for $(S+M-X)$ to equal I; the second term then becomes $\frac{\Delta Y}{Y}$.

Now, the equality between total domestic savings plus savings borrowed from abroad $(M-X)$, on the one hand, and domestic investment on the other, is nothing more than the application to an open economy of the Keynesian identity, always realized *ex post*, and necessary, *ex ante*, as a condition of equilibrium.

Let us note that in the case of an underdeveloped economy, as defined in the second part of this paper, we cannot equate the average and marginal capital coefficients. The formula only holds if the marginal capital coefficient is used instead of the average one.

upon an exogenous factor — the foreign demand for exports. One can say that the foreign demand for exports is a datum for national governments, and that consequently the foreign balance limits growth.

Let us now make three observations.

(*a*) Two international systems are possible. First, the true market system, in which growth is fully transmitted from country to country. Second, a system of macro-decisions by national governments; in this system national growth is partly controlled, each national government seeking to maximize national welfare. The contrast between 'transmitted growth' and 'controlled growth' brings to light two sets of optima. These optima are not comparable, just as two notions of collective welfare may not be comparable. They may also be incompatible.

(*b*) Tinbergen has formulated the general principle, according to which if two goals, subject to exogenous determinants, are being pursued, two measures must be applied at the same time to attain them. This principle has been applied to our hypothesis, that is to say, to the simultaneous quest for international stability and a certain rate of growth, by Lundberg in the paper we are discussing, by Kindleberger, and also in a very important article by Nurkse.[1]

(*c*) The relations entering into the determination of growth equilibrium present themselves differently according to whether one considers two developed economies or a world in which there is underdevelopment. In the real world there are underdeveloped economies, and it is consequently impossible to use a definition of international stability which does not allow for this fact.

Let us therefore discuss (1) the relation between international stability and national growth on the assumption that we are concerned with relations between developed economies; (2) the result of introducing a region of underdeveloped countries into this world picture.

I. RELATIONS BETWEEN DEVELOPED ECONOMIES

Since the idea of development is an arbitrary one, let us seek to give it a concrete meaning. There are several possibilities; the most useful for solving our present problem is to define a developed economy as one where the capital coefficient has reached a stable level.

The capital coefficient, k, is, in practice, determined by technical relationships (production coefficients within each industry) and

[1] *Loc. cit.*

by structural ones (the distribution of factors of production between different industries). An economy is 'developed' when it 'fully' uses the factors which it possesses; that is to say, distributes them in an 'optimum' way according to existing techniques. The coefficient of capital is, thenceforth, given.

Historical studies of the U.S.A. and the U.K. have shown that the coefficient remained relatively stable over a long period.

The discovery of a feature common to 'developed' economies does not imply that the situation does not vary from one country to another. No country ever represents the perfect type of a 'developed economy'. A technical revolution can always upset the factors determining the capital coefficient and throw even the most developed economy back into relative underdevelopment; two developed economies which specialize differently may have different capital coefficients; finally, and above all, we must, in the dynamics of the transmission of growth, take into account the essential distinction, analysed by François Perroux, between a 'dominant' and a 'dominated' economy.

The demand for the exports of dominant countries is weakly 'exogenous' and strongly controlled from within (mainly because of their direct foreign investment).

Consider, now, an economy of the Western European type. Let us assume that it cannot expect any transfer (inflows of capital or of overseas earnings) and must consequently achieve equilibrium in the balance of trade on current account. What will happen if exports tend to increase less rapidly than imports? The country can choose between the two systems of 'transmitted growth' and 'controlled growth'. But it *must* choose.

In choosing transmitted growth, that is to say the free world market economy, it forgoes the attainment of a predetermined rate of growth and takes the chance that its own 'national optimum' will be achieved through the pull of the dominant economy.

There is, then, only one aim in view — external stability. The use of a single set of means will suffice to reach it and to achieve, at the same time, internal stability and growth equilibrium.

Traditionally the best method was to have recourse to the gold standard in its most classic form. The supply of gold being relatively inelastic, an outflow led automatically to credit stringency, and so tended, in a free market, to reduce investment and hence the rate of growth. Consequently the automatic working of the gold standard enforced strict observance of the limits imposed on national growth by foreign demand.

But if, into the models of the welfare economy, one introduces the nation as a group, the state as a 'large unit' and its periods of expectation as variables, one cannot see any reason for condemning the adoption of a 'plan of growth' maximizing 'national welfare' over a period, subject to the free choice of nations. This device will be governed in each nation by its spirit of enterprise and its religion, its concern for the future, its inherited structure and the power exercised by this or that dominant group.

If the chosen plan is to be coherent and workable, if it is not to be defeated by inflationary pressures, if stability is definitely to be maintained, then the government, having chosen a certain rate of growth, will have to use the different means at its disposal to control the dependent factors.

The validity of such a 'controlled growth policy' is scarcely questioned. Western budgets clearly show that public investment plays a leading part, both as motive power and pilot.

Whatever may be the word — fundamental, structural or growth-conditioned — by which one qualifies the disequilibrium caused by a policy of 'growth', such disequilibrium does not often occur in a continuous manner. History does not follow a 'trend'. Consequently it is generally when there is a balance-of-payments crisis that the government has to decide what it is to do in order to achieve or maintain a certain rate of growth. Should the controls (in Meade's sense) at its disposal be used, which of them had best be used and to what extent ?

Let us suppose that an external deficit threatens a fully employed economy. Three types of solution suggest themselves.

(*a*) Complete reliance on external controls such as tariffs, quantitative import restrictions or devaluation. Domestic consumption is to be diverted from imported or exportable goods towards home production.

Professor Lundberg has just shown the futility of such an effort, its inability to control inflationary pressure, and its unfortunate results, which are not offset by any countervailing increase in the rate of growth. All in all, such an analysis restates, in 'modern' terms, all that was most valid in the traditional critique of protectionism.

(*b*) Reduction in the economy's rate of growth, which will 'induce' or 'entail' a diminution of the import surplus. This means that external balance will have priority over growth. The controls will have to be made to work in the manner of the gold standard; one needs a reduction in public investment, and a rise in the rate of interest which will tend to reduce private investment. If such measures are not to imply complete rejection of the policy of 'controlled growth', they will have to be meant as only temporary.

231

Domestic investment will be regarded as the 'shock absorber' for the foreign balance. The development effort will be 'suspended' until it can be taken up again at the end of the oscillation. It will be hoped that the 'trend' of growth can be maintained.

Is such optimism justified? Is it justified in all developed economies?

Any plan of growth represents an 'option' for a new structure. To abandon the drive for investment, or to slow it down, would modify the comparative advantage of the different sectors, and therefore the selective process of induced specialization. This would be even more true if adjustment to external compulsions had to be achieved by devaluation; the change introduced into the 'comparative advantage' pattern would be even more marked.

It would appear most unlikely that the 'temporary' acceptance of the structures of 'transmitted growth' could easily be followed by a rebirth of the structures of controlled growth. To slow down investment is easy; and this could perhaps justify its use as a shock absorber. But the difficulty of quickening up investment again on the former lines must also be considered.

(*c*) Rather than abandon controlled investment, it seems more difficult, but more desirable, in a foreign exchange crisis, to act on the controllable coefficients. One of these, the import surplus coefficient, affects the foreign balance; the other, the savings coefficient, affects internal spending. It is essential to act on both simultaneously, since there are two objectives, depending partly on exogenous factors.

One can then use only those controls, or groups of controls, which are apt not to divert demand from imported or exportable products, but to reduce this demand in absolute terms. Simultaneous action to reduce the import surplus coefficient and to increase the savings coefficient will make it possible to maintain a rate of growth which, in the absence of such a policy, would have implied an unbearable deficit in the balance of payments.

It follows that, if the 'defence of growth policy' is necessarily a savings policy, it must not lead to any diversion of consumption from domestic to imported goods; nor should import policy lead to the opposite diversion from foreign goods to domestic ones.

In particular, the effects of internal pressures on the prices of imported or exportable goods are important. We cannot here open a debate on types of 'linkage' or 'selection', but we can say that the best methods of control include a wage policy refusing to let wages absorb too large a part of the increase in productivity, highly selective taxes on expenditure and so on.

The question arises whether it is necessary to wait for a balance-of-payments crisis before imposing adequate controls? As against an anti-cyclical policy of controls over saving, we may speak of a 'stock-piling policy', both being capable of achieving the same practical results. In fact, rather than conflicting with the former, the latter completes it.

Stock-piling can build up reserves of 'productive capacity', of foreign exchange, raw materials or products. The intended effects of these reserves being very different from those of the classical gold standard, they are all interchangeable.

If we had to choose the least burdensome and most useful forms, I should be inclined to come down in favour of the recognized function of the public or private stock-piling of raw materials or products. This is not only because this function has shown itself to be so important and useful in the course of recent exchange crises, but still more because of the solidarity which it expresses between developed and underdeveloped countries.

II. Relations between Unequally Developed Countries

We shall say that an economy is underdeveloped if the necessary condition for its growth is an increase in its capital coefficient. Such an economy is habitually dualist; it is characterized by the co-existence of a subsistence sector, where the capital coefficient is almost zero, and a commercial sector with a substantial capital coefficient.

Integration of these two sectors involves a multiplication of 'capitalistic combinations', innovations in techniques, and a revolution in specialization and structures. This will set off the growth process.

The demonstration effect plays a major part in preparing growth plans for underdeveloped areas. It does so in the sense that such plans do not limit themselves to the aim of an absolute increase in total consumption, or even in consumption per head. Growth plans are considered adequate only if they can achieve some long-term narrowing of the gap between the standard of living in countries which are at present poor and those which are at present rich; that is to say, the rate of growth of the 'poor' country must not only be fairly strong in itself, but quite considerably above the 'rich' country's rate of growth.

Now the development of the 'poor' country is held back not only by this shortage of capital, but also through limitations imposed by its balance of payments. As H. J. Bruton has shown, these are two obstacles which must be dealt with simultaneously.

By taking the capital coefficient, k, as an alterable magnitude, one separates the rate of growth of investment from the rate of growth of national output. If the rate of growth of investment rises, all other things remaining equal, the capital coefficient will increase, and hence the equilibrium rate of growth of national output (g) will be reduced (by an increase in the denominator of the second term).

In an underdeveloped economy the foreign balance is much more greatly influenced by imports of machinery 'entailed' by investment than by imports of consumer goods 'induced' by the rise in incomes. The rate of growth of imports consequently tends to be more rapid than the rate of growth of the national product.

Inversely an argument which is still disputed, but which I believe is correct, suggests that in a developed country the rate of growth of imports (that is to say, exports of underdeveloped countries) tends to be slower than the rate of growth of national output.

It follows that an underdeveloped country has to face the following dilemma : should it first and foremost maintain external stability, equilibrium in the balance of payments and a stable rate of exchange ? It will then be able to achieve, without inflation, only a rate of growth that is slower than that in developed countries. Consequently, even if some growth continues, the poor country's total output will tend to fall further and further behind that of richer countries. *A fortiori*, its standard of living will fall even farther behind if population is increasing rapidly.

Or should the poor country persist with an ambitious plan for growth, but then face accentuated problems of external solvency and serious inflationary pressure ? Recourse to external controls alone will not be sufficient to absorb inflation and to sustain the 'desirable rate of growth'. Even 'heroic' action on savings will not be sufficient to maintain external solvency. Nor will even the most generous grants-in-aid from abroad succeed in filling the ever-growing gap.

Certainly (is there any need to repeat it ?) we know how arbitrary every model is; relationships between global quantities misrepresent reality, and there are many and various types of underdevelopment. Nevertheless, in its general outline, the method of analysis used seems right. It brings to light a conflict which would be unimaginable in the market economy, but which current experience shows to be very sharp, namely, the conflict between a heterogeneous collection of national development plans aiming at the maximization of national welfare over different lengths of time on the one hand, and on the other, the stability of a world economy beyond the control of these plans.

Let us try, in conclusion, to enumerate a few principles which may help to resolve this conflict.

(*a*) Growth, beginning from underdevelopment, implies a plan, the essential features of which are as follows:

(i) A deepening of capital that is so timed as to co-ordinate capital-saving and capital-using innovations, in order to keep a brake on the rate of increase of imports.

(ii) Modification of structures must proceed gradually in the hope of safeguarding the expansion of exports to a growing, underdeveloped economy. This requires, almost inevitably, selective measures such as multiple exchange rates within a system whose burdens grow heavier.

(*b*) This statement of basic truths is tantamount to saying that an underdeveloped country's whole 'plan for growth' may be bold in its overall ambitions, but must be wise in its specific devices.

The 'plan of growth' of developed countries must also be prudent. It would fail to be prudent in the long run if, whenever faced with a balance-of-payments crisis, it too often chose to slow down investment and not often enough to increase savings.

A slowing down of growth in developed countries is bound to have one of two consequences for underdeveloped countries: either their own growth must slow down, or they are compelled to modify their coefficients of structure and behaviour more quickly or more thoroughly than is feasible or desirable. In effect, this would tend to throw the 'poor' countries back either on autarchy or on authoritarian planning.

(*c*) Principles of wisdom are worthless if there is no 'discipline'. Escaping from the 'discipline' of 'transmitted growth', 'controlled growth' may yield to the temptations of a 'beggar-my-neighbour policy'; the 'Malthusianism of the developed' would be matched by the 'autarchy of the underdeveloped'.

We would then for ever have a conflict of plans which are incompatible because they are based, for equally serious reasons, on heterogeneous priorities — the priority of external stability for the 'developed' countries, that of a 'certain growth' for the underdeveloped ones.

(*d*) The merit of the post-war conferences and institutions was their quest for a new international discipline. But, perhaps, thought ran too exclusively in terms of restoring past patterns and not enough in terms of new ones, now that the emergence of 'Welfare States' had created an entirely new context. The attempt must be renewed and re-thought today.

We must reconsider the 'gift economy' both in its meaning and its techniques. The adaptation of different national plans over the same long period compatible with world-wide development, is quite a different thing from the sharing-out of an annually repeated 'dole'.

Without dismissing as negligible the foreign aid extended in the form of money loans, it must be realized that a policy for primary produce is at least as important. It can take the form, above all, of long-term purchasing contracts, covering the same period of time as the plans, and especially of a policy for building up reserves of raw materials and products.

By stabilizing the terms of trade of the underdeveloped countries, such stock-piling would weaken their inflationary pressures and would allow them to build up reserves capable of playing, in certain respects, the rôle traditionally assigned to foreign exchange reserves.

(*e*) However, any world policy would still appear insufficient or Utopian if it did not achieve the setting up of 'regional groups of countries'. 'Timing' comes in here too.

Many countries, especially in Western Europe, reject 'transmitted growth', because they consider that specialization, according to the present distribution of factors, is not optimal. But these countries are too small to compare with the United States as a zone of diversity, complementarity and external economies, or as a zone, above all, of receptiveness to innovation. Hence the European economies cannot fail to note a certain asymmetry between American 'external' behaviour and their own, which their growth leads them to adopt.

The setting up of much bigger areas, such as the European 'common market', could reduce such asymmetry and diminish the external tensions resulting from growth.

(*f*) Similarly the world-wide co-ordination of expectation periods and long-term plans between developed and underdeveloped countries would imply more international solidarity than is possible in the present state of the world.

It would, indeed, imply nothing less than that the developed countries adapted their plans to the underdeveloped countries' need for structural change, and that the underdeveloped countries accepted the limits of growth set by the external possibilities opened up by the developed countries.

All this presupposes that the two sets of governments would accept the same period of expectation for their long-term plans, and the same notion of a 'collective welfare' which would be common to them. That, in turn, implies solidarity or 'interdependence'.

We believe that, for the time being, we should not think on a world scale so much as of communities of the 'Commonwealth' type, possessing — to use François Perroux's expression — effective 'poles of development'. It is there that we may hope, in the near future, to see the achievement of a reasonably close co-ordination of capital movements, long-term purchasing agreements, commodity stock-piling and foreign exchange reserve pools.

Professor W. A. Lewis (U.K.) spoke next. He said : My purpose is not to offer criticism of Professor Lundberg's excellent paper, but merely to supplement it by making a few remarks about the cyclical problem in the smaller primary producing countries.

The fluctuations of the industrial countries are transmitted to these countries through international trade. Trade is very important to the smaller primary producing countries ; their exports may be as much as 30 or 40 per cent of national income. Their foreign earnings fluctuate much more than the level of employment fluctuates in industrial countries, both because world trade contracts in volume by more than industrial production contracts; and also because a wide price fluctuation is added to the output fluctuation. Because foreign trade is so large, its fluctuation is fully transmitted to the domestic economy. All domestic prices and wages soar during the boom, and have painfully to be reduced in the depression. Stabilization measures are even more important to these countries than to the industrial countries, partly because the fluctuation is wider, partly because they do not have the same network of social services to cater for the unemployed, and partly because racial and political difficulties are aggravated by the disputes to which these fluctuations give rise. Communism is boosted in Malaya every time that a cyclical fall in the price of rubber sets the various races quarrelling over whether wages are to be cut by 50 per cent or only by 25 per cent.

The primary producing countries have tried two kinds of measures to increase their stability : central banking and stabilizing the domestic price of exports.

The central banking measures achieve very little. Most of the banking is done by overseas banks, which keep their funds at head offices in London or New York or Paris. But even if the banks were all domestic, and amenable to control, the central banking measures which work in an industrial country would not work here. If a depression is due to a deficiency of home demand, or home investment, it can be cured by creating money. But if it is due to a deficiency of foreign demand, and of foreign exchange, the creation

237

of domestic money increases the shortage of foreign exchange. The central bank is therefore effective only if it can prevent the country from spending in the boom some of the foreign exchange earned in the boom. This it would do by discouraging the banks from lending money in the boom, and encouraging them to lend more during the slump. Attempts at doing this are not very effective. In the smaller primary producing countries the overseas banks are always very liquid anyway; they are reluctant to lend to domestic borrowers at all times, and there is not much to be achieved by trying to alter the time-pattern of their lending. Central banks are useful to issue currency, to do the government's business, and to discipline the rasher domestic banks, but they can do little to increase stability.

Governments have therefore sought to cut the link between domestic incomes and international trade by stabilizing the domestic price of exports. In a number of countries — Burma and the Gold Coast, for example — the government buys the farmers' surplus at a fixed price, with the intention of building up during booms reserves which will be used to subsidize the price during depressions. In this extreme form stabilization is bound up with a government monopoly of exporting. A less extreme method is to leave the marketing process unchanged, and merely impose a sliding scale export duty, which rises sharply as market prices rise — say, an export duty which is only 5 per cent when the price is £100 a ton, but which rises steadily to 50 per cent at £400 a ton. The proceeds of the duty must be held in reserve during the boom; in the depression they can be paid out to farmers, or used to maintain government expenditure above the level of tax receipts.

The fury with which some economists have attacked these measures is astonishing to me, but I do not wish to reopen the controversy here. It is obvious that any kind of stabilization measure calls for political wisdom and administrative experience, and that these commodities tend to be in short supply in the countries we are talking about. Hence mistakes will be made, and it will take some time to learn how to operate such measures. But I do not see how the governments of these countries can avoid trying to stabilize their economies so long as international trade continues to be as erratic as it is. My complaint would be rather that not enough try. In all these countries governments should do much more than they do to stabilize incomes, by levying heavy taxes during the boom, and sterilizing reserves which they will release during the depression. Sliding-scale export duties are excellent for this purpose, because they work immediately and automatically, as all good stabilizers should.

However, hard as these countries may try, we must recognize that it is extremely difficult for them to progress with stability in the face of wide fluctuations in foreign trade. Hence I am sorry that the Economic and Social Council of the United Nations has abandoned the effort to get agreement on measures to stop the transmission of depressions from one country to another through international trade. The effort was abandoned for two reasons : first, the resistance of some industrial countries, and second, the fact that there has not been a major depression in the past ten years. The second reason is more important than the first because, if there had been a major depression, the argument would have continued until resistance had worn down. I regret that the discussion has been shelved because I do not believe that we can take it for granted that we shall never again have major depressions. On the contrary, within the next four years the present residential building boom in Western Europe and North America will tail off, and the investment urge to clear the back-log left by the depression of the 1930s and by the war will also exhaust itself. If, in addition, peace breaks out, we shall need everything we can think of in the 1960s to prevent that decade from paralleling the 1870s, the 1890s and the 1930s.

The measures in question were of two kinds. First, measures to maintain the incomes of primary producing countries in the face of falling demands for their exports to industrial countries. Buffer stock schemes would have this effect, and so, to a lesser extent, would other forms of commodity price stabilization. The second kind of measure is an extension of credit to countries whose exports are contracting, so that their imports can be maintained despite a cyclical fall in their exports. This kind of measure requires some sort of fund from which an international authority — presumably the International Monetary Fund — would make loans as unemployment rose in the industrial countries, loans which would be repaid as unemployment declined. The difficulties mentioned by Professor Lundberg on page 221 would not arise if the use of the fund were tied not to the foreign exchange shortage of dependent countries, but only to the degree of cyclical unemployment in the industrial countries, as the United Nations experts suggested. However, the fund would only be effective if governments counteracted the fall in exports by creating credit, so that incomes and imports were maintained. By contrast, the buffer stock schemes would maintain incomes automatically, without individual governments having to take action.

The technical problems of these two kinds of measures have

been discussed exhaustively in the literature, and I have nothing to add. It cannot be said that it is technical difficulties which have prevented agreement. The obstacle has been rather the unwillingness of powerful industrial countries to incur the financial cost of stabilization measures, especially those countries who do not themselves depend much upon foreign trade. It took a long time to create a climate of opinion favourable to adopting domestic measures of stabilization ; it is taking even longer to create a climate in favour of stabilizing international trade, irrespective of domestic fluctuations.

If these fluctuations in international trade affected only the poorer countries, these proposals would probably be dropped altogether, since the richer countries seem to feel no compulsion to regulate their own behaviour merely to suit the interest of strident but powerless neighbours. However, some powerful and rich nations, notably the United Kingdom, have just as much interest in stabilizing international trade, so there is a good chance that this subject will return to the international agenda.

Finally I would like to consider for a moment the problem of balanced growth in the longer run. According to the Law of Comparative Advantage, each nation should specialize in those activities for which its resources are relatively abundant. This means that the countries where land is abundant should export agricultural products, whereas overpopulated countries should export manufactures. We have seen this principle working out as several overpopulated countries have developed — first Britain, then Germany, then Japan. We are certain to see it again as other overpopulated countries develop, and make their impact upon world trade — most notably India, who, in view of her shortage of arable land and her abundance of coal and iron, is certain to become a great exporter of manufactures and importer of food. Any idea that the poorer countries will always be net exporters of primary products is without theoretical foundation. The development of the overpopulated countries will create sharp disequilibrium in world markets unless their industrialization is balanced by an expansion of agricultural production in the sparsely populated countries, especially in Africa and Australia, and even more in North and in South America, and unless these countries are willing to export food and to receive manufactures in exchange. Both the Americas, North and South, show great reluctance to participate in this sort of exchange. If the sparsely populated countries are not willing to receive manufactures from Asia I do not know how long they will be able to resist the alternative, which is inter-continental migration.

This is a problem which will not become sharp for a decade or so, since Asia is only just beginning rapid industrialization. In the meantime there is the immediate problem of the foreign exchange needs of the poorer countries. These countries are urged to pull themselves up by their own boot-straps, whether by taxing themselves more, or by saving more, in order to pay for investments in human beings and in physical resources. But domestic saving does not necessarily release all the foreign exchange required to support a development programme, especially where the goods produced for home consumption differ from those which are produced for export. The amount of foreign capital going into direct investment in mining and in manufacturing is as large as ever, but the major requirement of poor countries is for making funds available to governments for public works and public utilities, without which framework all other investment is gravely handicapped. It is therefore most unfortunate that, whereas the supply of capital for direct investment is well maintained, the supply of loans to foreign governments has virtually dried up, mainly for reasons internal to the creditor countries.

There is a mounting crusade in the world to get the richer nations to help to increase the productive facilities of the poorer nations, especially by creating a fund from which to finance part of the foreign exchange requirements of development programmes. In our capacity as economists we have little to say about such a proposal. We point out to the poorer countries that they do not have the conditions required for economic growth, whether because their governments are bad, or their natural resources are poor, their consumption habits extravagant, or their customs and traditions unsuited to the modern world — as practitioners of a dismal science, economists have always been able to find plenty of reasons in defence of misery. We even ask the intriguing question, if there were capital to spare, would it not be more productively invested in the United States than in India or in Africa? And so, murmuring a few words of sympathy, in our capacity as economists we pass by on the other side. Fortunately very many Western economists are equally conscious of their capacity as citizens of the world, and are deeply ashamed that their governments continue to refuse adequate aid to the poorer countries. Such economists are to be found in the forefront of the crusade to get the richer nations to join the poorer in what will be the biggest task of the second half of the twentieth century — to abolish from the world poverty, with its companions ignorance, hunger and disease.

Professor Bonné (Israel) commented on the last section of Professor Lundberg's paper, and in particular the problems of under-developed countries. First, however, he wished to make a general observation. Almost all the contributions to the first four days' discussion had treated their subjects mainly from the viewpoint of advanced countries whose economists could look back on an accumulated theoretical tradition and a long experience in economic policy. As against this, not much consideration had been given to the points of view of observers close to the slowly growing fund of experience, and of new ideas tested by trial and error, in underdeveloped countries.

Professor Lundberg was sceptical about present methods of showing how divergent rates of growth in total productivity and income would permit, or prevent, stability in the world economy. Professor Lundberg's argument, which seemed to be directed mainly against the arbitrary use of theoretical models, would gain if more attention were paid to poor countries; important elements in the theory of international trade did not apply to economic relationships between richer and poorer countries. The theory implied that an international flow of goods, unhampered by restrictions, would lead to adjustments in levels of income and wealth and thereby improve living conditions in underdeveloped countries. Yet this reasoning applied only where conditions were favourable to adjustment. Such conditions did not exist today, and probably would not exist for some time to come, because of the differences in economic conditions between developed and underdeveloped economies. The absence of large-scale cyclical unemployment, the scarcity of entrepreneurs, the resistance to change, the absence of several of the acquisitive urges operating in fully developed economies; all these factors combined to prevent conventional economic analysis from yielding useful results when applied to poor countries.

There was one element whose importance was generally recognized at least in principle, namely, the need for investment. Yet the outlook for the free international flow of investment funds was not encouraging, and Professor Lundberg was not hopeful that the gap between the needs of countries with large development programmes and the means for supplying these needs could be bridged. However, if we did not insist on the complete and rapid elimination of differences in income levels between countries, Professor Bonné was not so worried as many other economists dealing with these problems seemed to be. First, rates of savings in underdeveloped countries were greater than was generally supposed. The findings of some recent investigations about rates of saving were surprising, and showed that in spite of the increased spending temptations savings were considerable. Indeed, as Professor Viner had stressed, the savings/income ratio seemed to be higher, for the same income levels, than in the richer countries.

Second, the size of the dwindling flow of purely commercial international investment depended mainly on political factors. Political stability had to precede economic stability — a commonplace conclusion, but one frequently ignored by economists. With political stability a large increase in investment flows could be expected. He was glad that Professor Lundberg did not exclude the possibility that long-term capital might continue to move to countries with insufficient savings. There was a tendency to regard the present outflow of public funds from Western countries as merely a philanthropic or political action. This might be one aspect of the matter, but some present-day capital movements to underdeveloped countries also meant investment in the market potential of the underdeveloped countries. They might pay dividends in foreign imports.

A further point was the desirable composition of capital formation. Capital formation in underdeveloped countries must necessarily include investment in training, education and health. Such investment was cheaper and easier than investment in capital goods, and yet was equally useful.

Professor Lundberg had hinted at the responsibility of the economist in attaining international stability. Surely Professor Lundberg was too modest in his estimate of the economist's rôle; he was inclined to give other social scientists pride of place. Their contribution was certainly important, but economists should be more courageous in devising new approaches to their problems and use more imagination, though not ignoring established economic teachings. The problem facing underdeveloped countries was how to develop their capacity for economic growth. He wished to quote a few words written more than a hundred years before, which had impressed him time and again : 'the capacity to create wealth is infinitely more important than wealth itself; it not only provides security of possession and increase of acquired wealth, but also replacement of losses'.[1] The economist dealing with underdeveloped countries had not only to advise on the administration, distribution and organization of existing resources of wealth, but also to establish conditions for creating new wealth.

Professor Todorovitch (Jugoslavia) thought that insufficient attention had been paid to the influence of the exchange rates between advanced and underdeveloped countries on world economic stability. He did not agree that exchange rates were merely a bridge permitting

[1] Friedrich List, *Das nationale System der politischen Ökonomie* (1904), p. 220.

trade between two countries. His own interpretation, a Marxist one, was that exchange rates depended on several economic factors, both national and international, and that it was by no means a matter of indifference whether the exchange rate was fixed or flexible. There was general agreement that the exchange of one currency for another was necessary, but perhaps not everyone would agree with him that the rate of exchange was a positive factor, influencing the relations between weak and strong economies. Professor Todorovitch said that the basis for his view was the labour theory of value. The strong economy, where labour productivity was high, exchanged its relatively dear currency for the currency of underdeveloped countries, who had lower labour productivity and whose currency had a lower value. That, at any rate, was the position with a fixed exchange rate. Such an exchange rate merely concealed the exploitation of weak countries by stronger ones. Part of the accumulation of the poorer countries was transferred to the stronger countries without any return. This had led Marx to say, in his speech on free trade at Brussels, that 'what the adepts of free trade cannot understand is how one country can grow richer at the expense of the other, and this should not surprise us, for these same adepts refuse to understand how, within the framework of one and the same country, a class can grow rich at the expense of another'.

The type of foreign exchange system might well influence employment and development in underdeveloped countries. It played a part in stimulating or depressing economic activity, in easing or hampering the redistribution of income to the stronger countries, and in determining the extent of the influence of stronger countries on weaker ones. That was why the less developed countries preferred flexible exchange rates, and the richer ones exchange control and a fixed rate. Stability could not be established in a world with different foreign exchange systems, or, to put the point another way, these different systems would continue while there was marked economic inequality between nations.

Professor Todorovitch was glad, however, that a certain number of economists had reached practically the same conclusions. He instanced the realistic theory of the rôle of dominant groups in the economic process, a theory expounded by Professors Perroux, James and Byé.

How could world instability be ended? Professor Lundberg had proposed various measures, but had, surprisingly, put little stress on material assistance. It was unrealistic to expect private capital to meet the needs of underdeveloped countries. After all, private capital had not been sufficient to ensure the recovery of

Western European nations after the war. It would be still less able to help the two-thirds of the world which was now anxious for economic improvement. International assistance was now a reality, and should not be ranked lower than long-term private investment. Professor Todorovitch said he put his trust in active co-existence between nations, a movement towards economic equality between countries, and the devising of new processes and mechanisms worked out and applied by an international body.

Professor Pitigliani (Italy) pointed out that Professor Lundberg did not think that exchange devaluation by individual nations would lead to stability in a world of much inflation or deflation, partly because of the dangers of setting off a chain reaction both in the international payments system and in individual economies. The purpose of his paper had been to consider movements towards, or away from, stability, in balance-of-payment relations. Professor Lundberg had not defined international stability, but identified internal disequilibrium with an excess or deficiency in the demand for goods as well as labour. This reminded Professor Pitigliani of Professor Lundberg's early studies of the degree of instability in an economic system, either in its normal functioning or when exposed to various shocks. Although he seemed to ignore time at first, Professor Lundberg later tried to analyse the relationship between stability in the international payments system and national economic development as a dynamic process.

The conclusions seemed to agree with the premises, and Professor Pitigliani confirmed that the best cure for instability in poor countries with large development programmes was rapidly increasing doses of long-term capital, possibly imported from richer economies. This, however, did not protect poor countries from other kinds of instability later on. Theoretically these conclusions seemed to follow the traditional approach of economists of twenty or more years ago.

This was not a criticism ; only a statement of fact. On the other hand, one would have liked to follow Professor Lundberg's process of thought, to see the keenness of his insight into modern theory. This would have been possible had he chosen to study the experience of individual countries in greater detail, or the more difficult problem of how to allow for unequal degrees of inflation in various countries during an international boom. Professor Lundberg's paper, therefore, suffered from his failure to define basic concepts, namely, national and international stability.

The main difficulty in attempting to combine the two concepts lay in the fact that international stability belonged to a different class of economic ideas from internal stability, as did stability in poor or in rich countries. The ingredients to be used to clarify these concepts were not all to be found in the economist's stock-room, some belonged to the political scientist and the sociologist.

Professor Pitigliani said that at the end of this important Congress he would like to summarize his impressions, as a faithful witness of its debates. He felt bound to say that the influence of modern mathematical theories had been less than he had expected. Also the influence of recent sociological and political studies had been, to say the least, small. Whether this fact was a result of the arrangement of the programme or of the present state of economics was open to debate.

Professor Weiller (France) thought that Professors Lundberg and Byé had shown clearly why it would be difficult to correct existing economic distortions in the world by devaluation. Their position took us a long way from the attitude of Bretton Woods, where the emphasis placed on 'fundamental disequilibrium' did not carry the analysis far enough. When Professor Lundberg spoke of the pressure of internal demand he blamed it for the plight of the balance of payments. However, the position was just the reverse when it was possible to talk of 'structural disequilibrium', along the lines already referred to.

About 1945 it was sufficient to stress discontinuity, or, if one preferred it, the danger of an interruption in growth, and secular stagnation. It was enough to admit, without ceasing to be 'classical', (1) the need for an international exchange system compatible not only with high employment but, above all, with tolerable levels of consumption and with renewed growth; (2) the consequent need to provide against a possible deflation. In 1946–7 inflation was therefore only a symptom of the existing distortion, whether this distortion was accompanied by direct controls designed to ensure priority for essential imports, or by means, including the Marshall Plan, for maintaining, if possible, what could be termed a 'necessary' deficit, until the return of normal structures. Much more was at stake at that time, therefore, than the mere inability of politicians to combat inflation in Professor Robertson's countries.

Professor Weiller felt it was harder to determine how classical theory ought nowadays to be modified in order to be applicable to underdeveloped countries with their rapid rate of population growth. It evidently appeared as though the traditional perspective had been restored. These countries could not retreat and wanted to develop rapidly. So the previous notion of 'structural disequilibrium' was no longer justified. But we could stress again, in their case, that a kind of distortion already existed, so that a distortion in the opposite direction looked better to them than an orthodox policy of maintaining the *status quo* by stabilizing devices.

Professor Weiller felt we understood this attitude better when a country adopted a development programme or a policy of long-term growth. They did this in order, as Professor Nurkse had said in very simple words (which we could not elaborate here, though a demonstration would be on the lines of Professor Perroux's analysis), to break the vicious circle of poverty.

Professor Lychowski (Poland) felt that Professor Lundberg's main analysis was correct. When he spoke of internal disequilibrium, and went on to consider its external implications, he was on safe ground. These problems were much discussed in capitalist countries, and, though there was no definite advice to be given in particular situations, there was much common understanding. But on international stability, as contrasted with the external equilibrium of a given economy, Professor Lundberg had admitted that even the elements of the problem were less clear. He said on p. 212 'we cannot expect any simple notion of the meaning of the term international economic stability', and did not seem satisfied with any of five or six different definitions.

The root of the problem was surely contained in Professor Lundberg's comment that the 'growth of the different economies, implying structural changes in the international division of labour, may have disequilibrating effects on international trade and flows of payments as between different countries or blocs of currencies'. Professor Lychowski suggested that what we had witnessed in the past forty years was the gradual disintegration of the old international division of labour, on the basis of which the capitalist system had expanded in the nineteenth and early twentieth centuries. We now had a new system, whose shape was not yet finally settled, but whose main elements were appearing in the shape of new productive systems. Forty years ago the capitalist countries had comprised over 90 per cent of the world market; now they made up only 70 per cent of a much bigger market. The remainder was in socialist countries. Even in the capitalist sector there had been big shifts, largely through the growth of the U.S. economy. If international trade had adapted itself to those changes, international stability might have retained the same sort of meaning as under the nineteenth-century gold standard, with its equilibrating effect on balances of payments.

According to all statistics, trade lagged behind production. This was not surprising when one remembered that trade between capitalist and socialist countries was only 2 per cent or 3 per cent of the world total. The well-known discrepancy between U.S. imports and exports helped to explain the existence of this abnormal situation. It was therefore not surprising that Professor Lundberg had concluded that long-term developments in the capitalist world must lead to balance-of-payments difficulties. And the equilibrating effects of capital flows were mere paper ideas. Professor Perroux had spoken of continual apprehension over the possibility of achieving stability. How could such apprehension be quieted if international stability, the bulwark of capitalism in the nineteenth century, was so shaky?

Professor Lychowski concluded by asking why so little had been said in the whole Congress on the delicate question of mutual relations between the two parallel economic systems, and their implications. The need for a new international division of labour was closely related to long-run economic stability, and he hoped that the growing contacts between economists of the two schools would start to fill the gap between the two systems. His own view was that the existence of this gap made it difficult to formulate any firm ideas on the relationship between growth and stability.

Professor Delivanis (Greece) said that when he first met Professor Lundberg, Sweden had just devalued. Professor Lundberg had shattered the currently optimistic forecasts with the kind of arguments he had used today, insisting on the dangers following in the train of devaluation. There was a tendency to assume that, with sticky wages, the only hope was devaluation, and that this would always help, despite bad effects abroad. The main quality of his paper was that in it Professor Lundberg had stressed the disagreeable consequences of devaluation for the world, and also for the devaluing country.

Professor Delivanis stressed Professor Lundberg's point that the development of backward areas required material help from abroad and the import of foreign capital. Private capital was not available on a large-enough scale, and in any case it was not desirable to have big private investments which might cause complications. Professor Lundberg was pessimistic about developing backward areas through inflation. We all knew its dangers, but underdeveloped countries could not accept stable exchange rates if they made development impossible. They could, however, limit the pace of inflation by slowing the rate of development.

Professor Gudin (Brazil) said he agreed with Professor Lundberg that many backward areas could have quicker economic growth, as a result of less distortion in the structure of production, if they

248

had less inflation (pp. 223-4). In Brazil there had been attempts to help economic development by inflation, but there had been no positive benefits. The few extra factors brought into production were more than offset by the fall in efficiency and discipline, besides the harmful distortions. In Brazil, there was a movement out of bonds into equities, then out of both into land and buildings, the capital-output ratio of which was around 10 to 1 instead of 3 or 4 to 1. Brazil had developed in the last ten years not with the help of inflation, but in spite of it.

Mr. Allen (U.K.) turned to the political problems of inflation in Western countries where, with the welfare state, there were 'no teeth' in class warfare. He raised five points. First, Professor Lundberg had stressed the lack of flexibility in modern economies, and the fact that this made the older monetary methods much harder to operate. But why did we need new international monetary institutions to solve our problems? He regretted the neglect of Pigou's *Economics of Welfare*, especially the parts dealing with the elimination of imperfections in the labour market. We needed far greater discussion of internal mobility, though something in this field had been achieved by the Dutch policy for developing distressed areas.

Second, surely one wanted to stress free trade as an important stabilizing factor, rather than on the grounds of ordinary comparative advantages. The U.K. showed excellent instances of the reverse policy. For example, the Australian import cuts had hit the British motor trade very hard at a moment when business was bad in any case.

Third, there was the underlying fear of organized labour, which was rarely mentioned explicitly. How far was it true that we were frustrated in economic policy because the trade unions opposed changes? So far as the U.K. was concerned, we tended to over-estimate the strength of trade unions, and to under-estimate the power of monetary and fiscal policy. The greater equality of incomes had made a vital difference by taking the edge out of the class struggle, on which trade unions had to base themselves. The importance of the growth of the welfare state in making labour less militant was shown by the relative ineffectiveness of union attempts to bring men out in the recent British motor strike.

Mr. Allen felt that Britain had recently been on a 'wages standard' because the monetary authorities had persistently retreated before trade union demands for higher pay. Yet it was his belief that if a tougher monetary policy were instituted the lack of support for the trade union leaders would become manifest.

Fourth, Professor Lundberg had stressed the high marginal propensity to import in the countries of Western Europe. In good years these countries should put aside larger reserves by pursuing a strong monetary or fiscal policy. Changes in exchange rates could also help. Here, he denied that the 1949 devaluation had failed. It had lasted for seven years so far.

Mr. Allen concluded by suggesting that we needed an 'intellectual schizophrenia', by which we could say exactly what we thought should be done. As yet, there was no unified lead from economists about how to deal with current problems. Surely such a lead could be given.

Professor Rugina (U.S.A.) expressed the opinion that, during the Congress, certain basic problems had not been debated sufficiently.

In contemporary economic theory, economists were devoting too much time to detailed problems, without having solved fundamental ones. Consequently, the world's economists produced a large number of 'models'; and yet very few solutions to basic economic problems had been generally accepted. This situation was serious since most of these results could not be incorporated into a unified logical system. Fundamental principles must be solved before problems of detail.

Professor Rugina appealed to all economists who still believed in a really free society to analyse a 'model' overlooked by most contemporary economists — the one consistent combination of a free society and an adequately free economy.

Professor Rugina said that individual freedom, like justice or truth, was indivisible. For example, it was illogical to say that individual freedom was desirable in the political field but not in the economic sphere. For when a citizen lost his economic freedom he automatically lost many political and social liberties.

If there were economic evils in capitalistic countries, this was because we had inherited from the mercantilistic era, which was by no means democratic, some obsolete institutions. Instead of accepting a magic formula, we should make a critical analysis of all our institutions and find out whether they would preserve a free and stable economy. After a thorough analysis, we might find that some of our monetary, banking and financial institutions did not do this.

David Ricardo, 150 years ago, had proved that credit money led to a permanent danger of inflation. In England it took about half a century to convince public opinion of this. But, finally, Robert Peel's Act of 1844 forbade private banks to issue notes. Other countries had passed similar legislation.

Unfortunately, far from being similarly controlled, bank deposits had remained unchecked. They were dangerous, because they were too elastic for a free and stable economy.

The modern gold standard, which was considered a stable monetary system, represented a combination of about 10 per cent gold and 90 per cent credit money, and consequently could not survive the 1929 depression. Yet, most authors of international reputation suggested that the modern gold standard was a stable monetary system with a mechanical operation. In reality, it was fundamentally unstable and was a decisive element which contributed to the failure of the liberal experiment of the nineteenth century, by nurturing the business cycle.

This led to the big question : if uncovered credit money did not fit into a free and stable economy, what kind of money should we use ? The answer was only commodity money or 100-per-cent-covered credit money.

Professor Rugina suggested some fundamental reforms necessary to reconstruct our economy.

(1) The reconstruction of all markets so that prices in all sectors (private and public) would be close or equal to marginal cost.

(2) The reorganization of the banking system so that the volume of investment would be equal to the volume of free savings.

(3) The equation of investment and savings by a flexible rate of interest.

(4) The introduction of 100-per-cent-backed currency. Gold or silver need not be used. Sound money could be achieved by using as collateral other non-perishable commodities like grain, rubber, coffee, steel, wine, olives, etc.

(5) The establishment of flexible foreign exchange rates so that the current price for a foreign currency would always equalize its domestic and foreign values.

(6) Completely free international movements of goods, capital or services so that balances of payments would always tend towards equilibrium.

(7) The forbidding of speculation on the stock exchange, and the commodity markets. (These so-called 'futures transactions' must be prohibited by law because they created artificial price fluctuations.)

(8) The limiting of the government to the administration of its own public sector.

(9) The reorganization of the public finances to permit monetization of the public debt.

(10) The presentation of the regular public budget with at least one alternative (*i.e.* allow a referendum on this issue).

Professor Rugina said that in this Congress the term 'liberalism' had almost been forgotten. However, the future of humanity depended on what was done by those who still enjoyed freedom of debate and the democratic ballot of the capitalistic countries. If they remain passive and indifferent to the great debate of our time — freedom versus slavery through central planning — then we deserved our hardships in the future. For, as the famous British historian Toynbee had put it, we should not have reacted intelligently to the great problems which had been raised in our time.

Professor Abay (Hungary) called attention to the fruitfulness of the 'holy trinity' — land, labour and capital. All satisfactions were derived from commodities originating in the land, that was to say, from nature. The resources of nature, in turn, could not be used without capital. Three main types of resource came from our material surroundings, aided by human discovery — energy, raw material and food. Similarly, three main types of capital resulted from human invention, namely, transport facilities, buildings and machinery. Labour might be a bad substitute for capital, as was the case in backward areas. But it could also be complementary to it, as happened in advanced lands. One could classify countries as poor, weak or rich in terms of capital on the one hand, or natural resources on the other, and, leaving aside (unwillingly) differences in enterprise and skill, they could also be classified according to density of population.

Thus the U.S.A. was rich in both capital and natural resources, and at the same time sparsely populated. On the other hand, the U.S.S.R. was rich in natural resources but weak in capital, with an even sparser population. The U.K. was weak in natural resources, strong in capital and had a very dense population. One could go on for a long time, but two major cases remained to be noted — Eastern Europe, weak in both resources and capital, with a middling population density, and China, with a very high population density, rich in natural resources but weak in capital.

The supply of factors of production affected stability and progress in each country, not according to whether it was poor or rich, but according to factor scarcities. Each different combination implied special possibilities, but also special problems. On the other hand, it was important to move from the situation where labour was a poor substitute for capital (as in poor countries) to one where it was complementary with it (as in rich ones). This was the only guarantee of a high living standard; so perhaps we should ensure that labour became complementary with capital everywhere.

Professor Abay felt that the theory of the factors of production

252

might have other uses. For the best classification of the epochs of economic history was that in socialist theory — the division of economic history into ancient communism, slavery, feudalism, capitalism and socialism; but only under just that condition which was not fulfilled by socialist theory, namely, that the distinction between the three production factors should be included. Feudalism without land as its outstanding factor, or capitalism without the stress on capital, was senseless. Similarly, ancient communism was nothing but a state where capital was not available, where land was available but covered with wild vegetation, and where labour was unproductive, crying out for co-operating factors. Under ancient slavery, labour was not highly productive, capital was scarce, and land abundant; so forced co-operation under a single rule seemed the best solution. In the case of socialism, the co-partnership of all workers seemed to be the ultimate aim, though capitalism was not outmoded as long as capital did not become superabundant.

But what about the framework of the whole social economy? The closed household was the original type of a full economy, but it became less and less important, though the total of individual units increased and covered the whole world. Now we had one world economically, if not politically. But how far was this one world an economic system? The inherited institutions were private property and free competition, with a continually evolving capitalism. The unequal distribution of private property could not be defended on grounds of social justice, and society's ultimate goal was not in doubt. Free markets would be the best way of allocating resources, if it were not for periodic crises. It might be argued that economic evolution proceeded by cycles, but this was not necessarily true. On the other hand, man was only creative when he was free, and economic freedom implied the maximum of political liberty.

The only rival to the free market was planning. What were the experiences of planned economies in the previous few decades? Everyone must admit that planning had gained a great victory. It was a perfectly feasible system, and it had advantages over other systems, especially in view of the difficult conditions in which it had been carried out. This might not be a final judgment; but planning had clearly experienced an initial success, if it had only become a rival to the free market. Both had to work with the same categories and definitions, both followed the same basic truths, and both were part of the same, single science.

Professor Lerner (U.S.A.) felt that Professor Lewis had missed one essential point. Help from rich to poor countries would not have the desired effect if it was taken out in an increase in numbers.

Otherwise, even if the rich gave away the whole of their difference in income, poverty would not be alleviated. Indeed, we should merely reduce the whole world to the plight of the poorest.

On Professor Lundberg's paper, Professor Lerner suggested a change in emphasis. Professor Lundberg had surely been too apologetic for devaluation. The limitations which he pointed out were equally applicable to all the alternative methods, which inflicted additional evils too. Deflation, for example, reduced income, because it worked via income elasticities as well as via the price elasticities used by devaluation.

On import controls, Professor Lundberg had stated the case clearly. One must remember that a system of import taxes and export subsidies, if it became universal, would be equivalent to devaluation. If it were not universal, then differential rates of tax and subsidy would distort the allocation of resources and would be the equivalent of trade controls.

Professor Lerner said he had been puzzled for some time over the reluctance of countries to use devaluation, where the local price level could not easily be adjusted. A major difficulty about devaluation was that it became associated in people's minds with the disease for which it was the remedy.

Professor Diatchenko (U.S.S.R.) said that, first of all, he wanted to express his satisfaction that it had been possible to meet in Rome and discuss very important and real problems. By the process of personal contact, we had increased that mutual understanding which was the main prerequisite of collaboration. He wanted to use his speech to thank the organizers of the Congress, and our deeply respected host, the Rector of the University of Rome, Professor Papi, whose hospitality was boundless.

Certainly, this, his first wide international meeting, had revealed important disagreements on many questions. The task of the Congress did not consist in eliminating all such disagreements. Many would still exist in the future. But there were different kinds of disagreement. Many of them arose because different points of view were based on insufficient information or insufficient knowledge. He felt we must take all possible measures to eliminate this source of disagreement. Such measures were, for instance, the organization of new international meetings of economists, exchanges of professors, reciprocal acquaintance with the work of research institutes, the exchange of literature, participation in periodic publications, and so on. Professor Diatchenko attached great significance to the growing membership of the International Economic Association, and the increasing scope of its activity.

In this connection, he wanted to call attention to the fact that very little had been said about the Soviet Union's economy in the papers of the Congress. And yet tremendous progress had been, and was being, achieved in his own country, in all branches of the economy and of culture, on the basis of socialist changes. This, today, was universally acknowledged. How this progress was being achieved, and what methods and resources were being used in the unprecedently rapid development of the Soviet national economy and culture, these were today questions of great interest to every economist. Admittedly, a few speeches in the Congress contained brief comments on the question of the planned economy. But these remarks were mainly the expression of a general doubt rather than the result of a profound and objective study of the facts. Professor Diatchenko said he appealed to everyone to study the facts; Soviet economists would help in every possible way. Then it would be clear to everybody that the planned economy in his country was not an expression of the will of the leadership, but was based on a profound study of the objective laws of development in Soviet society. For that reason, their plans had not been mere paper ones, unfulfilled, but had led to great and practical results. This was one reason why the ideas of planning were now spreading wider and wider.

Professor Diatchenko concluded, 'Wood is very light. But in the hands of an able chairman, a small wooden hammer is very effective. Therefore I am compelled to finish my short speech, and I want to finish it with an appeal. Let our contact, that has been started at this Congress, be constant and fruitful, in the interest of the development of economic science, and in the interest of the economic progress of all peoples.'

Professor Lundberg replied to the debate. He began by discussing problems of method. Professor Pitigliani had accused him of being thirty years out of date; there was doubtless some truth in this statement, partly because our present-day problems had something in common with those in the middle 'twenties. For example, then, the return to the gold standard had raised questions of how the price mechanism worked, and had shown the importance of the size of elasticities of import demand and export supply. But we also had new problems and new methods of analysis; for example, the target of full employment, combined with the danger of inflation on the one hand, and national income analysis on the other. He himself was surprised that economists were not farther advanced in mathematical and sociological thinking. To raise a problem from Professor Pitigliani's own country; how would backward villages in the south of Italy fare in the creation of new industrialized communities if all the enterprising people left ? On mathematics, it was worth noting that Professor Byé's formula was very useful for teaching purposes. Economists should usually think in terms of systems which had as many equations as they had ideas. His own system had too many variables and too few equations. However, the charm of economic life was, of course, that there was room for unexpected or irrational behaviour by entrepreneurs and governments.

Professor Lundberg suggested that the duty of the economist was not only to analyse and explain but also to point out complexities. He was glad that the participants in the discussion had policy proposals — for he had made few in his paper, and it was good for economists also to deal in value judgments. Professor Lewis had suggested two policy aims. First, he thought we should try to damp down depressions, or prevent their transmission to poor countries. Second, Professor Lewis wanted a world with a more equal income distribution. There were always differences of opinion on how fast such equality should be achieved, though it should be the concern of us all.

Professor Bonné had spoken of political stability as a condition which needed fulfilling before Western countries could lend to, or invest in, backward areas on a large scale. It was important that economists in the various countries should ensure that those taking part in policy discussions considered conditions in the outside world much more thoroughly than was usually the case. Politicians in Sweden, for example, were so concerned with the welfare economy and with social priorities that they gave too little thought to the outside world.

Professor Lundberg admitted that his paper was apologetic about devaluation. In the past he had pleaded strongly for flexible exchange rates, but, now that he knew more about the irrationality of wage policy and governments' economic policy decisions, he had less confidence in this method. In principle he agreed with Professor Lerner and would consequently have to disappoint Professor Delivanis. He would like to see a world where inflation was so well under control that a system of flexible exchange rates was possible and useful. The point in his lecture was that with conditions as they were in many countries, such a policy was unworkable.

Mr. Allen had mentioned the 1949 devaluation. It was quite true that in the conditions of 1949 — as they were known in September of that year — the devaluation of the pound sterling, the kroner and so on was correct. But had we been able to foresee the Korean inflation, we should have done better to wait. The real failure was not that we devalued in 1949, but that we did not revalue in 1950–1.

Professor Todorovitch had weighed inflation against progress and had decided that the latter was more important for the economy. Professor Gudin took exactly the opposite view. This was an interesting dispute, since both came from countries with much experience of inflation and development. But could they separate and evaluate the two factors? The reason why he himself had been relatively tolerant of inflation was that, in a 'developed' economy like Sweden, although savings were relatively high, much inflation had followed full employment and expansion. How, then, could he tell underdeveloped countries with much greater scarcity of savings not to allow inflation?

He had been glad to hear Mr. Allen on free trade as a stabilizing factor. The point was not made often enough. On this issue, one could dwell at length. The differences between Australia and Sweden, discussed in the paper, seemed to illustrate the stabilizing importance of foreign trade quite well.

INDEX

Abay, J., 252-3
Accelerator, the, 116, 118, 129, 140, 158, 160, 161, 163 n., 164, 165, 168 n., 176, 193, 197
Active sectors, 128, 129, 142
Adaptability of the economy, 46
Aftalion, 21
Agriculture, 11
    organized, 172, 181
Aid through trade, 83, 100
d'Alessandro, C., 139-40, 147
Allen, G. C., 133
Allen, George, 249-50
Amortization, 21, 110
Amzalak, M., 41
Anti-cyclical policy, 16, 20, 60, 110, 111, 118, 119, 120, 124, 130, 143, 147, 158 n., 170, 190, 233
    differences from policy to balanced growth, 111-16, 127, 130, 131, 144
Anti-depression policy, 156-7
Anti-inflation policy, 219
Armand, L., 121, 125
Australia, immigration policy, 144
    economic policy in, 220, 224, 249
Automation, 34, 106 n., 107, 117 n., 126 n.

Backward areas, see Underdeveloped countries
Balance in the economy, 16, 120, 130
Balance of payments,
    and deflation, 221
    and internal inflation, 194, 214-15, 216, 219, 246
    and the changing structure of the world economy, 247
    and unequal rates of inflation, 173, 174, 225, 245
    Canadian, 27
    deficits, 222, 224
    equilibrium, 190-1, 211
    improvement of, 218
    instability of, 173-5
    internal factors affecting, 213
    internal stabilization policy and, 219-223

Balance of payments—contd.
    in underdeveloped countries, 80-1, 92-3, 153
    of small countries, with rising world prices, 185
    problems, 17, 153, 231, 232, 233, 235
Balanced growth, 76, 106 n., 111, 113, 115, 116, 120, 124, 128, 129, 130, 145, 146, 147, 185
    and Socialism, 143-4
'Balanced' investment, 57, 58, 98
Banks, failures, 155, 164, 167, 169, 175
    lending policies of, 15, 34
Bargaining power of poor and rich countries, 54-5
Barkay, R., 86
Barre, R., 106 n., 146
Bastiat, 108
Baudin, L., 79, 95, 100, 143, 200
Beggar-my-neighbour policy, 235
Birth control, 89, 90, 91, 100
Birth-rates, 88-90
Blardone, G., 110 n.
Blocks of development, see Development
Blocks of investment and innovation, 122, 123
Bonné, A., 241-3, 256
Bottlenecks, 168, 192, 217
Brazil, inflation in, 249
Bretton Woods, 87, 246
Brewing industry, and development, 98
British Productivity Committees, 205
Bronfenbrenner, M., 171, 172, 173 n.
Browne, Dr. M., 85-6
Brus, W., 200-1
Bruton, H. J., 227 n., 234
Budget deficit, 158
    surplus, 12, 13, 158
Buffer stocks, 239
Built-in stabilizers, 136, 157
Buquet, L., 110 n.
Bureaucracy, as factor holding back poor country, 97, 99
Burns, A., 154 n.

Business decisions, factors underlying, 28
Byé, M., 123 n., 227-37, 244, 256

Canada, 31
  effects of U.S. tariff policy on, 26
  investment plans in, 26
  policy in 1955 recession, 16
  progress and stability in, 27
  Royal Commission on future develop-
    ment, 24
  variations in living standards in, 25
Cannan, 35
Capital, 252-3
  coefficient, *see* Investment
  deepening, 11, 168 n., 235
  formation, *see* Investment
  imports of, 25
  saving devices, 12, 28, 137, 235
  scarcity of, 46, 51, 72
  using devices, 235
  widening, 168 n.
  yield of, 98
Capital movements, international, 218,
    219, 230
  lack of today, 225
Capital-output ratio, 10, 11, 14, 29-30,
    34, 118, 176
Capitalistic attitude to wealth, 142
Cassel, 111
Ceiling, 117 n., 118, 168
Central banks, 143, 192, 194
  British and German in 1929-31, 165
  and stabilization in primary producing
    countries, 237-8
Chile, inflation in, 171
Church of England, investment policy
    of, 13, 33, 37
City of Glasgow bank, 34
Classical economics, 36, 46
'Clusters', 107, 113, 160
Collective bargaining, 216
Colonialism, 52, 82-3
Comparative advantage, 99
  and development in backward coun-
    tries, 240-1
Comparative cost, 101
  Lord Chief Justice, 18, 26, 61, 80,
    86
  theory reformulated, 61-2, 76, 84, 92,
    100
Competitive market, analysis of, 142
Confiscation of foreign assets, 92
Consumer choice, 144
  and growth, *see* Growth
Consumption coefficient, 110

Co-operation between Western and
    Communist economists, 88, 100,
    200, 201, 248, 254, 255
Cost-saving investment, 131
Counter-cyclical policy, *see* Anti-cyclical
    policy
Creative destruction, 177
  inflation, *see* Inflation
Credit control, 37
Credit money, danger of, 250-1
Cumulative historical period, 109
Cycles, *see* Economic fluctuations
Cyclical contraction, benefits of, 22, 112

Death-rates, 89-90
Decentralization, in Poland, 88
Deepening of capital, *see* Capital
Defence spending — effect on stability,
    and growth, 31-2, 118, 177
Deflation, 17, 24, 170, 175, 176, 184,
    220, 221, 254
Delivanis, D., 37, 99, 144, 147, 248,
    256
Demaria, A., 112 n.
Demonstration effect, 79, 84, 175
  and economic position of poor coun-
    tries, 55-6, 79, 233
Depreciation, 11, 21, 33
Depreciation of currency, 216
Depression, 166, 167, 180, 183, 237
Depression, great, 155, 156, 158 n., 164,
    178, 184, 195, 206
Devaluation, 218, 222, 223, 231, 245,
    246, 248, 250, 254, 256-7
Developed countries, savings in, 34
  trade policies of, 52, 65
Developed economies, defined, 229-30
  relations between, 229-233
Development, blocks of, 99
Devons, Eli, 9, 10
Diatchenko, V., 254-5
Differential rates of growth, 99
Disequilibrium in the economy, 211,
    213-14, 231
Disguised unemployment, 50-1, 67-8,
    70-2, 77-9, 86-7, 99, 170
Disproportions in the economy, 134
Distortions in the economy, 114, 246-
    247
Dividends, 12, 23
  restriction of, 13
Dollar shortage, 174, 215
Domar, E. D., 11, 33, 115
Dominant economy, 230
Dominated economy, 230
Doyle, N., 33-4, 37, 205, 207

Index

Duesenberry, J. S., 55, 73
Duesenberry effect, 79
Dupriez, L., 19-24

East India Co., 47
Economic development, effect of income
  distribution on, 49-50, 199
  rich landlord and, 50-1
Economic fluctuations, 4, 20, 24, 36,
  109, 111, 113, 116, 127, 129, 131,
  132, 140, 141, 142, 145, 152, 153,
  157, 158, 159, 160, 161, 162, 163,
  173, 175, 176, 177, 179, 185, 189,
  190, 191, 197
  definition and measurement of, 154-5,
  187
  theories of, 15, 105, 138, 140, 155,
  159, 160, 161, 162, 163, 164, 165,
  167, 168, 169, 176, 189, 193, 201,
  253
  transmission from rich to poor countries, 87
Economic fluctuations and growth, 156,
  189-91, 197, 199
Economic growth, theory of, 76
Economic planning, 7, 76, 143
Economic planning, theory of, 5, 88,
  108 n., 136, 146
Economic progress, and tropical climate,
  91-2
Economic reform, 251
Economic system, structure of, 94-5
Economic theory, 139
  modern innovations in, 47
Ellis, H. S., 72, 92, 137-8, 146, 211
Endogenous factors, 154, 155, 159, 160,
  161
Entrepreneurial ability, 96, 99
  decisions, 132, 134, 135
Equilibrium, 4, 36, 143, 223
  theory of, 5
Equilibrium growth, paths, 111
  rate of, 227
European Coal and Steel Community,
  124
  Common Market, 236
European Unity, 122
Excess population, see Population
Exchange rates, 17, 212, 218, 221
  and exploitation of poorer countries,
  244
  free and fixed, 17, 34-5, 38
  multiple, 235
Exogenous factors, 116, 128, 136, 154,
  155, 229, 230, 232
Expectation, period of, 231

Expectations, 129, 165, 214
  greater confidence of, 26
  long-term, 99
Export duties, 238
  premiums, 216, 221
  subsidies, 254
Exports, foreign demand for, 229, 230
External economies, 27, 56, 57, 61, 92,
  100, 122, 123
  and protectionism, 56, 57-8

Factors of production, effects on pro-
  gress and stability, 252-3
'Favourable events', 5, 188, 189, 191
Federal reserve policy, 206, 207
Fellner, W., 92, 137, 146, 227 n.
Fels, R., 166 n.
Firm, economics of, 139
  theory of, 140
Fiscal policy, 25, 26, 33, 37, 113, 137,
  157, 197, 202, 219, 220, 249, 250
  action, 120, 191, 198
Fisher, I., 159, 179
Floor, 117 n., 118
Fluctuations, see Economic fluctuations
Forced saving, see Saving
Foreign aid, 42, 83, 87, 93, 97, 126 n.,
  236, 241, 244-5, 248, 253-4
  lending, 64, 76-7, 219
  lending, private, 243, 244, 248
Foreign exchange, see Exchange rates
Foreign Trade, see International trade
France, inflation in, 47
  savings and investment policies in,
  28, 37
Free goods, 43, 44
Free trade, as a stabilizing factor, 249,
  257
Frickey, E., 155
Friedman, M., 158 n., 173 n.
Frisch, R., 161
Full employment, 114, 119, 138, 145,
  180, 182, 184, 185, 192, 198, 219,
  220, 255
  and capital exports, 225
  and the level of income, 187, 191
  and rate of growth, 132, 133, 156,
  157
  theory of, 140
Functional finance, 158 n.

Gayer, A. J., 109 n.
General Staff of industry, 120
German banks, lending policy, 5, 34
German foreign exchange problems,
  29

Germany, deflationary dangers from, 220
  inflation in, 47
  under Hitler, 35
Gestrich, H., 132
Gift economy, 227 n., 236
Gilfillan, C. S., 117 n.
Gold, general shortage of, 166
Gold reserves, British, in nineteenth century, 165
Gold Standard, 174 n , 186, 205, 230, 231, 247, 251, 255
  breakdown of, 164, 175
Government, and incomes, 135
  and pressure groups, 135
  control, 107, 231
  economic decisions of, 141
  effects of efficiency of, 45-6
  expenditure, 33
  investment decisions, 29
  policy, 173, 215, 216-23
Growth, and consumer choice, 138, 200
  and foreign exchange problems, 17, 29, 34-5, 134, 231-2, 234-5
  controlled, 229, 230, 231, 232, 235
  definition of, 106 n., 151-2, 186, 198-199
  divergent rates of, in different sectors, 131, 132, 134
  interruption in, 99
  in underdeveloped countries, *see* Underdeveloped countries
  rate of, 9, 13, 22, 24, 25, 28-9, 108, 116, 119, 121, 156, 230, 231, 234
  stable, 110, 131
  transmitted, 229, 230, 232, 235, 236
  unbalanced, 212
Gudin, E., 86-8, 200, 206, 207, 248-9

Haberler, G., 7, 13, 32-3, 37, 119
  lecture, 151-78
  discussion on lecture, 179-207
Hahn, A., 140-1, 146
Harriss, C. Lowell, 31-2
Harrod, R. F., 126 n., 128, 132, 145, 167, 227
Harrod-Domar model, 170 n.
Hawtrey, Sir Ralph, 11, 159, 160, 179
Hayek, F., 159, 162, 166 n., 167, 206
Heertje, A., 200-1, 207
Hershlag, Z., 198-9
Hicks, J. R., 99, 115, 116, 118, 127-30, 134, 135, 142, 143, 145, 162, 163, 164, 165 n., 167, 180, 201
Hicks-Harrod-Domar models, 138

Historical measures of growth, 37
Hoffmann, W., 30-1, 37, 109 n.
Hofmannsthal, E., 92
Hollander, Jacob, 138
Hoover, H. H., 82
Hot money, 175
Hydro-electricity, 85

Immigrants, 44
Immigration policy, 24, 144, 224. *See also* Migration
Import regulation, 212, 216-18, 222, 224, 231, 254
  and exports, 218
Import, propensity to, 214, 220, 250
  surplus coefficient, 227, 228
Impulse industries, 114
Impulse problem, 177
Income, growth of national, 4, 8, 94-5
  per capita, 5
  redistribution, 185
  redistribution, international, 253-4, 256
Industrial revolution, and British living standards, 100-1
Industrialization in backward areas, 240-241
Infant industries, 56
Inflation, 11, 13, 14, 15, 17, 24, 33, 36, 37, 74, 115, 135, 153, 170, 174, 175, 177, 180, 181, 182, 190, 192, 195, 196, 214, 215, 217, 219, 246, 250, 255
  and devaluation, 218, 222, 223, 231
  and growth, 14, 119, 171, 191
  and investment, 48, 182, 183, 192
  and political problems in developed countries, 249–50
  and savings, 48, 171, 188
  caused by fear of recession, 14, 26
  chronic, 38, 47, 119, 171, 184, 192
  continuous, 25
  controlled, 115
  cost, 194, 197, 198
  creative, 127, 189, 191
  demand, 194, 198
  income, 181, 183, 184, 192, 198
  in richer countries, 48, 91
  in underdeveloped countries, 47, 68-69, 91, 223-4, 236, 248-9, 257
  'little', 13, 28, 33, 34, 37, 38, 182, 183, 205
  planned, 182-3, 184, 192, 203-4, 207
  profit, 181-2, 192
  secular, 119, 153, 170-3, 195
  suppressed, 48
  wage, 192, 193

Innovation, 5, 105, 106, 108, 109 n., 110, 112, 114, 115, 116, 117, 118, 119, 133, 135, 136, 137, 138, 144, 160, 233, 236
complementary, 122
creative, 20-1
Instability, degree of, 23
meaning of, 152-6
in poor countries, *see* Underdeveloped countries
Institut National d'Études Démographiques, 90
Institutions, 105, 106, 107 n., 119, 125, 141
Insurance, 23
Insurance companies, investment policies of, 15
Interest rates, 14, 37, 115, 141, 159, 160, 161, 163, 191, 196
high, 51, 212
low, 203, 206-7
Internal economies, 57
International comparisons of income, 100, 101
International monetary institutions, 235-236, 249
drawing rights on, 221, 239
International payments system, 220, 246
and development, 223
post-war, 222
stability of, 221, 245
'International Public Services', 125
International trade, 4, 5, 17, 52, 53, 58, 59, 75-7, 80-1, 83
fluctuations in, 240
lagging behind production, 247-8
patterns of, 199
theory, 124
Invention, 5, 11, 117 n., 128, 146, 160
period before industrial use, 110, 112
Inventories, 159, 214
Inventory liquidation, 141
Investment, 8, 10, 12, 14, 15, 25, 44, 65, 123, 135, 219
active, 129, 130
and balance-of-payments difficulties, 232, 235
and defence spending, 31-2
and increasing output, 28, 97, 118
and inflation, 28, 31
and progress, 140
autonomous, 15, 16, 116, 128
coefficient, 110, 117 n., 136, 176, 227, 228, 229, 230, 232, 233, 234
distortion of, 217

Investment—*contd.*
gross, 21, 22, 34
induced, 116, 117, 118, 119, 129, 160, 168
lumpiness of, 16
net, 11, 21, 22, 23, 24
opportunities, exhaustion of, 168
passive, 128, 129
problems in France, 27-9
semi-autonomous, 128, 129, 145
Israel, development in, 86, 96, 197-8
Italy, 3
development in, 96, 187, 255-6
inflation in, 47
poor or rich country, 96
Iversen, C., 66

Jaffé, W., 142-3, 147
James, E., 244
Jannaccone, Senator, 7
Japan, development of, 93
population problems, 35
Johnson, H. G., 227
Jöhr, W. A., 19, 134-5, 147

Kaldor, N., 160, 163 n.
Keirstead, B., 24-7, 35, 37, 109
Keynes, J. M., 21, 23, 87, 95, 98, 115, 138, 166 n., 172, 175, 180, 193, 201
General Theory, 192
Treatise on Money, 181, 192
Keynesians, 49, 99
Kindleberger, C., 75, 76, 175 n., 229
Kitagawa, K., 92-3
Kombinat, 122
Kondratieff cycle, 109, 153, 155
Korea, war in, 32, 155
Krengel, R., 29-30
Kurihara, K., 171
Kuznets, Simon, 11, 14, 29, 30, 38, 109 n.

Labour, scarcity or abundance of, 43-5, 252-3
Labour-saving devices, 12, 137
Lags, 116
Land, 252-3
Land reform, 50
Latin America, inflation in, 47
Laugier, H., 125
'Leader' industries, 125
Leduc, A., 91-2
Leisure, 25-37
Leontieff, W., 123
Lerner, A. P., 34-5, 38, 197-8, 206, 253-4, 256

Levi-Strauss, C., 109
Lewis, W. A., 237-41, 253, 256
Lindahl, Erik, 179-86, 192, 196, 198, 203
Lipinski, E., 88, 100, 201
List, 98, 99
Lundberg, Erik, 7, 17, 151, 161
  lecture, 211-26
  discussion on lecture, 227-57
Lychowski, T., 247-8

Managerial ability, 46
Manoilesco, M., 86
Marchal, J., 227
Marrama, V., 145
Marshall, 56
Marshall Plan, 246
Marx, 244
  Das Kapital, 200
Marxian view of monetary and real factors, 200
  of foreign exchange rates, 244
Matrix-multiplier, 15
Meade, James, 35, 71, 231
Medical progress, 89
  in nineteenth-century Europe, 90
Merleau-Ponty, M., 147
Metzler, L., 168 n.
Migration, 69, 99, 240
Mill, James, 46
Mises, 159, 163
Mitchell, W., 154 n.
Models, Harrod-Domar, see Harrod-Domar
  long-run, 30
  macro-economic, 133, 138, 161, 162, 201-2
  short-run, 114
Modernization schemes, 21
Monetary authorities, 196
Monetary factors, 151-207
Monetary factors and growth, 187-91
Monetary instability, 165, 193
Monetary nature of great depression, 164-6
Monetary policy, 25, 26, 33, 36, 113, 137, 157, 158, 159, 164, 167, 168, 169, 172, 178, 184, 185, 186, 190, 191, 193, 194, 195, 196, 197, 198, 199, 202-4, 206, 207, 219, 220, 249, 250
  ineffectiveness in downswing, 202-3, 206-7
Monetary policy after 1945, compared with after 1918, 159 n., 200, 206
  reason for special position of, 36-7

Monetary reform, 36, 115, 169, 251
Monetary system, types of, 179-80, 186, 196
Monetary theories of economic fluctuation, 159-61, 162, 164, 169-70, 179
Money, passive rôle of, 163
Monopoly, and technical advance in poor countries, 54
Morton, W., 173 n.
Mossé, R., 27-9, 37
Multiplier, the, 158, 161, 163 n., 164, 168 n., 176

Nakayama, I., 35
Nasr, Z., 84-5, 100
National Bureau of Economic Research, 54, 121 n., 123, 153, 154, 155
National income, statistics, 13, 108
  analysis, 255
Neutral money, 162, 196
New Zealand, immigration policy in, 144
Non-classical linkages, 107
Nuclear energy, 85, 106 n., 117 n., 144
Nuisance commodities, 43-6
Nurkse, Ragnar, 57, 69-77, 78, 98, 113, 143, 227 n., 229, 247

Occupational structure, 120
Okyar, O. F., 141-2, 146
Oligopoly, 107, 115, 117 n., 121, 127
Open-market operations, 196, 207
Organized labour, see Trade Unions

Papi, U., 3-6, 108, 135-6, 146, 186-91, 192, 196, 206, 207, 254
Pareto, social constants, 21, 22, 23
Passive sectors, 128, 129, 130, 142, 145
Pedersen, J., 195
Pension funds, investment policy, 15
People's democracies, 126 n.
Perroux, F., 151, 156, 227 n., 230, 237, 244, 247, 248
  lecture, 105,-126
  discussion on lecture, 127,-147
Pigou, A. C., 163 n., 167, 176 n., 200, 249
Pitigliani, F., 96-7, 245-6, 255
Planned economies, 7, 35, 36, 144, 200-1
  stability in, 36, 88, 201
  unemployment in, 88
Planning, 108, 110, 118, 119, 120, 136, 137, 187, 252, 253
  long-term, by industry, 26, 119
  See also Economic planning
Plasticity of structure, 146
Ploughing-back of profits, see Self-financing

Index

Poles of development, 120, 121, 125, 227 n., 237
Poorer countries, *see* Underdeveloped countries
Population, 105, 106, 138, 253-4
ageing of, 119
Dutch, 10
excess, 69-70, 72-3, 77-8, 85
experience in richer countries as compared with poorer ones, 62-3
growth, 24, 110, 137, 141, 144, 188, 202, 224
optimum, 35, 43
problems in poorer countries, 62-4, 65, 66-7, 68, 69, 70, 72-3, 79, 88-91
U.K. Royal Commission on, 10
U.S., 10
Poverty, 79
non-economic causes, 42
vicious circle of, 42, 43
Power resources, 11, 85-6, 117
Price level, and productivity changes, 184-5, 193, 194
Prices, stable, 184-5, 198, 203, 206
Primary products, 153
fluctuating demand and prices, 80, 87, 215, 237
price stabilization of, 60, 238, 239, 240
Production functions, 22, 106 n.
Productivity, low level in backward countries, 21-2, 86-7
Profit, 119
Progress, and cycles, 140, 141
defined, 107 n.
measurement of, 144-5
rate of, 19-21, 23
Propagation problems, 177
Propensities, 21, 23, 119, 175
Protectionism, 224, 231
Psychological factors, 16, 21, 129, 134, 140, 142, 147, 160, 168 n., 176, 189, 197, 228
Public intervention, 121
investment, 27, 116, 117, 118, 119, 136, 231
ownership, 102
policy, 128
sector, 86, 108, 117, 144

Quotas, *see* Import regulation
Qureshi, M., 80-1

Ramsey, Frank, 8, 9
Real factors, 105-48, 151, 158, 159, 161, 162, 164, 167, 168, 173, 174, 177, 188, 191, 193, 197, 199, 200, 206

Real factors—*contd.*
and theories of fluctuation, 162-4, 169-170, 180
correlation with monetary factors in the short cycle, 157, 186-7
Recession, 22, 155
Rent, producers', 22
Replacement costs, 33
Research, 11, 112, 116, 117 n., 118, 123
Resources, scarcity of, 43-6
'quality aspect' of, 44-5, 85-6
Resta, M., 93-5
Reynaud, P., 95-6
Ricardo, 98, 99, 166 n.
Richer countries, *see* Developed countries
Rigidity of prices and wages, 140, 158, 165, 176, 189
Risk taking, 31
Rist, C., 165
Rist, L., 97-8
Robbins, Lionel, 105
Robertson, Sir Dennis, 41, 61, 62, 88, 105, 127, 134, 135, 137, 138, 142, 151, 156, 193-4, 205, 206
lecture, 7-18
discussion of lecture, 19-38
Robinson, Mrs. Joan, 132, 137, 146, 201
Rome, University of, 3
Rostow, W. W., 109 n., 113
Rubinstein, M. L., 81-4, 100, 138
Rueff, J., 151
Rugina, A., 35-6, 143-4, 147, 250-2

St. Lawrence Waterway, 27
Samuelson, P. A., 121 n., 201
Sauvy, A., 90-2, 110 n.
Saving, 8, 12, 13, 15, 34, 35, 44, 120, 135, 136, 140, 182
and inflation, *see* Inflation
coefficient, 117 n., 227, 232
forced, 25, 48, 65, 74
individual, 14
in underdeveloped countries, *see* Underdeveloped countries
net, 11, 22, 23
private, 24
shortage of, 12, 28, 225, 233
voluntary, 13, 25, 160
Savings-investment and rates of progress, 21, 29, 95, 138
Sayers, R. S., 146
Scarcity, 43-6
Schneider, Eric, 130-4, 145
Schultz, T., 78

Schumpeter, J. A., 20, 107, 109, 111, 113, 117, 131, 133, 141, 154, 155, 156, 158, 160, 168, 177, 191
Schwartz, A., 109 n.
Scitovsky, T., 92, 113
Scotland, hydro-electric schemes in, 27
Second best, theory of, 33, 153, 178 n.
'Secular stagnation', 164
Self-financing, 23-4, 25, 28, 115, 117
Shareholders, 13
Shift work, 22
Shone, Sir R., 138-9, 146
Singer, H. W., 85
Slichter, S. H., 173, 192
Smith, Adam, 63
Social yield, 98
    costs, 61, 84, 98
Sommer, Dr. L., 36-7
Specialists, shortage of, 95-6
Spiethoff, 131, 133, 156
Stability, 36, 141
    future prospects for, 26-7
    indicators of, 211-13
    meaning of, 19-21, 95, 145, 247
Stabilization of primary products, *see* Primary products
Standard of living, 85-6
    and population, 89-90
    rising, 10
    space and service, 10, 31, 37
Stationary state, 22
Statistical measures of growth, 37
Sterling, revaluation of, 166, 169
Stock piling, 233, 236
Stone, J. R. N., 8
Strasbourg, Research Centre, 96
Structural disequilibrium, 99
    shifts, 131, 132
Structure and growth, 120, 232, 233, 235
    preference for national, 120
Sukarno, President, 82
Suppressed inflation, *see* Inflation
Suranyi-Unger, T., 136-7, 146-7
Sweden, price policy in, 184
Swinfen, T., 204-5

Tabah, L., 88-90
Tariffs, 53, 135, 212, 216, 221, 231, 254
Taxation, 232, 238
    avoidance of, 28
    for capital construction, 12, 33, 37
    high, 174, 220, 221
    of windfall gains, 48
    pressure for low, 219

Technical change, 11, 45, 117, 126 n.
    discovery, 44
    innovation, 14, 176 n., 177
    knowledge and poorer countries, 64, 81
    progress, 22, 34, 131, 132, 140, 184, 195
    progress and capital-output ratio, 30
Teilkonjunkturen, 145
Tensions, 115 n., 130, 133
Terms of trade, 53, 54, 75, 76, 153, 175, 215, 236
'Thresholds', 79, 96
Time preference, 8
Tinbergen, Jan, 145, 147, 229
Todorovitch, D., 243-5
Toynbee, A., 252
Trade cycle, *see* Economic fluctuations
Trade unions, 174, 193, 198
    and leisure, 25
    fear of, 249
    wage policy, 33, 171, 172, 173, 178 n., 181, 183, 184, 193-4, 206
Training Within Industry, instructor, 205
Transfer payments, 119
Transport, 11
Trends, 113, 231
    and cycles, 154, 155
Trial and error, 142, 143

Underdeveloped countries, defined, 233
    development of, 20, 65-77, 80-1, 91, 96-7, 99, 174, 226, 245, 247, 248
    differences between, 41-2
    economic organization of, 66-7, 233
    effect of richer nations' trade policies on, 52, 53, 65, 76, 80
    effects of usurious interest rates on, 51
    foreign trade and, 52, 53, 58, 59, 75-7, 80-1, 99, 226 243-4
    imports of, 59, 93, 234, 235
    industrialization in, 240-1
    instability in, 58-60, 153, 237
    investment in, 49, 53, 97, 141, 243, 245, 256
    'islands of wealth' in, 50, 84, 100
    monetary problems in, 159
    need for rapid growth, 233
    price of growth in, 199, 223-5, 234
    rate of growth in, 85, 86
    relations with developed economies, 233-7
    savings in, 30, 38, 48, 79, 81, 86, 91, 97-8, 224, 226, 233, 241, 242-3, 257

Index

Underdeveloped countries—*contd.*
  stabilization of prices of exports, 238
  'trial and error' in, 242
Underdeveloped regions of advanced
  countries, 25, 83
Underemployment equilibrium, 138
Unemployment, 180, 185, 198, 220
  benefits of, 205, 207
  in planned economies, *see* Planned
    economies
  in rich and poor countries compared,
    67
  of intellectuals in poor countries, 85,
    95 n., 96
  unwillingness to tolerate, 170, 172
United Kingdom, 17
  and foreign trade, 17
  average standard of living, 25
  economic policy in, 139
  inflation in, 33
  lending policies of banks, 15
  position in 1920s, 166
  Royal Commission on Population, 10
  saving in, 93
  terms of trade, 53
  1952 recession, 16
United Nations Organization, 82, 84
  Economic and Social Council, 239
United States of America, 37
  and foreign trade, 17, 121 n., 215
  capital-output ratio in, 11, 29-30, 37,
    118
  deflationary dangers from, 220
  effects of changes in defence spend-
    ing, 32
  foreign lending policy, 87-8
  lending policies of banks, 15
  monetary policy of, 206, 207
  overseas investments, 121
  policy in 1927 recession, 206
  policy in 1953-4 recession, 207, 220
  population, 10
  position in late nineteenth century,
    166
  savings in, 14

United States of America—*contd.*
  stabilization policy in, 185-6
  tariff policy in recessions, 26
  variations in living standards in, 25
United States Congress, 82, 121 n.,
    126 n.
Upswing, monetary factors in, 166-9
U.S.S.R. aid to underdeveloped areas,
    83-4, 126 n.
  economic position in, 83, 96, 138,
    255
  planning in, 184

Vakil, C. N., 66-69, 78, 79
Valéry, P., 111
Value judgments, 33, 256
Vanoni Plan, the, 187
Veil of money, 193
Veit, O., 195, 206
Vickrey, W., 202-4, 206, 207
Viner, Jacob, 7, 138, 142, 151, 165 n.
    192, 198, 242
  lecture, 41-65
  discussion of lecture, 66-101
Voluntary saving, *see* Saving

Wage determination, 216
  policy, 232
Wage-price spiral, 211, 215
Walrasian system, 36
'Watchdog Policy', 20
Weiller, J., 98-9, 120, 246-7
Welfare, collective, 229, 237
  state, 236
Wheatley, 166 n.
White, Harry, 87
Wicksell, 131, 143, 159
Wooley, H. B., 121 n.
Work study, 204-5
World Bank, 87, 97, 98

Yeager, L., 170 n.

Zero marginal productivity of labour,
    see Disguised unemployment

THE END

PRINTED BY R. & R. CLARK, LTD., EDINBURGH